Waterlily

Ella Cara Deloria

Biographical sketch of the author by Agnes Picotte

Afterword by Raymond J. DeMallie

University of Nebraska Press: Lincoln and London

The paper in this
book meets the
minimum require-
ments of American
National Standard
for Information
Sciences – Perma-
nence of Paper
for Printed Library
Materials,
ANSI Z39.48-1984.

Library of Congress
Cataloging
in Publication Data
Deloria, Ella Cara.
Waterlily /
Ella Cara Deloria;
biographical sketch
of the author by
Agnes Picotte; after-
word by Raymond
J. DeMallie.
p.   cm.
ISBN 0-8032-4739-7
alkaline paper
1. Dakota Indians –
Fiction.   I. Title.
II. Title: Waterlily.
PS3554.E44445W3
1988 813'.54 – dc19
87-21462CIP

Second printing: 1988

In Memory of Ruth Fulton Benedict, Who Believed in Waterlily

Contents

Publisher's Preface

Waterlily is a novel of Indian life—of the Dakotas, or Sioux. But apart from dealing with an actual people at a more-or-less-identifiable time and place, it has little in common with the conventional historical fiction centered on famous people and major events. For the book was written by Ella Deloria, herself a Sioux and an accomplished ethnologist, who sought to record and preserve traditional Sioux ways through this imaginative re-creation of life in the camp circle. It is of special value because it is told from a woman's perspective—one that is much less well known than the warrior's or the holy man's. More fully and compellingly than any ethnological report, and with equal authority, it reveals the intricate system of relatedness, obligation, and respect that governed the world of all Dakotas as it takes the protagonist, Waterlily, through the everyday and the extraordinary events of a Sioux woman's experience.

In *Speaking of Indians,* a more analytical description of Sioux culture published in 1944, when she had completed at least a first draft of *Waterlily,* Deloria states explicitly a goal that applies as well to the novel: "We shall go back to a time prior to white settlement of the western plains, when native custom and thought were all there was, and we shall examine certain of the most significant elements in the old life." White Americans appear only peripherally, providing in their first tentative contacts with the western Sioux a counterpoint to the native values.

Deloria goes on to point out that "the ultimate aim of Dakota life, stripped of accessories, was quite simple: One must obey kinship rules; one must be a good relative. No Dakota who has participated in that life will dispute that. In the last analysis every other consideration was secondary—property, personal ambition, glory, good times, life itself. Without that aim and the constant struggle to attain it, the people would no longer be Dakotas in truth. They would no longer even be human. To be a good Dakota, then, was to be humanized, civilized. And to be civilized was to keep the rules imposed by kinship for achieving civility, good manners, and a sense of responsibility toward every individual dealt with. Thus only was it possible to live communally with success; that is to say, with a minimum of friction and a maximum of good will."

Deloria was an ideal intermediary between the predominant American and traditional Dakota cultures, and she took that role seriously. She was born in 1889 the daughter of one of the first Sioux to become an Episcopalian priest. The Delorias belonged to the Yankton group of Sioux, those who were situated geographically between the Santees, the easternmost, and the Tetons, the westernmost. But Ella came to know the Tetons, the subject of this book, intimately because she was raised among them while her father served as a missionary on the Standing Rock Reservation. After 1928, when she began to do anthropological research for Franz Boas on a regular basis, she conducted fieldwork among them. Her biculturalism is manifest in her career: that she revered the old Dakota ways, studied them, recorded them, and could defend them eloquently in English as a member of the American scientific community, is illustrative.

A letter from Ruth Benedict to Ella Deloria dated November 7, 1944, which Deloria preserved with the manuscript of *Waterlily*, makes it clear that Benedict had at that time read a completed draft. Although she found it eminently publishable, she recommended cuts to bring it "down to the usual size for such a book." Benedict wrote: "We must get together and go over them, so that, when the war is over and publishers are taking books that dont have to do with the war effort, the manuscript will be ready to submit to them." But the book was not published in Deloria's lifetime, even though she did shorten the manuscript, reducing the length by half or more in the interests of making it a better story, and she and Benedict expended a good deal of effort in refining it for publication. It is published here for the first time—an immensely readable, enjoyable, informative story that transcends easy categorization.

The present edition of *Waterlily* reproduces the manuscript in its entirety. Beyond the usual copyediting to systematize spelling and punctuation and to clarify style, inconsistencies in characters' names—the result of Deloria's combining drafts written at different times—have been regularized. Occasional redundancies have been eliminated, and a few dated slang expressions and turns of phrase out of keeping with the tone of the story (set in the days of early contact between the Teton Sioux and the whites) have been revised editorially: for example, "the eternal question in a man's heart" (referring to courtship), "sweet young thing" (a young girl), "sinful" (evil), "thank heaven" (thankfully). Similarly, occasional terms whose meaning has changed since the manuscript was written have been revised to forestall confusion: for example, "migration" (for a formal move of the camp circle), "routine" (ritual actions), "superstition" (common belief). Some terms common in the anthropological literature on the Sioux in Deloria's time have gone out of fashion today, but they have been retained in this work: for example, "Dakota" (referring to all the divisions of the Sioux people), "magistrates" (the camp-circle officials), "social kinship" (relationship based not on the Western concept of blood relatives, but on the Dakota cultural concept that relationships can be based on patterns of thought and behavior and be equally as binding as relationships of blood). Finally, to clarify cultural features an occasional explanatory phrase has been added, based on other of Deloria's writings. Throughout, the effort has been to retain the author's style and tone. Although she occasionally used Sioux terms, they are explained in the context. The character *s̓,* conventionally used in Sioux orthography, is pronounced like the English *sh*.

A fuller account of Deloria's life and career, of how *Waterlily* relates to her professional work, and of its ethnographic value may be found in the biographical sketch of Deloria and the afterword at the end of this book. The University of Nebraska Press is deeply indebted to Father Vine V. Deloria, Sr., for graciously permitting the publication of his sister's manuscript; to the Dakota Indian Foundation, Chamberlain, South Dakota, for their care in preserving the manuscript, which had been entrusted to them, and for making a copy available; to Agnes Picotte, director of the Ella C. Deloria Project, Chamberlain, South Dakota, for bringing the manuscript to the Press's attention and for generously sharing her knowledge of Ella Deloria's life; and to Raymond J. DeMallie, professor of anthropology and director of the American Indian Studies Research Institute at Indiana University, for so kindly giving of his time and expertise to provide crucial assistance with the editing as well as an afterword that splendidly illuminates the broader significance of *Waterlily*.

Waterlily

CHAPTER I

The camp circle was on the move again. Whenever one site wore out and became unsanitary, or whenever it was time to go elsewhere to hunt deer or to gather the fruits in season, the magistrates whose duty it was to think and plan for the people ordered this move. And at such times everyone must obey. To remain behind was to be without protection.

The day was oppressive, hot and heavy. The air was filled with dry dust that rose only so high and then hovered there, enveloping and moving with the line of march—fine dust, continually stirred up by the feet of humans and animals and by the ends of travois poles that scraped along behind the packhorses. Up hill and down dale the column crawled, picking its way over the trackless land.

The young wife Blue Bird could scarcely sit her horse another instant. Oh, to dismount! But the kinship rule of avoidance kept her silent as long as it was her father-in-law who walked ahead leading her horse. At last, mercifully, he handed the rope to his wife and dropped behind to walk with a friend.

"Now I can speak. She too is a woman; she knows how it is with me." But even then Blue Bird waited as long as she dared before saying, "Mother-in-law, let me get down. I must walk."

"Very well. If you must you must. But say when you want to ride again," the older woman replied, then added, sighing, "Ah, child, we do you wrong to travel today—but try to bear up. Already we have made the three stops, so the next will be the last. It can't be far now." That was all. The respect customary between two persons in their relationship made them hesitate to discuss freely the cause of their mutual anxiety.

Blue Bird stepped out of the line and walked along beside it, determined to keep up. But she fell steadily behind and soon her mother-in-law, who continued in line, was far ahead, talking to herself. "It is my daughter-in-law's own concern. If she wishes to walk more slowly, that is her right." It was not for her to question her son's wife as though doubting her common sense. But she consoled herself with the likelihood that there would be relatives back there who would be with the girl if she needed help. And so, with shaky optimism, she plodded on, trying not to worry.

And now the line was moving along the crest of a ridge, still at the same snail's pace. Far ahead the four magistrates who always led the moving camp walked with the Peace Pipe extended continuously before them in propitiation of the Great Spirit. It was they who set the pace, always bearing in mind the aged and the infirm, the women with burdens on their backs and the short-legged children who trudged along beside them.

As for the men, they were out on scout duty. All able-bodied men and all responsible boys were on horseback, convoying the column. Some rode far ahead of it and others far behind, while still others were spaced along the line on both sides. They kept out of sight so that the line seemed to be moving alone, but actually they were ever on guard, one or another of them dashing out to some distant peak from time to time to scan the country beyond.

Blue Bird looked about her in anguish. Over at the left where the ridge fell sharply away she saw the tops of trees. That meant water—or seclusion at least. She must go now, right now. She dared not wait another instant, for this was her hour.

Turning aside, she walked swiftly and disappeared over the slope, but her going drew neither attention nor comment. Decency compelled adults to leave the line and go temporarily out of sight whenever it was necessary. Only small children, and sometimes the very aged to whom nothing mattered much any longer, were not so scrupulous, nor were they expected to be. The Tetons were a modest but also a reasonable people.

On the young girl's brow stood beads of sweat icy cold. Against a spinning world she struggled to think coherently. Just what was it her grandmother once told a woman—something about the best position to induce an easy birth? Or was it quick birth? What was it, anyway? She groped for it in her confused mind. Suddenly it came like a flash. And with it something else the grandmother once said: "No woman cries out like a baby; people ridicule that. To carry a child is an awesome thing. If one is old enough to bear a child, one is old enough to endure in silence."

Blue Bird clung to those words with desperate tenacity and allowed not a moan to escape her, though she was alone. An eternity passed—and then, the child was a girl. Of that she was vaguely aware as she picked it up from the soft grass on which it lay and fumbled for her knife in its case hanging on her belt. Cleanly and quickly she cut the cord, as old wives said it should be cut. She herself had never beheld such a thing. Unmarried young women did not witness births.

Still dazed, she wrapped her child in a fawnskin, which she had prepared in secret, working it long hours at a time to render it white and pliable and soft. She had kept it with her against this hour. Next she changed to a fresh gown, wrapped the placenta and cord in the discarded one, and tied it in a neat bundle. Then, stretching with superhuman effort, she settled it securely into the fork of a tree, well beyond the reach of desecrating animals. You should always do this, for every newborn child, that it might grow up straight-limbed and clear-minded. Everyone knew that; it was the ancient law.

At the water's edge she knelt to wash her stained hands. Then, hardly knowing why, she rained a few drops gently on the little face that fitted nicely into the hollow of her hand. But, try as she would, she could not concentrate on the wonder she held there. All around the waterlilies in full bloom seemed to pull her eyes to them irresistibly, until she turned to gaze on them with exaggerated astonishment. How beautiful they were! How they made you open your eyes wider and wider the longer you looked—as if daring you to penetrate their outer shape and comprehend their spirit. She glanced from one to another, and suddenly it was impossible to distinguish them from her baby's face. A new sensation welled up within her, almost choking her, and she was articulate for the first time. "My daughter! My daughter!" she cried, "How beautiful you are! As beautiful as the waterlilies. You too are a waterlily, *my* waterlily." She sobbed with joy.

Shocked by the cool water, the baby struggled vigorously, moving her head quickly from side to side. And then, wonder of wonders, she looked up at her mother and smiled—Blue Bird was certain of it. Forthwith Blue Bird forgot every care, even her unhappy life with a foolishly jealous husband.

Pressing her baby against her heart she rejoined the line. With supreme effort she retained the composure and the placidity conventional to women, for even her lingering pain was itself a pleasure. Her return to the group attracted no special attention. After all, young women with babies in their arms were the rule rather than the exception. Moreover, the people near the end of the line were not the ones who had seen her leaving it earlier.

By now the sun hung low. Blue Bird walked quietly alongside the line as if looking for her people, until a woman who was a social cousin noticed what had happened and took charge of her. After sending her family on, she turned her packhorse out of the line and settled the mother and child on the travois seat behind and began leading the horse at an even slower walk so that its delicate burden should not be jolted by hidden bumps and stubble.

They pulled into the new camp circle at dusk. Everyone else had arrived and swung into position. Some tipis were already up and others were rapidly being erected all around the circle. The men and boys who had ridden all day to guard the people now appeared at their tipis, gladdening their wives or mothers with such small game as they had come upon. Soon an unbroken ring of campfires twinkled in the growing darkness and pungent smoke rose like incense from every hearth. Camp life was readily resumed after a march.

Increasingly Blue Bird felt her weariness. She was grateful when her cousin invited her to stay until she should regain her strength. "You have been through much today," the cousin said. "It is not easy to give birth on the march. Stay here with me and let me take care of you. I will do the work and cook the food while you feed your baby and rest. If you were to go home now you would feel you must work."

News traveled swiftly round a camp circle, from tipi to tipi, and in no time at all it completed the circuit. When Blue Bird's mother-in-law heard the baby had come and that mother and child were safe in a cousin's tipi across the common, her relief was boundless. Early next morning she came to see them and heartily agreed that her daughter-in-law should remain where she was for a time. To her simple mind (for she was not a very imaginative woman) this seemed an ideal arrangement, at first. It was not until she was halfway home that she found herself muttering, "My son will not like this. He will be angry that his wife does not come directly home with the baby." And she began to dread telling him, knowing how ready he was to misinterpret whatever Blue Bird did, and knowing, too, how ill-tempered he had always been and how morose he had grown since this gentle girl became his wife. It was a disturbing thought.

CHAPTER 2

Blue Bird had never been entirely happy either in her marriage or in her life in a camp circle that was not her own. It was not that the people were unkind; quite the contrary. But she could not feel satisfied there. She never ceased to yearn for her own people. It was almost four years now she and her grandmother had been staying there. Sometimes she wished they had risked everything and struck out alone in search of their own camp circle. Even if they had perished on the way, it would have been worth trying.

Her childhood among her own many loving kinsmen was a happy one, but that time was like a dream vanished. Try as she would, she could never recapture the feel of that carefree life, so cruelly ended in a day. Tonight for the first time, with her infant, Waterlily, asleep beside her, she was again completely happy. This was a different kind of happiness, satisfying, if subdued. But it was good. She lay idly reminiscing in the dark tipi of her cousin, who was out somewhere. With singular detachment she was able for the first time to recall in detail the events of that tragic day that had robbed her of her family. Tonight it seemed remote, like something that had happened to someone else long ago in a far-off place.

She had been fourteen years old at the time. Her father had decided to leave the camp circle for a few days of deer hunting because their supply of meat was dwindling fast and no buffalo had been sighted in a long time. He took his wife and his mother and his three children, Blue Bird and her brothers, ten and six years of age.

The family made their temporary camp near a wood and immediately went out to cut the poles and boughs needed to set up their working arrangements, drying racks for the meat, and an arbor of leaves. Soon the father was bringing in deer and other game at such a rate that the two women had to work steadily from dawn to dusk caring for the meat, for they were a frugal family and saved every bit that could be used.

But busy as they were, the old grandmother took time out one afternoon for a walk under the tall cottonwoods nearby. The next day she announced, as they sat eating, "There is a large cache of earth beans over yonder, where many little paths under the matted grass come together from all directions. The field mice, too, have been busy preparing for winter."

"Well, that is indeed good news," her son's wife said. "Now maybe we can take back earth beans as well as meat. I hope you can remember where the cache is."

"Oh, yes. And anyway I set up a stick to mark the spot," the old woman assured her, adding, "I could easily have thumped in the dirt roof right then with my club and brought the beans home. But of course I waited."

The younger boy, who dearly relished them, pouted, "Oh, Grandmother, you should have! Then I could be having some beans now."

Blue Bird cut in, "You can't do that, silly! Don't you know that you have to leave a return gift for the mice when you take away their food? They have to have something to live on, too."

That was no way for a girl to speak to a brother, and few adults would fail to correct such a slip. Blue Bird's mother said gently but firmly, "Daughter, one does not call one's brother 'silly.'" And then she turned to her mother-in-law, saying, "I have some dried corn in that rawhide box. Will it answer?"

The old woman was delighted. "Of course. It will be just the thing. Too good, I should say. For who are they, to have green corn dried for them? They should be too happy with it to think of bewitching me—I hope." She said this laughingly, but it was plain she half feared the common belief about the powers of resentful mice.

Blue Bird went with her grandmother to open the cache and they found an abundance of beans, unusually large and meaty. They would cook up rich and sweet, the old woman said. She found more caches and went to work at once, happily drawing out handfuls of the black, earth-caked store and piling it on her blanket, spread out to receive it. For each handful she religiously returned a handful of green corn that had been parboiled and then sundried, a treat for the mice indeed. When she was through, she and Blue Bird grasped the corners of the blanket and tossed the beans high to winnow out the dirt. The loose, fine dust was carried off on the breeze. The clumps settled to the bottom and could easily be removed later.

The old woman gathered the blanket to form a bag holding the beans and tied a thong around it tightly, bending over. When she straightened up, she groaned a bit over a kink in her back, as was her habit. Then, shielding her eyes with one hand, she studied the sun. "Come, child, we must be going now. It is getting on," she said. But she could not resist hurriedly picking up a few dry sticks. "We can always do with more firewood." She made a bundle of them with the pack strap she always wore for a belt. From a lifetime of practice she flung the bundle expertly onto her back. At last she and Blue Bird started home, carrying the beans suspended between them.

Out of the woods and into the clear they came, but when they looked toward their camp, it was not there. Everything was in ruins. How could it have happened so quickly, so quietly? It was unbelievable that in the short time since Blue Bird and her grandmother had left it, any enemy war party had raided their camp. Yet that was the case.

The destruction could hardly have been more thorough. The skin tent was slashed beyond mending, the poles were all broken or askew, and the drying racks filled with jerked meat were completely dismantled. The two boys lay dead, flat on their faces, not far from the tipi. They had been shot while running away, impaled by arrows in their backs. The parents had vanished without a trace. Whether they too had been killed or were taken captive the two survivers were never to know.

They hurriedly covered the bodies of the boys, but this was no time to mourn. Shocked as they were, they could not entertain both grief and fear at the same time. One emotion must wait, and fear took precedence. Lest the marauders return and find them, the grandmother decided they must hasten into hiding. She and Blue Bird did so, lying concealed under bushes and behind rocks by day and traveling by night. Under an overcast sky they lost their way and wandered blindly, with no idea of their destination.

The second day at dawn they happened upon a large camp circle, though it was not theirs. But the people were their kind and spoke their dialect, so they knew they had found refuge. On learning of their plight and their recent tragedy, the magistrates sent the crier out from the council tipi to announce their arrival and rally the people to their aid.

The response was quick. Someone gave the newcomers a tipi to live in, while public-spirited collectors carried around the circle a great bull hide into which contributions were placed. Women came running out of their tipis to add their gifts, such items as clothing and food. And thus all in a day Blue Bird and her grandmother were equipped to start life anew. From time to time the wives and mothers of hunters brought them meat, and at the next several feasts they were invited as special guests. In such ways did the people help them establish themselves in their new camp circle. And when at last, in the privacy of their newly acquired home, the two could give way to their grief and wail at leisure, their women neighbors came in to wail with them in sympathy, as was the custom. And the members of the camp circle adopted the newcomers as relatives.

It was true enough that here Blue Bird and her grandmother fell into the category of the humbler folk of the community. Without any male relatives to give them backing, they made no pretensions to importance in the social life of the camp circle. Nor were they expected to. Nevertheless, their lowly station in no way degraded them in the popular esteem. The Tetons did not have to put on airs in that way. If one's circumstances did not allow it, one did not need to give feasts or take part in the conspicuous give-away ceremonies. The grandmother and grandchild, accepting their situation, were content to remain quietly in the background. Since they could not return to the camp circle where they did have position, and with it certain social obligations, it was enough that they had fallen in with their own kind of people and that they had been taken in as relatives in social kinship.

As the seasons passed, the young men of the village could not fail to see that Blue Bird was maturing and that her growing beauty was remarkable. But this fact troubled her grandmother greatly, and she felt the need of someone with whom to share the responsibility for the girl until she should be safely married.

Knowing well how some reckless young men played at court-ship, she feared for Blue Bird. She must be warned at once that many a girl had come to ruin by taking their smooth wooing seri-ously, and the grandmother was the only one to tell her. "I shall have a talk with her tomorrow." But each day she put it off, dreading the ordeal. "I am too old for this; would that her mother were here," she said to herself. "Or perhaps I should simply give the girl away in marriage now, to some kind and able house-holder, to be a co-wife. Then she can be honorably married before any trouble can befall her. Yes, that would be best."

But just whom to give her to was a puzzle. And what wife would want her? Being co-wife was not necessarily bad, pro-vided the man was kind. She had been a co-wife herself. But then, she was the wife's sister and therefore was well received. In fact, as she remembered now, it was that elder sister who had offered to take her into the family. Ah, but Blue Bird had no sister in this camp circle. A head wife might resent her. That too must be considered. Slowly and timidly the old woman turned the problem over in her mind many times. But she had not yet acted when Blue Bird said to her one day, "Grandmother, one of the young men at the courting place has been urging me to marry him. His name is Star Elk."

The old woman shook her head emphatically, "No! No! Not that one. It would be good for you to marry, grandchild. We are so alone and helpless without a man to provide for our home. But not that one. Only last night the women around the campfire were talking about him. 'He is no hunter,' they said. 'He takes no interest in anything. Always he has been headstrong and un-friendly, even as a boy,' they said. That is not the kind of man for you, grandchild."

"But I have told him I would marry him, Grandmother."

The silence that followed was ominous. When the old woman again found her voice, she said, "Ah, if only you had told me he was courting you so I could have warned you, grandchild. Since you have promised already, there is nothing I can do. Once she gives it, an honorable Dakota woman does not break her word to a man. Those who make false promises are ever after derided. To give your word is to give yourself." With that she stumbled out of the little tipi and began to wail in a quavering voice the following lament: "Ah, my son! Ah, my daughter-in-law! You have left me alone to struggle on. What can I do, frail and full of years as I am?" Far into the night she wailed.

Blue Bird's marriage was inevitable now. But even after resigning herself to it, the grandmother went about with a heavy heart. "If only I had had someone to help me arrange a suitable marriage for her," she muttered to herself from time to time. That the girl might run off with Star Elk was a dreaded possibility, even while there was a feeble hope that perhaps the young man had been misrepresented as altogether undesirable. Perhaps he was not that bad after all, and perhaps he would soon do the honorable thing—marry the girl openly, with tribal approval.

The most glamorous kind of marriage was by purchase. A woman who married in that way was much respected, for it meant that she had kept herself so unattainable that the man, who wanted her at all costs, thought nothing of giving horses for her, even at the risk of her rejecting him publicly. "I do not aspire to that for my poor orphaned grandchild," the grandmother said. "All I ask is a valid marriage, and then I should die happy." He might come to live with them or take her to his people openly. Whichever way, it should be planned and above board, and then Blue Bird would be respected.

But Star Elk lived up to his reputation. He lured the girl away, the very thing her grandmother had feared. What a gamble that was! A Teton girl who accepted marriage on such shabby terms took the supreme risk with her honor. How did she know that the man was not just trifling with her? Too often an elopement ended disastrously for the girl, while the man always went free. Momentarily the old woman looked for the girl's return, after the man tired of her. She would of course receive her back; was she not her grandchild? But the disgrace would be lasting.

As it happened, though, Blue Bird was lucky. Star Elk did not dally on the way but took her straight home to his people. And for her grandmother that was the one mitigating fact. Soon the new relatives-in-law came for her and placed her tipi in among their family group that they might care for her. Thus, even though Blue Bird had married in the least honorable way, the material condition of her grandmother was bettered, and that was something.

Because Star Elk had taken Blue Bird home to his people, the marriage was accepted as tolerably valid, and in due time the foolish step was forgiven the girl. The usual sharp censure of the eloping woman was toned down considerably by the circumstances. Condoning it, women began saying, "Well, what could you expect since the girl is very young and pretty and lacks a mother to guide her? What could a tottering grandmother do, anyway? It is good that the girl did not get into real trouble and bear a fatherless child." Thus Blue Bird, by not being "discarded in the wilds" (abandoned far from the camp circle) or bearing a "fatherless child," came in time to be counted among the blameless women of the camp circle. By the slimmest of margins—but she was in.

Even so, things were far from ideal. Star Elk was lazy and petulant and given to jealous fits. It was his relatives who received her kindly and treated her well, partly for their own reputation as correct in-laws, and partly to compensate for his failures. This made up in a measure for the poor bargain Blue Bird had made. But, kind as they were, it might have been better if they had been remiss in some details, or even outright hostile to her, if only her husband had been more satisfactory. The marriage had been unfortunate from the beginning.

The tipis of skin were opaque at night. Unless the fire was flaming, occupants must feel their way about. The cousin entered the tipi at a late hour and moved with caution toward her place. Perhaps Blue Bird was asleep. Nevertheless she spoke to her softly, "Cousin, are you resting well? We shall be by ourselves. I have sent the children and their father to sleep in his mother's tipi. Wake me at once if you need anything."

"I am quite all right, cousin, and I think I can sleep now. I was just thinking of the past; that is all."

The two women said nothing further. There was in the language no formality equivalent to "Good night." One quite well indicated one's goodwill and good wishes by tonal quality. After a little, Blue Bird reached out drowsily and touched her baby, smiling in the dark as she did so. "This is all I want," she murmured. "Let him do his worst!" And presently she slept. How could she guess to what lengths he would go to spite her for staying away?

CHAPTER 3

Star Elk had grown more and more ill-tempered each day of his married life. The truth was that he was tormented with jealousy over his wife. He continually imagined that other men looked upon her with desire, and accused her of encouraging them furtively. She used to enjoy looking on at the celebrations and dances, but after a time he even forbade her to do that. And when she was with child, he once declared in a rage that it was not his. That was pure nonsense, as was nearly everything he said of or to his wife.

And now that the baby was born, he behaved still more outrageously. When he learned that Blue Bird was staying away for a while, he pouted and refused to see her and the baby. It was reported that all day and late into the night he lay out in the tall grass, among the horses that were picketed behind the cousin's tipi, and watched to see who went to call on Blue Bird. When this was rumored around, people laughed at him. "How shameful, to pout like a woman," the men said. "He has always been a queer fellow . . . without close friends . . . even as a boy he had none. . ." "His kind do not take to fasting or warfare—but if at least he were a tolerable hunter."

But neither the disapproval of the older men nor the ridicule of his contemporaries spurred Star Elk to be more dutiful as a husband. If anything, the effect was to make him more and more active in finding ways to hurt his wife. He reached the limit when he decided to "throw her away publicly."

During a great victory dance, attended by many visitors from neighboring camp circles, he waited until the crowd was biggest, and then, at an intermission, he forced his way in, snatched one of the highly decorated sticks used by the drummers, and stood motionless, holding it high. That was the way to gain an au-

dience's full attention when one wanted to take part in the ceremonial give-away. Only persons of social standing were qualified

to do this, because of their past record of hospitality, generosity,
war achievements, or the like. But here was Star Elk, who had no
such record. The crowd waited in silence. What was this fellow
going to do?

Arrogantly he held the stick high for one dramatic moment
and then cried out, "This is that woman! Whoever needs a woman to fetch his fuel and water can have her!" He flung the heavy
drumstick into the crowd. Fearful of being struck, the people
pushed back in waves. Nobody scrambled for the stick. He knew
nobody would; all he wanted was to hurt and shame Blue Bird—
and that he did.

It was a foolish and uncalled-for act but wholly characteristic.
Instead of enhancing the man, as it might if he had cried, "This is
a horse for the needy!" what he said only lowered his already low
standing. Moreover, Star Elk had insulted a victory dance.
"Throwing away a wife" was a custom, to be sure, but this was
not the place. If it must be done at all, it should be at some social
dance where the mood was properly light and reckless. Even
then it was a custom shunned by men of standing, who considered it beneath them to air their emotions publicly. The way to
leave an unfaithful wife was to send her away or to walk out of her
life without so much as a backward glance. Only vain and weak
men gave vent to their temper in public as Star Elk had done. It
was also wrong because Blue Bird had not been unfaithful, and
this was generally known. Star Elk not only succeeded in losing a
good wife and making a fool of himself; he earned such public
disfavor that he could not remain in the camp circle. He left
immediately, his destination unknown.

Naturally, Blue Bird was hurt by that undeserved public insult. But she was not nearly so crushed as Star Elk had intended
her to be. The fact was that at the time of the festivities in the
center of the camp circle she sat in her cousin's tipi, sick at heart
over something infinitely more vital to her even than her honor,
for her baby was dying.

Do what she would, Blue Bird could see that the little Waterlily was growing steadily weaker. All that day she had lain mo-

tionless and refused to eat. Nor did any of the medicinal roots the cousin brought from neighbors help her. When a mother from the opposite side of the circle heard of the symptoms, she came hurrying across with a powdery substance obtained in the badlands and known as "earth-smoke," saying, "Try this next. It always cured my children—a pinch of it in a little water." But Waterlily could not swallow it.

All hope was dwindling fast. In a few hours the child would die unless something was done. Blue Bird must pray. Inexperienced in such holy matters, she nevertheless determined to make some kind of appeal for divine aid. But how to proceed?

Mechanically she thrust her hand into the flat rawhide bag which was her purse and which contained her personal effects and a small otterskin very evenly painted a brilliant red. She had hurriedly salvaged this one object from her father's belongings that fatal day and had prized it ever since. She was sure it must be potent with supernatural power, although her father had never said so. She only knew that he had venerated it above all else. Perhaps, possibly, it would save her baby.

Then she took some smoking mixture of tobacco and red willow bark and tied a bit of it into squares of deerskin, making ten tiny bundles no bigger than her thumb. She knew she must make some sacrificial offerings. Fumbling in her haste, she muttered to herself, "Is that right? Alas, what do I know about it? Those who know tell of the Something Holy—*Taku Wakan*—that has supreme power, but I never understood. It is so remote. What right have I?" All the while she worked in a desperate race with death.

Throughout the Great Plains and the wooded country near the Rockies, wherever the people moved, she had seen here a rock or there a tree with red paint on it, and sometimes a once beautiful blanket or other gift rotting there. She knew what that meant. Everyone knew. Those rocks and those trees had been set apart and consecrated; they were individual altars where people had prayed in times of stress. She was going to make her own altar now.

Taking up the baby and clutching in her free hand the bag with its special contents, Blue Bird left the tipi and walked away unnoticed. On and on she walked, until the noise of the festivities died away and the camp circle was no longer in sight. She stopped in utter stillness beside a great rock in the midst of an empty plain. She studied the rock and saw that though it was well embedded in the earth, the exposed part was nearly as tall as she. It sat apart from any other object as though already reserved for her. It sat on virgin ground. Surely no human had ever stood where she now stood.

She carefully laid the all but lifeless infant on her wrap spread on the ground and set immediately to work, covering one side of the rock with red ocher face paint. Then she carefully spread her father's hallowed otterskin on the top of the rock, like a covering for its head. Next she planted a stick upright in front of it. (The painted side had become the rock's face. She had personalized it.) To the top of the stick, which stood waist high, she tied the ten little tobacco bundles. They were on short strings of uneven lengths and dangled, now clustering and now separating, in the faint breeze that came and went. In descriptions of sacrificial altars where men fasted and prayed in some lonely spot, the essential property was unvarying: one hundred bundles of tobacco. But ten was all she could manage; it would have to do.

The hot summer sun beat down in all its fury. The earth danced in continuous ripples around the rim where it met the sky. Once the baby whimpered weakly. Everything was as ready as Blue Bird could make it. Now for the prayer, which was of utmost importance. "Prayer should be audibly released into the infinite" she had heard somewhere. She began speaking to the Great Spirit (*Wakan Tanka*) in the rock. Aloud but haltingly, fearful lest she not pray correctly, she said: "O, Grandfather, Hear me! Since the very beginning you have been here. Before there were any men you were here. And it is certain that long after we are all gone you will remain. Hear me, Grandfather, and pity me. I want my baby to live."

Right or wrong, that was her prayer. Overwhelmed by her daring, she stood motionless, waiting—for what, she did not know. Presently someone said in her ear quite clearly, "*Hao!*" It was the Dakota word of approval and consent.

Quickly Blue Bird covered her face with both hands and bowed her head for whatever was to follow. A man must have stolen up from behind while she was praying, maybe an enemy, ready to kill her. So be it. Inert and without clear thought she waited a long time, but nothing happened. Very slowly she raised her head and uncovered her face to look about her—behind her and then farther off and finally to the whole round horizon. In that vast emptiness she stood alone.

"I have prayed aright and my prayer is heard! My baby, my baby will live!" A strange lightness, an unearthly joy, seized her, and a new boldness born of confidence swept away all her girlhood diffidence. Holding her hands to her mouth like a trumpet, she first called out, then shouted, and finally screamed her enraptured thanks: "Grandfather, you have made me thankful!" Screaming this over and over until her throat ached, she whirled about, throwing her voice in all directions in a frantic aim to reach the whole of space with her thanks.

But that sort of elation could not last. Soon enough she was back to reality and began to contemplate her unhappy lot. Through no fault of her own she had just been cruelly shamed in public. It was so merciless, so unfair. Feeling sorry for herself, she wailed aloud. In the customary way she addressed all her dead relatives in turn, her parents, brothers, aunts, and uncles, ending with the forlorn question no one can answer, "Where have you gone? Where have you gone?"

It was always good to let sorrow out and bad to hold it in. She felt much better when she had had her fill of unrestrained weeping. She dried her eyes, fitting the base of her palm into her eye sockets as all women did. She picked up her child, but its limp body no longer distressed her as she departed, leaving the rare otterskin to be the Great Spirit's forever. To no one less would she ever have relinquished what her father once venerated.

Everyone was at the dancing when she reentered her cousin's tipi. She was glad it was vacant, that she would not have to account for herself. What she had been through was not for common telling. Once more she offered the earth-smoke and Waterlily was able to swallow it this time. Gradually the infant seemed not to be in such pain as before. She fell asleep and after a while was recovered. Blue Bird was not surprised. She had prayed for that and had her answer already.

Elated about her child, she heard almost without emotion that visitors from another camp circle had recognized her old grandmother as one of the family who had never come back, and would take the news of her and her granddaughter back home. "Your grandson Black Eagle has long mourned for you," the grandmother was told. "As soon as we get home he will be coming for you." And so he did, and at last Blue Bird, her child, and her grandmother were back where they belonged, where their many relatives welcomed them with tears of grief for the dead and of joy for the living.

CHAPTER 4

Any family could maintain itself adequately as long as the father was a good hunter and the mother an industrious woman. But socially that was not enough; ideally it must be part of a larger family, constituted of related households, called a *tiyospaye* ("group of tipis"). In the camp circle such groups placed their tipis side by side where they would be within easy reach for cooperative living. In their closeness lay such strength and social importance as no single family, however able, could or wished to achieve entirely by its own efforts.

In the atmosphere of that larger group, all adults were responsible for the safety and happiness of their collective children. The effect on the growing child was a feeling of security and self-assurance, and that was all to the good. Almost from the beginning everyone could declare, "I am not afraid; I have relatives." To be cast out from one's relatives was literally to be lost. To return to them was to recover one's rightful haven.

It was to such a haven that Blue Bird finally came back. It was where she belonged, and where her child belonged. It was important for her daughter to grow up with backing, in informal association with the girls—her cousins and sisters—and in a respect relationship with her brothers and male cousins, who would stand back of her, ready if she should need help.

There was every reason for Blue Bird to rejoice, but at first she wept several evenings in her tipi and women relatives came in to weep with her, then to dry her tears. She wept because now at last she knew for sure that her parents were dead. "If only I had seen them, too, lying with arrows in their backs, I would have got used to it long ago," she told her old grandmother. "But I always imagined them to be back here waiting for us."

"Now you know, child. So accept it and try to be happy always. With your child and your relatives, what more should you ask?"

However, the few years since they had left the camp circle had wrought considerable change in their larger family. Some had gone to live far away among their spouses' people; others who had been away had returned with their families, in some cases bringing a retinue of their husband's or wife's relatives. Except for these newcomers, all the grownups were familiar to the old grandmother, but Blue Bird had forgotten some of them and had to get reacquainted with many. Yet she remained in her tipi day after day until her grandmother said to her, "Grandchild, go about and see everybody; they are all glad you have returned."

But Blue Bird was reluctant. "Grandmother, you go visiting and bring me the news. And as for my seeing our relatives, you know that there has been no stop to their coming to welcome me and bring me courtesy food. I think it is better that way—for them to come when they wish, for me to be here to receive them. You see, Grandmother," she went on, "Because I was bereaved and then shamed in public during my years away, it is more becoming to me to be quietly happy when relatives come than to hurry out to interrupt their lives. You know what they say of one who does that, 'like a dog greeting familiars,' rushing at them too eagerly before sensing their mood and situation—perhaps they are upset, perhaps they've just had bad news—and 'leaping up their frame' as an untrained puppy will, soiling the gown with its clumsy fat paws. No, I don't care to be a puppy, even a friendly one."

"I suppose you are right, and anyway we have much to keep us busy here, what with all the meat your brothers and cousins are bringing to us. It was your cousin Black Eagle who started that, by reminding them of their duty as your male relatives. Black Eagle, my first grandson! He was manly, even as a boy, and now wise enough to lead our group. You are fortunate to be in your cousin's care, granddaughter."

"I know it. But I feel I hardly know him yet. I only barely remember how he looked as a young man, and the time he married and went south to live in his wife's camp circle. I was around nine or ten at the time, I guess. And now he is back to stay. I met his wife and we exchanged gifts, but the rest of his family I have yet to see."

"Yes, your cousin has returned and is the recognized head of our *tiyošpaye* now. My little Black Eagle!" the old woman lapsed into memories and tears came to her eyes. Wiping them away, she said, "And his relatives of marriage grew so fond of him that they all followed him here and will stay with us always. The parents are 'child-followers,' but their child's husband as well as their child drew them here. Altogether, the number of your cousin's wife's people living here is said to be seven or eight, including children."

Blue Bird did not know it yet, but this was the family with which she was to be allied for the rest of her life, this outside family, rather than one of the same blood as she. But they were still strangers. It was through a friendly little boy who took a special interest in the winsome Waterlily that she came to know them intimately.

The months passed unnoticed, with the daily activities of the relatives and with the ever-changing Waterlily for a preoccupation, and almost before Blue Bird realized it, her child was in the creeping stage, very active, into everything, and requiring constant watching. But one day when the grandmother was out and there was outside work for Blue Bird to do, she placed Waterlily in the center of a huge spread-out buffalo robe and barricaded her all around with long, hard pillows of skin stuffed with deer hair. She handed Waterlily her wooden playthings, the ring "teeth-maker" and the little turtle with its entire back worked in colors to simulate the design on a real turtle. In a peculiar sense this was Waterlily's very own turtle, for was she herself not inside of it? Somewhere in the stuffing of down was the bit of withered navel that fell from her shortly after her birth. When she was old enough to wear an elaborately decorated gown, this turtle would be attached to the center back of her belt both as an ornament and as a talisman ensuring long life to her. Until then it was a toy.

In no time at all Waterlily had lost all her trinkets in the shaggy fur and tossed her beloved turtle overboard and then climbed quite easily over the pillows to retrieve it. But on the way she stopped to put a bit of charcoal into her mouth. Luckily, the fireplace was cold. She first examined the charcoal minutely, while a little boy of perhaps six years stood watching her at the entrance, smiling but anxious, seeing what she was about. The instant she took the charcoal to her mouth he moved swiftly to her and fell on one knee, coaxing her to give it up. Waterlily quickly clamped her lips together—for keeps.

"Ah! That's bad. Here, spit," he entreated her, cupping a hand under her chin to catch it. She looked at him genially and her round cheeks curved up in friendliness, but her mouth remained tightly pursed. "Well," he said, "I'll make you laugh and then you will open your mouth." He made funny faces and funny noises while the child stared at him in wonder. No use. He must try another tack. He would be a wild pony.

Like all little boys, he loved horses and knew their actions well. He could imitate them, in his own fashion. Suddenly he was a most spirited one, a wild bucking horse that could throw and maybe even kill his rider. He assumed a four-footed position and jumped unbelievably high, straight up, and landed on all fours in almost the same spot. Then he reared; he raised his forelegs high; he humped his back menacingly and turned round and round very fast. Let any rider try to stay on!

Waterlily was charmed but she did not give up the charcoal. Maybe she had already swallowed it. But try one more thing. The boy stopped directly before her and looked at her fiercely and then shook his wild, disheveled head from side to side and up and down. Finally, breathing very loud, he neighed just like a horse. It was the neighing that did it. Waterlily screamed merrily and the charcoal fell out.

From that day on the two children were fast friends. The boy came to see her often and played with her, patiently sitting by and picking up her toys, only to have her hurl them out again. It was a game with them.

The boy, who said his name was Little Chief, was an appealing child with gentle ways that pleased Blue Bird. She might have guessed what she later learned, that he was "grandmother raised," for his language was precocious and amusingly quaint, copied from the talk of elderly people, who often used obsolete words and phrases. He used his kinship terms readily and well, a sign of good manners. Obviously he had been carefully trained, as only painstaking grandparents could train a child—with quiet suasion. "That is not done, grandchild," they said quietly, or "Nobody does that," meaning "and neither ought you." No cross words, no whipping, just those simple words of correction, in kindly tones, were remarkably effective. The very calmness of grandparents soothed a child and made him inclined to obey.

One day the children went wading after a rain. Meantime Blue Bird took a pattern from the boy's moccasins left in her tipi and amused herself by making a pair of handsome moccasins for him. When next he came to play with Waterlily there they were, waiting for him in the honor-place opposite the tipi entrance, all embroidered in bright red and yellow and violet porcupine quills that made them very gay. Little Chief stared at them until she said, "Try them on; I am sure they are just your size." And as he did so she said, "I am sure Waterlily must have made them for you, because she was saying, 'I'd like to make some moccasins for Little Chief because he is so good to me.'"

The boy knew she was joking lightheartedly though she spoke quite seriously. Mothers often did so—putting words into a baby's mouth before it could speak what they would themselves say. It was a custom. His grandmother used to do the same thing. He was speechless with delight but at last he managed to say, "I will show them to my grandmother," and slipped out of the tipi, smiling shyly.

Not many hours later the mother-in-law of Black Eagle, a tall, vigorous woman of middle age, came to see Blue Bird, bringing her some special delicacies. With complete deliberation she settled herself in the caller's space, immediately to the left as one entered the tipi, and calmly and methodically wiped the dampness from her brow, cheeks, and neck, remarking what a warm day it was. Blue Bird sat waiting.

When Black Eagle's mother-in-law was ready, she began talking thus: "I have come to see you because I have something to say. To make moccasins for a child is not only to honor him but to honor his people also. His grandfather and I are deeply touched that you should do this for our little one who is our very heart. What though he is an orphan who never so much as sampled his mother's milk, and whom we have raised with great difficulty? Even so, or just for that, we have tried to raise him with honors— with feasts and with gifts to others in his name. And so, because you have honored him, a stranger to you, my old man [long-married women often fondly referred to their husbands thus] sends this message. He says, 'Among my horses is a beautiful white mare three years old. From this day on it is no longer mine. It is that little girl's.'"

It was Blue Bird's turn to make a formal answer. "It was a simple thing I did, because he played so nicely with my child. It was nothing. But it gladdens me to have your husband's message. You see, I too like my child to be honored. Doubtless you have already heard of my sorrow because of her father's unfair treatment of me. Single-handed I am trying to raise her with such honors as I am able. Therefore whoever honors her with a gift honors me."

After that, the two women chatted pleasantly without asking personal questions. It was bad manners to be curious. "I will remain silent; when and if she chooses she will tell." Usually the very things one would like to know would eventually come out in the conversation, unless they were secrets purposely withheld.

Blue Bird had wondered about Little Chief—where he came

from each day and who his parents were and whether or not he had brothers and sisters. Before the visit was over she knew all about him and much more. The mother-in-law of Black Eagle discussed her children quite openly. "I have three," she said. "The eldest is your cousin's wife and her name is First Woman. Her sister, who also lives here, is Dream Woman. You have already met them both. Dream Woman and her husband have two girls, named Leaping Fawn and Prairie Flower. You have seen them playing about.

"I shall tell you more about my daughters. First Woman, you will find, has a soft heart but it does not show. Really, she is a tender grouch. From habit she speaks too directly and sometimes she wounds. Now, her sister is very different. Always she was a quiet girl and even now nobody knows what she is thinking, for she never has much to say. But she is kind, inside and out. She too, like you, does very beautiful art work with porcupine quills. Yes, she has great ability, supernatural ability everyone says.

"When your cousin decided to come home and bring his family, we all came and now this is our home."

Blue Bird hoped she would account for Little Chief, but she said no more about him until she was preparing to go. Then she said, as if by the way, "I have a son also, you know. Little Chief's father, Rainbow. How I wish he would return."

"Is he living elsewhere?" Blue Bird thought she ought to ask.

"He lives nowhere. He is a rover. Right now I think he is staying with some cousins in a far-off camp circle. So restless he is. When his young wife died in childbirth, he went away. Oh, he returns now and then, but never for long. We—his grandfather and I—have cared for our grandson all his life."

"And how well you have cared for him," Blue Bird said sincerely. "We are great friends now, you know. He comes to see us regularly and it is good to have him."

"Yes. And it gladdens us that he has you and your little girl for his friends. Thank you again for being nice to him."

And with that the woman departed. Her name was Gloku, which means "She comes home bearing her own"—a reference to children. That evening, when her old man came in from his daily confab with his cronies, she confided in him. "I cannot get her out of my mind," she began. "She is as nice as she is pretty."

"That so?" he said, indifferently, not even bothering to ask who.

"I speak of course of the lately arrived cousin of our son-in-law."

"Ah, yes," and the old man dismissed the subject.

But a woman with a plan is persistent. Later, as they prepared for bed, she tried again to plant her idea.

"Old man, our son should make an end of his wandering one of these days."

Her spouse yawned. "He should indeed. I am getting too old to hunt or tend the horses." Thus settling the question, he turned laboriously toward the tipi wall to sleep, coughing and groaning from habit. Almost at once he was snoring away.

"Stupid old thing," his wife said under her breath, "if I had a knife handy I could hack him"—knowing she never in the world would, for they were a happy pair.

But before Blue Bird could even think of remarrying she was to lose her faithful old grandmother. The woman had aged noticeably in recent years. Though she was never actually sick she was growing too feeble to do anything. For that reason both Blue Bird and Black Eagle had forbidden her to go after water and fuel any more. There were others in the *tiyošpaye* still active and able to supply all the tipis with such necessities. There was no need of her doing so.

Blue Bird said to her, "Grandmother, I know you are happiest when you are working, but why don't you visit with your old friends instead, now. Everyone wants you to take things easy." And truly the old woman began to find it her greatest pleasure to sit with some aged contemporary and talk all day. There was nothing like the mellow society of those who knew and remembered and loved the same things. There they would sit, alternately indulging in reminiscences and then in quiet and deep meditation. Suddenly one would startle the other out of her reverie by asking with the urgency of the immediate, "Just how was this or that feast (or ceremony) carried on, cousin? Do you recall?" And the other would arouse herself and consider the question with serious concentration as though it mattered, some trivial detail of bygone days, of no possible interest to anyone else alive.

All summer this went on until one day, after a severe storm, the old grandmother was found lying dead in the woods, a sharp stick driven deep into her temple. Evidently she had been struck down by a dead branch that gave way in the high wind. So, after all and unknown to anyone, she had gone wood-gathering again after she had promised to leave off. The lifelong habit had been too strong.

It was at her burial that Blue Bird first saw the man who was to become her second husband. Rainbow, the father of Little Chief, had returned for another visit that day and had immediately taken charge to spare his brother-in-law, who was mourning for his grandmother.

The tipi where the dead woman was laid out in ceremonial dress was the scene of continuous wailing. From everywhere women came to weep aloud and were given presents for coming. Men came too, but did not wail. The younger men paid silent tribute simply by coming, but the old men left the death tipi and sang dirges outside long after, and the blend of sounds—of wailing and of singing—made the surroundings dismal enough to be satisfying to the bereaved and complimentary to the deceased. "Do you remember her passing? It was so fitting, so many were moved to mourn her," women would recall in afteryears. But when men bore away the body for burial only Blue Bird and a few close relatives followed, for in those days a funeral was no public function. A scaffold had been set up on a knoll within sight of the camp circle but remote enough, and on top a platform for the body.

Despite her sorrow, Blue Bird could not help seeing the stranger working with the other men. He knew what to do every instant. When it was time to mount the scaffold he did not wait to be asked or shrink from the responsibility until someone else should assume it, but sprang lightly up onto the platform and proceeded to do what must be done, with sober efficiency. It was his sureness and smooth timing that she particularly appreciated.

No awkward pauses to confer on what to do next, who must do it, and so on, which could take the dignity from a solemn hour.

When the shrunken body encased in a buffalo hide was hoisted up to him, the stranger received it from the men below and laid it gently in position, as though it were the body of a child. Then without haste he placed around the body the few simple belongings the old woman was to take with her, and at the last he covered body and platform with a great hide, carefully, while those below waited with coils of braided thong to bind the whole together as one, securely, to withstand the wind.

So sympathetic yet businesslike he was, so mature. By comparison the peevish Star Elk whose childishness had made life insufferable to Blue Bird seemed even more inadequate. But Blue Bird must bring her wandering thoughts back to the immediate. It was not easy. As for the stranger, Rainbow, he worked with such concentration, was so indifferent to those about him, that if the very attractive chief mourner affected him at all, none could see it. None could say he so much as glanced at her.

But one evening, after a long day of traveling to another location, as Blue Bird was putting up her tipi where she now lived with only her child, Rainbow came by and offered to water her two horses along with his own and his father's, since the young boys of the group, who usually helped her, had not yet come in. At dusk he brought back a rope he said he had not needed after all, and the two chatted over simple and impersonal things. Gradually he brought up what was on his mind, as was evidently his way.

"I have something to ask you. It may or may not appeal to you. But however it strikes you, it is for you to say, and that will settle the matter for all time. If you say no, then I shall never again bring it up. For, look, we are no longer children; we know our own minds. I will never offend you by attempting to change yours for you by urging, or by tricks such as young men sometimes use. I am too old for that."

Blue Bird knew exactly what he meant. He wanted to marry her. And that was perfectly legitimate, for he was her cousin's wife's brother, and a marriage with him would have tribal sanc-

29

tion. But she did not express herself at once, and they talked again of other things. Sometime during their chat he said that when the people reached the spot where they always hunted in the fall, he was going out after deer.

When he turned to walk away, she said softly, "Did you say you were going hunting?" He swung around and replied, "Yes. I said that." "Oh." He had not gone many steps when he heard her call, "I am going with you." And that was her acceptance. "All right," he said, "if you really want to." Going home he laughed a little in triumph. It was all they said but it was enough. Blue Bird had consented to become his wife, for under no other terms did a woman go hunting or camping in the sole company of a man not her husband.

Next morning Rainbow and his father sat on the men's side of the fire in the tipi while his mother prepared their morning meal. After a time she said, "Why so silent? Can't you two make a little talk while I am busy? Is someone dead that you sit speechless?"

That, evidently, was the old man's cue. He cleared his throat and began, "Well, well, well! So Little Chief is off again so early. What ails that boy, anyway? Has he lost all taste for his own tipi? It seems to me he is eating even his morning meal away from home."

His wife's turn. "It is because he likes to play with that little girl. He can't wait to go over there. And her mother is so kind to him."

Rainbow rose to the bait. "What little girl, Mother?"

"Why, son, the child of your brother-in-law's cousin, a cute little girl she is, too. That cousin whose grandmother died not so long ago." As if Rainbow did not know. And then his mother, no longer able to hold back, came straight to the point. "Oh, son, she is a fine young woman. I confess it—I covet her for my daughter-in-law. It is her babies I would happily carry about on my back." And swiftly she enumerated Blue Bird's assests: she was beautiful, she was virtuous, she worked efficiently, she had such pleasing ways.

The father too was talking along the same lines, having chimed in somewhere in a blundering effort to reinforce his wife's arguments, until both old people were talking incoherently at once. It was plain she had been coaching him carefully for this moment but that he had not learned his lines well.

Rainbow laughed aloud. "Just what are you two trying to say?" he asked. "Don't go picking a wife for me; I can get my own." As he was leaving after their meal he stood halfway out the door and remarked, "By the way, Mother, you used to have a little travel tipi."

"I still have it. Why?"

"We shall need it when we go hunting, that woman and I." And then he walked on, leaving the crafty old pair bowed with chagrin. Neither said a word for a time. All that work, all that anxious maneuvering, for nothing—it was amazing! It had already been settled without them. And to think how they had discussed it and planned and argued and even come close to blows over the subtlest way to bring it about.

The old man looked up from under his eyebrows and grinned foolishly. "Well, wife, we were not so clever. The joke is on us this time."

"So it is, old man. But the real matter is that everything is as we wanted it. That is the thing to rejoice over," she said, and he agreed thoroughly.

CHAPTER 5

Two more days of traveling brought the people to their destination in the vicinity of Box Butte, where it was planned that they would remain for a time before going into winter quarters, so as to enable the men to hunt deer.

Box Butte was well named. It was a solitary rectangular elevation rising tall and clear above the surrounding land, so prominent that on clear days it could be seen two or three days' journey away. The land south of it, where the camp circle was to be made, was smooth and appeared to be level, though in reality it sloped very gradually toward the river that ran eastward on the south. It was an ideal campsite, offering the three requisites for a camp circle—thick grass for the horses and plenty of wood and water for the people.

Farther to the south, beyond the river, were other buttes, shaped much like Box Butte, as nearly perfect rectangles as though they had been made with a rule, but smaller, each one curiously aloof from the rest. The hand that set them around had been guided with taste, you might say. All alike yet at the same time so scattered as to avoid monotony and in a manner not to block out the landscape. One could see between and past them into long distances. Men were grateful for that. It was good for the eyes to look long distances occasionally.

As soon as their tipis were up, the small hunting parties of congenial companions began radiating from the circle into the wild country farther out. For Blue Bird and Rainbow this was their marriage trip as well. They expected to be away many days and to return with enough meat to supply their immediate relatives, the families of Rainbow's parents and his sisters, First Woman and Dream Woman.

As a courtesy to their new relative, Blue Bird's mother-in-law and two sisters-in-law had prepared everything for her trip and packed the small travel tipi and other camping needs on the travois platform behind the horse that dragged the poles. Blue Bird rode that horse while Rainbow rode a faster one, though he held it in check to the pace of the more plodding packhorse so that the two might ride side by side and accustom themselves to each other. At intervals Rainbow rode out for a quick survey of what lay ahead before they came to it. All travelers did this as a precaution.

Blue Bird had no idea where they were going but her new husband had in mind just the place. His people had returned to this campsite regularly every two years as far back as he could remember and he and other youths had often explored the surrounding country. He had in mind a certain spot hidden down a deep valley, close to a stream. It was always peaceful there and solitary. It would be an ideal spot for a tranquil stay. They would make their tipi under the tall cottonwoods and watch the golden leaves glisten in the sunlight. There only nature's sounds would reach the ear—the murmur of the water, the twitter of birds overhead, the call of coyotes in the hills—all pleasantly new and wild.

Back home Waterlily did very well without her mother. Already she was used to playing in Little Chief's tipi, and now she slept and ate there. From now on it was going to be as much her home as the tipi of her mother and new father. At night she slept on a tiny pallet laid at right angles across the head of the grandmother's bed, while her companion, Little Chief, who was now her brother, slept near his grandfather, on the men's side of the tipi, beyond the central fire.

At every meal the grandmother served the children first and then any adults present, including guests. It was the custom to put children first in all things. And as they ate she gazed fondly on them and murmured from time to time, nearly unconsciously, "Come now, grandchildren, eat. Eat so that you will soon grow tall and strong. Eat first and then play."

Waterlily was a rolypoly and needed no urging, but Little Chief, who was tending to slim down of late, ate his meals desultorily. Often he forgot to eat at all, remaining outside at his play. This worried the grandmother, Gloku, and she never missed a chance to speak of it so that she could then explain it away. "My grandson does not eat, though I urge and urge him. He is getting tall now. That is why. When children suddenly shoot upward they will not eat no matter what you say. I guess everyone knows that."

This was purely in self-defense, for skinny children were a reproach to their parents. Women sometimes said of such a child, "Just look at him! Poor thing, he must have fathers and uncles who are stupid hunters, or lazy. His womenfolk must be stingy with food. Ah, the poor child." She had said it herself about other puny children. Now imagining it said about Little Chief made her uncomfortable.

Waterlily was suddenly surrounded with so many new relatives, all making a fuss over her, that it was quite bewildering after her quiet life with only her mother in their tipi, but she soon took it in stride. From that day when Little Chief came to visit her, the two children had been as devoted as though they were brother and sister, and now they were really that and it was no different. In spite of the gap in their ages they always played happily together. Little Chief took much credit from the fact that

Waterlily learned to walk under his tutelage, and now he was trying hard to teach her to talk. It was high time she did, being nearly three winters old, yet she preferred to remain mute. This distressed the boy greatly, and he complained to his grandmother, "I don't think my little sister is ever going to talk. I think she is going to be like Ieśni [Doesn't Speak], the old man who has to talk with only his hands because he refused to learn when he was little. I don't want that for my sister."

"You must be patient. Waterlily has a voice and she will talk soon, when she is ready. You shall see. No doubt she is teaching herself in her mind and trying out new words where nobody can hear her. She does not want to make mistakes and be laughed at. As for Ieśni, he could not talk because he had no voice," his grandmother told Little Chief.

And she was right. Suddenly, overnight as it were, the child was talking, glibly and well, to the surprise of everyone. Little Chief was triumphant. "I guess she was learning in her mind all the while, when I pointed to you and said, 'Grandmother,' and to the puppy and said, 'Dog,' and to the pony and said, 'Horse.' She was learning because I was teaching her." "Yes, you were a good teacher," his grandmother assured him.

Gloku was herself an excellent tutor. She had trained her own children well, so that they had good manners and were respected in the tribe. Then she had helped with her grandchildren's training and now she was starting in again with Waterlily.

The first thing to learn was how to treat other people and how to address them, she said. You must not call your relatives and friends by name, for that was rude. Use kinship terms instead. And especially, brothers and sisters, and boy cousins and girl cousins must be very kind to each other. That was the core of all kinship training. But Gloku did not lecture all the time. Instead she stated the rules of behavior toward one another and pointed out examples. When the right opportunity came up she never failed to take advantage of it.

For example, there was the time during her mother's absence when Waterlily in high spirits flung a handful of dirt into Little Chief's face and was sharply corrected for it. They were playing with their cousins, Leaping Fawn and Prairie Flower, when it happened. Waterlily had meant no harm, certainly. She was only trying to be funnier than the rest, who were having a hilarious time of it. But when her grandmother spoke suddenly in warning, it frightened her, and she began to cry and scream in sympathy when she saw the tears streaming down her brother's face from the stinging hurt.

"No! No! Don't do that, grandchild, ever again. It is not done, and he is your brother. One must not hurt a brother!" The severe words were entirely unexpected from the always gentle grandmother. But in afteryears Waterlily could say that this was the only time she was stern with her. Turning to the boy, his grandmother said as sharply, "Do not take on so. Your sister meant no harm, you know that. She is too little to understand that it would hurt. See how your crying causes her to be unhappy. For shame! You should restrain yourself at all costs for a sister's sake—and for a girl cousin's, too," she added. Might as well teach the whole lesson at once. "You are big enough now to know that a brother does not embarrass his girl relatives but strives only to spare them and make them happy; this I have told you often already. Now go and wash out your eyes."

And so she settled the matter by first correcting the children and then explaining why. And then she took them to the creek to play and soon they had forgotten the bad time and were happy together again.

Both grandparents were patience and gentleness itself. All day long and in the evenings, as long as they were alone, they humored the two children and bore their noisy play with unvarying affection, in the selfless way of grandparents. But when company came the situation was changed. The children sat off to one side and played quietly there as they had been told, so as not to disturb adult conversation. They learned to do this from one another, the younger ones copying the older ones. Children were not actually repressed, but they soon learned to repress themselves, when they saw that it was the approved way for them. If a little one in their group was too young to understand, the grownups always corrected the older children instead. That was the general practice.

Gloku was especially skillful at this and Little Chief learned to cooperate with her for Waterlily's sake. One evening when there was an important man visiting the grandfather, Waterlily made a disturbance by laughing and screaming merrily at the shadow pictures the older children were making on the tipi wall to amuse her. Each time, the grandmother called gently to them, "Play quietly, grandchildren," addressing them together as though she did not know where the fault lay. But when that did not suffice she turned on Little Chief and deliberately blamed him. Waterlily was too little to be reprimanded yet, so he must take it for her. In time, when this happened often enough, she would realize and improve so as to spare her brother. In time she would learn, and this was the grandmother's way of teaching her—by indirection, by examples of correction aimed at someone older who could take it.

"Play quietly, Little Chief," Gloku said. "You know better than to laugh and scream when there are visitors. And what a racket you are making, anyway! Supposing this were enemy country we were camping in; supposing a scout were stealing up to our tipi in the dark. We should not be able to hear him for all the noise, and he could look in and count our strength. So play quietly now."

Little Chief knew he did not deserve these rebukes, but he was used to the practice and knew why his grandmother employed it. Because he loved his little sister very much he was content to be scolded in her place. He simply lowered his voice to a bare whisper, and when it came time to laugh he put his hands over his mouth and went through the motions of keeping back a laugh that he would not permit to escape. But Waterlily went on being noisy. It would take time.

The child was humored all around. Her new aunt Dream Woman dropped all her work to make playthings for her, a little tipi and tiny bags and other furnishings such as a woman would own—perfect replicas and beautifully decorated with quillwork that women stopped to admire. The tipi was only as tall as the length from her elbow to fingertips, but still too much for Waterlily to manage yet. Leaping Fawn, who was older, set it up for her and placed the furnishings about inside, and the little people one finger long, made of skin. Dream Woman did things like that, quietly making her relatives happy and saying little. That was why she was named Dream Woman, because, like one who dreamed or saw visions of beauty and then remembered them, she worked such designs as nobody else imagined or originated. Women said she had supernatural help or she could not be so skilled in art. Be that as it may, Dream Woman was not one to divulge any secrets though she was often teased to say where she got her designs.

And then one day the children went to pray. The evening before, Dream Woman, having already fed her family, came into her parents' tipi for a little while. They were eating still, but Waterlily was playing with her tipi and her little people, having quickly finished her supper. Little Chief had not yet come in from throwing rocks for distance with other small boys, back of the tipis, though his grandmother had called him several times. But after a little he stood outside the doorway and called in, "Grandmother, we can see a great big man up there, a giant."

"Where is 'up there?'" Gloku asked. "Come in and eat your supper while you tell us all about it."

"But I'm not hungry, Grandmother. And that giant is standing on top the butte—over there, at the sunset end."

His grandfather said, "Nonsense, child. Even a giant away up there you could hardly make out from here. Better come in now. Maybe the giant is only some dirt on your eyelash." And he chuckled at his own jest.

Dream Woman spoke up. "I believe the pile of prayers up there is what my nephew sees. It is such a clear evening that everything is plain. I noticed how close Box Butte seemed as I came in."

And that is what it was. When the boy came in, his grandfather explained it to him. "Child, the pile of prayers is holy. Ever since there were men, I suppose," he began, "they have gone up there to pray and have left their prayers in a great pile, until now it is much taller and bigger than any giant, and that is what you saw." A minute later a thought struck him and he turned to Gloku.

"Old woman, take them up there before we move away, the boy and his sister. It is everyone's right to relate himself to the Great Spirit. Let them do that and leave their prayers."

What he said about Box Butte was entirely true, for Box Butte was a holy hill, a shrine where people went to pray for all sorts of blessings, but mostly for a long, good life. Many made such prayers there and at other hallowed places. They regularly ended their prayers for all sorts of things with the same refrain, "And, Great Spirit (or Grandfather), may I live long," for the Dakotas passionately loved life while at the same time they met death without panic when it came.

The day being pleasant and fair, right after the noon meal the grandmother packed some pemmican into a parchment bag and poured water into a skin container, saying to herself, "The day is hazy and pungent with autumn smoke, very agreeable, not too hot nor too cold. It is a good day to pray. We shall visit the holy hill." She called Little Chief in from play, telling him, "Grandchild, as your grandfather said, we are going up there now" (indicating the direction with a characteristic lift of her chin toward it). "You and your sister shall leave your very own prayers today." She handed him the water-skin to carry, lifted Waterlily up onto her back, and pulled her blanket up over her and drew it tight to hold her firmly in position there. Then she reached for the boy's free hand and they started out.

It proved a considerable walk. Box Butte, always so deceptive, seemed to move back constantly as they approached it. Occasionally Gloku sat down to rest and let Waterlily down to play near her. Meantime the boy darted about everywhere, expending his boundless energy recklessly, visiting now this rock and now that tree to see what was behind it and then racing back, only to dart away again. When his grandmother called that they must be off again, he skipped and bounced about continuously as she got up and put Waterlily on her back once more. It wearied the grandmother just to watch him. And while she plodded up the steep ascent with the aid of her staff, he ran, nimble as a mountain sheep, straight up to the tableland on top and then came running down again to join her. This he did effortlessly two or three times. For Gloku with the child on her back it was hard climbing, yet she would not think of putting Waterlily down, so used she was to carrying grandchildren on her back that they seemed part of herself.

At last they reached the level top of the butte and sat down near the sharp rim of it. From there they traced the river winding its course toward the east, a shining streak that disappeared and reappeared through clusters of trees as it went. "Where does it go, Grandmother? On and on—to where?" Little Chief was always asking questions. She told him that by and by it would empty into the Roiled Water (the Missouri), which men said was the chief of all rivers in the world.

Beyond it they could see many other buttes like Box Butte, more and more purple as they grew smaller and smaller the farther away they were. Looking nearer, they saw their own camp circle in the foreground, going about its business unaware of their watching from their high station. It was like a plaything, a miniature camp circle of little tipis, like Waterlily's, set in a ring, little men and little women moving hither and yon like ants, little horses in a scatter, feeding around the circle.

They had climbed the south side, about the middle of the butte. The pile of prayers was at the west end, the "sunset end." But first they must have their lunch and drink their water. The grandmother touched the children's wrists and faces with water to refresh them and patted some of it on the crown of her own head. Of pemmican, one's own handful was one's sufficiency, so rich and sustaining was it. Each one reached into the bag and came up with a handful of the tawny stuff, which the grandmother had made that morning by parching some very dry jerked meat, then dampening it and finally pounding it with her dull wooden mallet until it was light and fluffy as cotton.

"Come now, children," she said at last, "we shall leave our food and water here till we come back." And so, with the grandmother holding each child by the hand, the three approached the shrine. Innumerable stones were there, of every size and description, each chosen according to the taste of the petitioner. Many were tiny pebbles, baby prayers. Here and there the stones were red with paint, some still vivid, others now dull. The rest had been washed clean of any paint by the snows and rains of many years. It was plain at last why Gloku had helped Little Chief to select a nice round stone on the way, all white and smooth, to bring along. At the same time she had found one for herself and a very small red one for Waterlily that just fitted her palm.

Near the pile she sat down. At once the little girl began backing up to sit on her lap as usual, but Gloku put her off gently. "No, not now, grandchild. You and your brother sit there facing me, for I have something I must do."

They watched her unfold a bit of painted deerskin and spread it out. It contained ceremonial red paint. With a little of it on her fingertips she carefully painted each child's right palm. "Before you handle holy things you must have sacred paint on your hands," she told them. Then she painted their stones and instructed them to place their prayers where they would stay. So, standing on tiptoe, they put them as high up the side as they could reach, fitting them into convenient spaces between the larger stones.

Waterlily did not question anything and allowed the grandmother's hand to guide her. But Little Chief found the whole procedure very bewildering, for never before had anything made his grandmother act so strangely, so solemn and so aloof that she could forget him. Nor could he tell from her face whether this was really in fun, after all, and not so serious as she was making it. Unable to decide which it was, he prudently prepared for either, frowning a little while at the same time smiling cautiously as he placed his stone. His confusion only increased when Gloku turned abruptly away from the pile of prayers and walked a few paces south until she stood at the very edge of the butte, tall and straight and with head tilted back a trifle, and her chest high, and eyes fixed as though on something very far away, beyond the farthest butte. And then came the strangest moment of all. She was calling out to someone there, throwing her voice, half wailing, in a mighty prayer.

"Great Mystery . . . !

"See these little ones . . . !

"They have become your relatives today . . . !

"Treat them as such . . . !

"Pity them; be kind to them . . . !

"Grant them to live long and good lives . . . !"

Little Chief would never forget this—his grandmother's unusual behavior, her prayer in their behalf, and the way she remained standing a long time as if frozen, unaware of her surroundings, oblivious to the brisk wind that whipped her buckskin skirts smartly against her and blew her hair in her face, or to Waterlily wandering off too far, or to Little Chief himself, staring in wonder up into her face. Something had surely come over his grandmother.

But suddenly she seemed to snap somewhere and return to the immediate. Back at the pile of stones she carefully painted her own—her hands were red already—and placed it nearer the top, being able to reach higher than even Little Chief.

They returned to the spot where they had first rested, and ate more pemmican and drank more water. Gloku remained sitting there while the children played, Little Chief hurling rocks into space with all his might, thinking to hit the camp circle maybe. Compassionately Gloku watched the children. "I have done all I can," she said. "If they are to enjoy long life, that is up to the Great Spirit."

As the sun lowered, the day grew cooler and it was time to descend the butte and go back home. The children were reluctant to go, but soon forgot about that, when they found that their parents had returned during their absence, bringing much food for feasting and for their winter's fare. And everyone was happy.

CHAPTER 6

After traveling away from the region of Box Butte for many days, the people settled down into winter quarters in a deep valley with a high ridge on either side. There it was protected and cozy. Let the blizzard do its worst over the deserted uplands, it could not hit them broadside down there, even though they could not entirely escape it.

As usual in winter they dispensed with the regulation camp

circle and broke up into small communities occupying the sheltering bends of the winding creek. The very large *tiyośpayes* preempted entire bends while small groups that were congenial gathered together to occupy others. Thus, a series of villages were strung along the creek, on both sides. To go visiting one must follow the timberline instead of cutting across a common or following a curving line of tipis, as in summer.

It was a most sociable winter, for another camp circle had joined that of White Ghost by prearrangement, thus doubling the number of people. Such an encampment was always to everyone's liking. "That winter it was most agreeable—so many people!" the oral historians would be saying for years to come.

Each tipi was so placed that there was room to build a stockade of willows around it, with a runway between, where it was always somewhat milder than outside the stockade. The willows, set very close together, served as both a shelter for the tipi and a stable for the horses during severe storms. The people always went to great lengths to make their homes secure against winter. The tipi poles were all planted into deep holes, except for the hoisting pole by which the tent was raised. It was left resting on the ground, as always. And the entire framework of poles was anchored by guy ropes fastened to the top. These could be carried around and tied to heavy stakes in case of bad weather to brace the tipi against the prevailing wind. And finally, a single rope was dropped from the top into the tipi and left tied loosely to one of the rear poles where it was out of the way till needed. Then a stake was driven into the center of the tipi back of the fire, and to this the rope was tied very tautly to hold the tipi down solid.

Blue Bird took great pains to make her home both comfortable and ornamental inside, with an elaborately decorated dew-curtain that went completely around the room and was tied to the poles, to the height of her shoulder. It hung straight down and its lower edge was tucked beneath the fur rugs under the bed spaces. The space between the tipi itself and the dew-curtain provided a circular storage place where she kept surplus food and robes. It was always noticeably colder in this storage place than in the tipi. Thus further insulation was provided.

Backrests with fancy robes thrown over them, saddlebags, and other containers filled with the nicer gowns and other apparel, standing smartly around against the dew-curtain, and long, narrow Teton pillows, plain on one side for night and worked with porcupine quills of many colors on the other for daytime— all these touches helped to enhance the tipi. Such touches were a woman's pride, for they reflected her industry in preparing skins and her artistry in decorating them.

On the left side as one entered the tipi was where the men sat, ate, and slept, and the right side was where the women of the family belonged. The space across the back, behind the fireplace, was called the honor-place, for there all special guests were seated. As one entered, the first space to the right of the entrance was for fuel and drinking water, while the corresponding place on the left was for casual callers who dropped in for a little while and did not care to be settled too far in because they must leave shortly.

It was this callers' space where Little Chief sneaked in his pet dog during stormy nights and kept him hidden. Grownups frowned on the practice of letting dogs stay inside and the old grandfather was especially firm in the matter. "Grandson, do not harbor your dog inside," he would say. "It is not done. Dakota dogs should be as hardy as their owners. It weakens them to be kept in." And each time Little Chief would comply, only to repeat the practice when again his heart melted with pity for his shivering dog. Perhaps it was already unfit for storms.

Quite different were his grandmother's sturdy wood-gathering dogs. They were as important and useful as packhorses, eight noble and intelligent creatures that did all but speak. Gloku had provided a small travois for each one and made a set of harness of rawhide for pulling it. All day the dogs stayed on duty, for they knew their responsibility not to stray beyond call. When she announced her intention to go after wood they were ready. "Ah, my friends," she would talk to them, "you never fail me!"

The lead dog was especially fine, a huge wolflike animal by the name of Burnt Thigh, because Gloku got him from the Burnt Thigh, or Brulé, band of Tetons. In the morning she would call, "Burnt Thigh, where are you? Today you and I are going after fuel. Come!"

Soon Burnt Thigh would crawl into the tipi and sit up on his haunches in front of his mistress to be decorated. With her ceremonial vermilion paint she would first make a round circle on his forehead and then a thin line down his nose to its very tip. He would close his eyes and submit willingly, even proudly, to this little rite as though he knew what it meant. "There. Now we are relatives and won't be disloyal to each other," she would say half-solemnly. "Let's start!"

Outdoors the other dogs would be assembled and waiting, their tails wagging vigorously and their feet dancing, all eager to be off. She would harness each one in turn, talking to it all the while and calling it by name as she worked. Soon she would walk away toward the wood with her dogs in single file behind her, often to be gone the greater part of the day. Late in the afternoon she would return, the little procession following her, each dog dragging a disproportionate-looking load of fuel. Unhitching and feeding them was also a ceremony. She offered them food as generously as her store allowed and thanked them in formal speech.

It had been a late fall this year. The weather did not get noticeably colder for a long time even when all the natural indications, like the position of the stars and the behavior of birds and animals, said it should be winter. A great deal of life was still being lived in the open; women tanned hides pegged to the ground outside and men went out daily to hunt small game, while the children found themselves new playmates among the villages nearest their own and joined in games.

Black Eagle's group was an especially happy place. Everyone was delighted over the marriage of Rainbow. His mother was particularly pleased and said so on all occasions, feeling quite sure that it had been largely her doing. "Have you met my new daughter-in-law?" she asked her women friends. "She is a truly fine woman, so capable, and withal so kind, gentle, and respectful to her in-laws! One who knows her kinship obligations deserves nothing but respect in turn."

And then one night Gloku had a dream that for the time at least put an end to her preoccupation with her new daughter-in-law—a dream so vivid that she could not shake it off. She dreamed she stood on a great butte and looked eastward. Far off on another butte exactly like the one where she was, a huge man stood looking at her. She knew him at once though there was a distance of four days' journey between them. He was a certain Yankton Dakota medicine man and diviner who had once treated and healed her father. This man was famous throughout all the Dakota bands because he used no herbs. He was so holy that he healed merely by the spoken word. Everyone revered and feared him.

Gloku and he stood looking at each other, and the thought came to her, "Can it be that the holy man has a message for me?" whereupon the man nodded slowly to indicate yes.

While she wondered what that message might be, four immense crows flew past her in a line, and she said, "Can it be that after four nights I shall be in danger?"

And again the man nodded yes. But now she could see him only dimly, for a sudden fog moved over the land between them. And she said, "Can it be that I shall be rendered invisible?" For the last time the holy man nodded yes.

After that she wakened with a heavy heart and was bothered all day. She went about her duties mechanically until her eldest daughter, First Woman, whom she described often as being direct and outspoken, remarked brusquely, "What ails you today, Mother? You are acting very strangely." But Gloku denied that anything ailed her. "If I tell my dream, it will surely come to pass, by other minds' dwelling on it to induce it," she told herself.

She lived through some wretched hours, and now it was the fourth day, *the* day. "If I can somehow get through this day safely, then I shall be free and I can laugh at that dream," she said to herself. But she was not laughing yet.

She stayed close to people, and though she ordinarily shunned idle gossip she actually sought it now; it was so normal and human. It looked as though she would get by—until a certain old woman who gadded about regularly came to see her and invited her to go and pick rose berries. "Cousin," she said, "I did not come merely to eat and pass the time but to have you go with me to the ravines yonder. You should see the rose berries now, so plentiful and so big and fleshy they are. Let's get in a good supply while we can."

Gloku wanted nothing so little as to venture from home. "Oh, who wants that common stuff?" she said. "Not while we are all well supplied with buffalo meat—the only real food."

Her caller pretended to scold her. "Don't spurn them so, cousin. There always comes a time when the meat is gone and we are glad enough for a pudding of rose berries. And who can ever say when a famine may overtake us?"

Gloku gave in and went with her. It was as her visitor had said: the berries covered all the rose thickets like one continuous red blanket. They were able to fill their containers rapidly and were soon safely back home. Gloku sighed. "Well, that's over and you've had your way. Now sit down and eat some of my best corn cakes before you go."

The old woman was ready enough to eat the delicacy but had no intention of going home yet. "I thought we might also go to the big river to get some real water," she said. "It is so much better than the salty creek water."

And somehow they were again on their way, past several clusters of tipis along the creek that flowed eastward to empty into the big river. After the last camp they still had to cross a lonely stretch of bottomland, where coarse slough grass grew tall and thick and useless all summer, to die each fall, only to send up new shoots each spring until an accumulation of the crops of countless years formed hard clumps that made walking very difficult.

Gloku complained as she went. "What a place to walk, today of all days. I wish I had never come. How headstrong you are!" but her companion feigned not to hear, quite satisfied to have had her way.

They found that the bank was high and steep and they had to make a path of sorts to reach the water. The nights had lately grown more than chilly and thin sheets of ice had formed along the edge. After drinking some water, Gloku hurriedly filled her container and climbed back to wait on the bank, but her companion took her time down at the water's edge. "Hurry up! Let's get home. The sun has already set," Gloku kept urging her in vain.

At last they were starting back when suddenly some terrifying war whoops filled the air as three men appeared on the bank upstream and made a dash for them, brandishing their toma-hawks as they came. "This is it!" Gloku cried. "I was warned of this—run for your life! You wanted so badly to come!" And then, hardly knowing what she did, she grabbed up a handful of sand and tossed it behind her as she ran. Leaping over the huge clumps with miraculous ease she literally flew. Not until she had reached smoother ground did she dare look back. The men had her companion down and were beating and scalping her.

Gloku stopped at the first village and gave the alarm. The men who immediately went out brought the injured woman in and said the enemy had already left without a trace. The woman died that night. For days the members of the soldier societies formed scouting parties and went carefully over the surrounding coun-try, but the first snowfall that night covered all tracks.

In afteryears this was Gloku's prize adventure story. When-ever she told it she began with the graphic dream, which she was sure was a prophecy. And in describing the way she threw sand behind her she would explain, "I was led to create a fog like the one in my dream and it rendered me invisible." She never failed to conclude with an extraordinary report that came out of a neighboring enemy tribe some years later, during a truce. "Some of our warriors claimed that a Dakota woman vanished before their eyes." That, she was morally certain to the day of her death, clinched her story.

That harrowing episode ushering in the winter might have been an evil omen for the days ahead, but it did not turn out that way. With many tribesmen living together and with plenty of food to last the winter, the people looked forward to a good season, and got it. There were always storms and blizzards, of course, but they were milder than on the flats and could be en-dured, as they always had been.

Winter was not the season for great gatherings; there were no big feasts, no ceremonials, little if any dancing. All of those activities were better suited to the milder seasons when the peo-ple lived in camp circle formation with the council tipi in the center. As always, there was still plenty to do. There were the usual winter sports, with target shooting and hurling the wooden snow-snake over the ice or snow as the men's principal games. Bowling on the ice with round stones was for women and especially for young girls. The moccasin game, a guessing game requiring skill in sleight-of-hand, was played by both men and women, though not in mixed groups. It was enjoyed in the tipi during winter though better outside in good weather, when great crowds could stand around and try to follow with the eye the lightning movements of the players' hands as they shuffled the hidden markers back and forth to confuse their opponents.

Indoors, women players in pairs engaged in toss-and-catch with deer hooves and sometimes in the plum-pit game, a favorite of old women particularly. It was something like dice. The tiny markings on the pits and the almost always limited vision of old women, especially in the dark tipis, made the accuracy of the points claimed a matter of doubt. But they enjoyed it anyway; enjoyed, too, occasionally wrangling over the score. In both the toss-and-catch and the plum-pit game, and for that matter the ice bowling and the rest, both players and spectators indulged in betting trinkets.

Boys spun cedar tops on the ice, whipping them to keep them spinning as long as possible. Smaller boys dramatized the old owl myths. Dressing up fantastically and wearing masks to resemble the owl spirit as they imagined him, they went around from tipi to tipi and from camp to camp, dancing. The audiences asked them to foretell the weather—assuming they had come from the north where winter weather was made—and then gave them sweetened corn cakes and pemmican mixed with wild fruits and similar treats. Little girls played their own dramatic games, some with singing, while small tots like Waterlily tried to understand the very simple games outgrown by their immediate predecessors and passed along to them.

Women visited around as they found time during the day and in the evenings congenial men gathered in the tipi of some person of prominence whose personal charm drew others to his company. There they sat sometimes long after midnight, smoking and talking and lunching occasionally amid much laughter and gaiety over funny stories and jokes. All kinds of talent came out. There were those who clowned cleverly on purpose, and those whose behavior, comical by nature, unintentionally sent the company into roars of laughter; those who could entertain by singing, and those who told stories professionally.

Of the last group the most famous was one called Woyaka (He Tells). Woyaka was a raconteur of exceptional skill and had a phenomenal memory. He was known everywhere, in every camp circle, for he sojourned in one or another as it pleased him. When he joined White Ghost's people for the winter everyone was delighted, looking forward to the time when he would come to tell stories, for he went the rounds as the heads of various groups of families invited him.

Meanwhile, in winter no less than in summer, the constants of life went on. Men and women worked, children played, old men sat dreaming of their youth and their past glories in war, and old women fussed over their grandchildren, for whom they would give their life if necessary, caring for them continuously and forgetting themselves in so doing. Always the young people went about subtly, with an eye for one another. And some people were marrying and some were dying and some were being born—all the natural and expectable things that happen wherever humans live together. It was a good winter all around.

The day came when there was great commotion in Black Eagle's group because Woyaka had finally got to them and sat in the tipi of Black Eagle on his special invitation. "It is important to me," that good leader said, "that the children of my relatives sit at the feet of a master and learn tribal lore from him. They must hear the myths and the legends; they must know our people's history, and to that end they must listen to the winter count," he said.

The winter count was a dramatic calendar of years that began with the previous winter and worked back in reverse chronological order. Woyaka was the man to give this, for, it was said, he alone could recite it farther back into the dim past than anyone else—three hundred winters and more. Each year was named after the most important event. Not only could Woyaka name off the years; he could, if asked, give the full story of the event referred to. "They hold a buffalo-calling ceremony," "Many expectant mothers die," "A man afflicted with sores kills himself,"

"A bear spends the winter with people" were some of the arresting titles that made the listeners wish they dared interrupt the

flow of Woyaka's recitation to ask, "What killed the mothers with their unborn children?" or "How cold was it that a bear moved in?" or "Was it from shame or pain that the poor man killed himself?" or "How were the buffalo summoned? By whom? Did they answer?"

There was no denying Woyaka's gift as a storyteller and historian. How he became that, he told his youthful audiences. "Regard me, my grandchildren, and observe that I am very old. I have passed more than eighty winters. Many a man of lesser years finds his eyesight fading, his hearing gone, his memory faulty, while I retain all my powers and remember everything I hear. That is because my grandfather had a plan for me and he never rested in carrying it out. The day I was born he looked on me and vowed to make of me the best teller of stories that ever lived among the Tetons. And to that end he never gave up training me. I was, you might say, my grandfather's prisoner, for I did not have the liberty enjoyed by other boys; I did not go about at random; I did not run with my own kind or engage in idle play.

"Well might you think my childhood was austere, for at any instant and without warning my grandfather would grip me firmly by the shoulder until I winced, he being a powerful man. 'Now tell me,' he would say, 'what was that you heard last night?' And woe to me if I could not give it step by step without a flaw! Gravely he would then tell me, 'Grandson, speech is holy; it was not intended to be set free only to be wasted. It is for hearing and remembering.' Since I did not like to disappoint him I refused to trifle my time away on nothings. If I wakened during the night or too early to get up at dawn, I fixed my mind on rehearsing a new story or in going over what I already knew or in recalling some incident in all its details, just for practice.

"Did other boys find life easy? Could they daydream all they liked and fritter their time away? Then it was because their elders had no plan for them. My grandfather had a plan for me and that was why he had to be stern—to carry it out. In truth I was his very heart, and he was a kind man by nature. But he wanted me to be a storyteller and he spared no means to make me one. 'You owe it to our people,' he would say. 'If you fail them, there might be nobody else to remind them of their tribal history.'

"So determined was my grandfather that he even took me back to the very spot where I was born that there he might pray for me to have a clear mind. It was a long and hard journey and we walked all the way. Whenever I grew weary—being only eight years old—he carried me on his back. It rained every day, but we pressed on.

"The place was called Sandy Bend, on the north side of the beautiful Kampeska [Shell] River flowing eastward, far to the south [the Platte River in Nebraska]. I have visited it since. That lonely day my grandfather and I were the only humans in those parts. We came to the exact spot, on a little hill overlooking the river. It was smooth and hard-packed with white sand, a round spot like the inside of a tipi. The rain stopped and the morning sun came out, dazzling and blinding me.

" 'Come, stand here, grandson, in the very center,' my grandfather said. 'This is holy ground, for it was where you came into life.' And so I stood in the center of the round white spot while my grandfather moved a short distance away and there sent out his cry in my behalf: that I be enabled forever to hold captive everything I heard."

Some men were great warriors, some were seers and some hunters, some doctors of the sick, some workers of miracles and some diviners. It was believed that all such men were holy and that they succeeded in their undertaking in proportion as they enjoyed supernatural help. Of Woyaka the people said, "Surely he must enjoy more supernatural help than any other storyteller, for he is the greatest of them all."

Woyaka was a strange man in certain respects. He did not enter freely in the bantering and good-natured joking that went on about him. His eyes were fierce and searching and he went about with a great preoccupation that everlastingly set him apart and made ordinary men uneasy in his company unless he was telling a story. Then he came to life and both he and his hearers were lost in the things he so skillfully related. Otherwise he walked alone. Ordinary human comaraderie was not for him.

Nevertheless he held a universal respect that was close to veneration. He was showered with gifts and welcomed into any camp circle where he chose to stay for a time. He had no desire for things and promptly passed such gifts as moccasins and wearing apparel to others who needed them more. He seemed to prefer being unencumbered by things other than his mental possessions. People boasted, "Did you know that Woyaka is staying in our tipi at the present time?" Women from everywhere brought such dishes as were considered delicacies for him to feast on, though everyone knew that he ate only to live. Many went further: whenever they wished to act as handsomely as possible, they made a public feast and there announced to their guests that it was Woyaka who was feasting them, though he had had no hand in it. In such ways did the camp circles manifest their appreciation of so famous a man in their midst.

After the evening meal, which the children of Black Eagle's group could hardly eat, so great was their excitement, they hustled around getting ready for their first story hour. "What shall I take to the grandfather?" "What shall I?" "And I?" they asked, pulling on their mothers' skirts to gain their attention. Even Waterlily—copying the older ones as they insisted—wanted something to take along. A gift was no prerequisite. Though Black Eagle would certainly reward Woyaka at the end, however, it was customary to greet newcomers with a gift, and Woyaka was no ordinary newcomer, a fact that the children sensed.

Teton children loved to give. As far back as they could remember they had been made to give or their elders gave in their name, honoring them, until they learned to feel a responsibility to do so. Furthermore, they found it pleasant to be thanked graciously and have their ceremonial names spoken aloud. For giving was basic to Dakota life. The idea behind it was this: if everyone gives, then everyone gets; it is inevitable. And so old men and women preached continually, "Be hospitable; be generous. Nothing is too good for giving away." The children grew up hearing that, until it was a fixed notion.

The girls met in the grandmother's tipi for a final briefing. Always bent on making well-behaved women of them, she directed them thus: "Now, as you enter the tipi where the great man sits, move so quietly as not to attract attention; there are men sitting with him. Say nothing, and keep your eyes well down. At the same time, observe from under the eyelid just where to step. Do not be clumsy and trip over people's feet. It is rude even to step *over* any part of a human's body, even if your feet do not touch it. Go straight to the honor-place and there present your gift." She turned to the eldest granddaughter, Leaping Fawn, saying, "Grandchild, you know the proper side of the fire to walk in on—the left-hand side—and the proper side of the fire to walk out on—the right-hand side. So you lead the way, holding your little cousin by the hand.

"Sit like women. Never cross your legs like men. And be sure to keep your skirts pulled well down over your knees." To Leaping Fawn again, "See that your little cousin, young as she is, does the same. She must begin learning now. Above all, sit up straight; do not loll. Remember that no woman reclines in the presence of men, unless she is too ill to know."

All this had been told the girls many times but it was only by tireless repetition that proper habits could be fixed. Cautiously, as they had been instructed, the girls entered the tipi and approached the guest. One after the other they murmured, "Grandfather, for you," and made their gift. Then they took their places, barely aware of the man's quiet thanks or the exclamations of praise over the pretty gifts—moccasins and such things—from the adult guests present. They were far too busy in seating themselves correctly and tucking their skirts about their legs with only the tips of moccasins showing. And thus they sat all evening, composed and prim and quite different from the pile of irrepressible small boys in continuous motion on the other side.

Leaping Fawn was a well-bred girl with a sense of propriety. "How tractable she is," women said of her often. "Such a good girl!" She was called "good" because she fell into pattern easily, the exact opposite of a girl named Alila, from the neighboring settlement, who had been coming regularly of late to play with the girls of Black Eagle's camp. Though she was likable and friendly, Alila was at heart a young rebel who deliberately broke little rules of etiquette just for the fun of it. "There!" she seemed to be saying, "I've not conformed—and where is the dreadful result?"

Leaping Fawn had her troubles in trying to keep Waterlily still and in the proper posture. Her short legs would not stay flexed right and her skirts slipped up each time she moved, which was often, exposing chubby knees. Fortunately, she fell asleep almost at once, and Leaping Fawn was then free to fix her whole attention on the stories.

"I shall first tell you how our people caught the buffalo in the days before they had horses," Woyaka began. Then he smoked a while in silence, until his youthful hearers were wondering just how, and growing more eager by the minute to find out.

"When the people could not find any meat, when all the deer and other animals conspired to hide, until all food was nearly gone and a bad famine was certain, then they called upon a buffalo dreamer to help them.

"A buffalo dreamer was a man who, when he went fasting on some lonely butte, was visited by the spirit of the buffalo, who promised to be his brother for all time. 'Call me when you are hungry,' he said, 'and I will come. Sing this song I am about to teach you, and then I shall know you.' And he taught the buffalo dreamer a beautiful buffalo song, to be his alone. In afteryears, if another man wished to sing that song to entertain his friends, he must first say, 'This is the holy song of Such-an-one, a buffalo dreamer with greater power.' Then his listeners could not say he had stolen it.

"Now, when the buffalo dreamer had to call upon his brothers, he first made himself ready and worthy to receive power, by purifying himself in the sweatbath, by fasting and praying all night in a special tipi, and by abstaining from all physical appetites, so that he might keep his pending task sternly before him, for that was the only way to be sure of obtaining the gift he sought.

"Next day, all the people went out on open ground, away from their tipis, and there set up the small travois poles that their pack dogs dragged with loads bound to them. These poles were set up as tripods, close together, like the frames of tipis around a circle. Now every woman and child took a place behind this circle, each one armed with a stout club with which to strike the travois poles when the time was right. Meanwhile, all the hunt- ers stood back of the women, with their arrows ready on their bows. And so they stood waiting, hoping, though as yet there was no sign of the buffalo anywhere.

"Then the holy man emerged from his tipi of preparation and made his way toward them. Outside the single opening to the circle he stopped and 'talked mystically.' That is to say, in sacred language he related his vision wherein he and the buffalo spirit became brothers. 'Do you remember? It is I, the man to whom you made that promise,' he said aloud. 'My children are hungry; they cry for food. I have no choice but to trouble you, my brothers. A vow is a vow. Keep it, then!' So he flung out a challenge.

"Then he sang his holy song from his vision; over and over he sang it, and paid attention to nothing but his song, a crying chant that had no ending. And as he sang he walked to and fro in front of the entrance, looking like a buffalo rampant himself, for he was wearing the head and skin of a buffalo and for the time he *was* a buffalo, talking to his own kind.

"And did they come? Most certainly they came. Looming large through the falling snow, they appeared over the hill and headed in a long, black line straight toward the circle. A magnificent buffalo bull led them; with eyes aglare he approached, frightening the people. But they knew they must stand their ground. Without their share of the responsibility the undertaking would fail; everyone must cooperate, for that was where the power finally lay.

"Hurrying past the holy man, who still sang and walked to and fro without seeing them, they entered the circle and began moving in a mass around inside, to the accompaniment of the continuous clatter, clatter, clatter of wood on wood, which the women and children made, striking their clubs in rhythm on the dog-travois poles. The singing of the holy man, the clatter, and the pace of the buffalo never slackened. Meantime each hunter picked out his animal and shot it from over the women's shoulders, aiming to kill by hitting the animal in the right spot. Arrowheads were priceless; let every one count!

"And soon the tribal leaders called a halt. 'Stop! It is enough. Our friends have kept their vow; once again they have given themselves to save us; once again they have extended hospitality to us. Let us kill no more than we need. It is enough.'

"And suddenly all was still, even the holy man's singing. And then, in the deafening stillness, the lead buffalo came to his senses; he had seemed to walk in his sleep before. The next time he came to the opening, which he had passed by time and again, leading the others after him, he turned and went out, and the rest went also. On and on in a single line, as deliberately and surely as they had come, they went until they disappeared over the hill. They knew they would not be shot at from behind, for they and the Dakotas were friends.

"And then came the ritual. The holy man cut off the tip of the tongue of the largest bull, the finest cow, and the prettiest calf, and reverently tied them into a bit of buckskin painted red. These, symbols of the buffalo's sacrifice, were buried while the people wailed ceremonially, as for dead relatives.

"Thus did our ancestors get food, when all else failed, with the help of the Great Mystery. Thus early they learned that man cannot manage alone. And, hungry as they were, nobody touched the animals until the ritual was decently finished. And then there was happy feasting again."

After this, Woyaka repeated some short myths, long familiar to the children, who never tired of them. And then he dismissed them, saying, "That will be enough for now, grandchildren. There will be many evenings that I shall sit here. Whenever you want to hear stories, come, for I have many to tell."

As they rose to go, and while Leaping Fawn was trying to rouse the sleeping Waterlily, Alila startled everyone by asking, "What will they be about, Grandfather?" for Alila never minded speaking out.

"They will be about many different things: of how the birds taught the Dakotas to play; of how West Wind and North Wind struggled for supremacy until West Wind emerged victorious. You shall hear also the story of Iron Hawk, the wonder-man of the east, and of Falling Star, the hero, and of the first man and woman to inhabit our world." He added, with one of his rare chuckles, "And such a time as their son had in managing his wives, Corn-woman and Buffalo-woman! For they were jealous of each other. It is from the son of the Buffalo-woman that we roving Tetons come. Is it any wonder that we love our buffalo brothers who sustain us so patiently? While they live we shall not die."

And the children went home singing, "While the buffalo live we shall not die!"

CHAPTER 7

After such a tame winter the people felt it extra keenly when it suddenly turned very cold toward the end of the season; when blizzard followed blizzard with scarcely any respite. Nobody cared to venture out into the whirling snows, knowing that in weather like this it was not unheard of for even a grown man to lose his way while going from one village to the next. The adults watched their children's every move lest they slip out unobserved and some tragedy befall them. It had happened to children in the past; it could happen again.

Days and days of monotonous waiting passed while both adults and children chafed under the tension. But of course it must end in due time, and it did. Suddenly one morning it was spring again. You could feel the balminess of it. Surer still, you could tell it from those tiny birds called *skibibila* chirping in a brisk, competitive chorus that resounded the length and breadth of the valley. And that always meant spring, for they were the harbingers of it—premature harbingers all too often, for they were frequently caught in a belated blizzard and paid for their early arrival with their lives. But still they came first, and that marked a turning point in the year. It was no wonder that their chirping was hailed with joy.

For this particular year the winter was dead. There were no more storms, no more snow. Each day the sun rose a little sooner than the last, with increasing warmth and brilliance, and old men and women stood outside to greet it with their private petitions as it appeared. In no time at all the snow would be entirely gone.

Already it lay only here and there in dirty patches while in between, the soaked earth looked blacker than remembered after being hidden so long. Now at last the children could be turned loose safely, and they went out through the string of villages in hilarious droves, making the most of their liberation.

For some time now it had been realized that during the summer there would be a new baby in the lodge of Rainbow and Blue Bird, and already his sisters, First Woman and Dream Woman, were busy making handsome portable cradles for the child. This was their traditional privilege as its aunts, and even if other women made one also and presented it as a friendly gesture, it would not have the same significance. Although of course it would be happily accepted, it would not have social importance.

Rainbow's father, whose eyesight had been giving out slowly, was at least able to go about seeking out-of-season foods that his daughter-in-law might relish and Gloku was constantly on the alert for her welfare. Secretly she prodded her daughters to be dutiful toward their brother's wife. "Daughter, set up your sister-in-law's tipi for her when we make camp; drive the anchoring pegs for her. That wooden mallet is none too light," she would say to one of them as they journeyed, when the people were moving about again. To the other one she suggested, "Why not cook enough for your brother's family as well as your own tonight. Your sister-in-law seems tired."

"Grandson," she said to one of the youths of the group, "your uncle is still out hunting and your aunt is trying to care for the horses. You are lively and practically live on horseback anyway. It is nothing for you to drive them to water for her," and that was enough to send the boy off to translate his kinship obligation to his uncle's wife into a helpful deed for her. And thus it went, although actually none of the relatives needed urging. It was a pleasure to help Blue Bird, whose own agreeable and correct kinship conduct toward one and all merited their full consideration.

Such pampering this would be, if Blue Bird would allow it. But she was too wise to demand it—least of all from Rainbow. Women were quick to deride the pregnant woman who wanted to be babied by her husband. "Why," they said, "what is so special about her that she makes such demands? Any woman can be with child if she is with a man." And others said, "You are right. How much more becoming for a woman to be independent."

Blue Bird knew this was the prevailing attitude; that one who expected special consideration, thinking herself unique, was in for murmured criticism. She for one would not invite it. So while she was grateful for the solicitous attention of her husband's womenfolk, she was prepared to face her situation with independence. She knew that if need be she could go through with her ordeal by herself; she had done it once and could do it again. But she also knew she would be well attended here in this group of loyal families, where all the members were ready to stand by her. She was sure of them.

Particularly she was sure of Rainbow's mother. It was her kinship duty to devote herself to a son's wife. She would even scold her own son if she thought him remiss in his care of his wife—no matter who that wife was, no matter how inadequate she might be. That was the role cut out for mothers-in-law, and few women would neglect it, at least in the open, for fear of censure. But as it happened, Gloku was truly fond of Blue Bird.

It was Rainbow's sisters that Blue Bird must be cautious with. She watched herself very carefully, knowing she could irritate them unless she conducted herself with extreme tact. If she should be so stupid as to mistake their tenderness as a personal tribute to herself rather than for what it was—their way of honoring their brother and his coming child—and if she should overstep her bounds by making absurd demands on their brother, they would instinctively shift their loyalty from her to him. "Oh, how she enjoys adding to our brother's normal anxiety," they would whisper, "acting like a baby!"

The sisters could not help it; it was the way they were trained: brothers and sisters must always place one another above all else. Blue Bird knew that in their place she would do the same. A smart wife conducted herself circumspectly so that her sisters-in-law would approve of her entirely and would defend her. If she did so, they could then afford to be very generous in their praise of her: "How fine and mature she is—truly a real woman!" and add even, "I trust our brother realizes what a fine woman he has." But that was only so long as their sister-in-law did not antagonize them. Blue Bird said to herself, "A mother-in-law stands by you. But sisters stand by their brother. You cannot expect them to humor a whimsical wife who gives him needless trouble."

Here then was Blue Bird's delicate role: to accept the attention showered on her by Rainbow's sisters with appreciation and grace, and at the same time with tact and restraint. These intense loyalties between collaterals of opposite sexes were deep-seated, the result of lifelong training. They had been going on long before her time and would continue long after she was gone—as long as Dakotas remained Dakotas and their kinship sanctions endured. Everyone knew and accepted them and aimed to play his or her part within their framework, and then relationships remained smooth.

Gloku now took sole charge of Waterlily and kept her from annoying her mother. But because Gloku was often busy with many things, it became Leaping Fawn's assignment to assist her grandmother by guarding her small cousin and keeping her entertained. That was no small order, for Waterlily had whims of late and was given to whining over everything. But Leaping Fawn was the one to see it through.

Old wives who prided themselves on a thorough knowledge of child behavior explained Waterlily's actions as perfectly normal. "It is always thus. A child whose baby status is about to be usurped by another seems to sense what is coming and to rebel against it by being difficult. Waterlily is acting as must be expected." And whenever adults could gain the ear of the child they whispered to her, "Hush, you must not cry. Why, look at you; you are a tall girl now. Soon your mother is going to give you a little sister or brother. It will cry often because it won't know any better. But you know better; you are tall now. Only babies cry, because they cannot talk."

The boy Little Chief, becoming noticeably less of a child and more of an independent personage, no longer clung to his womenfolk and paid less direct attention to Waterlily. It was doubtful that he had any inkling of the coming event, for he went about strictly with boys his age and interested himself only in outdoor activities with "the crowd." This he did unaware of the subtle steering of him by the grownups into that very direction. At no precise moment did they decide and then announce to him, "It is now time for you to leave off playing with girls. From now on you must play only with boys." That would make him self-conscious, something the people prevented by a cautious handling of adolescents. This was done principally by taking no conspicuous notice of the natural changes in them. For instance, it was considered inexcusable for an adult to laugh at, or even just comment on, a boy's changing voice.

The tribe's concern was that its girls should become women and its boys men through normal and progressive steps without complications. And in the case of boys, this was a peculiarly delicate matter because of the belief that a boy who was allowed to play girls' games and wear female dress was liable to come under a spell that would make him behave in a feminine manner all his life. To guard against any possibility of this, Little Chief had been carefully steered, and now it seemed clear enough that all his inclination was in the right direction. It was well, therefore, to let him go and come as he pleased, and his grandmother and aunts and his new mother, Blue Bird, were quite happy to have him desert them and stay out, except to eat and sleep. By now he was quite able to be independent.

It seemed that he had even deserted Waterlily, but he had not actually done so. Rather he had begun making her needs the drive for his adventures, according to his grandmother's teaching. "Your sisters and cousins depend on you, and you must never fail them," she had said. And so he was beginning to imitate the older men's behavior toward their women relatives, and to dramatize himself as the invincible mainstay of his sister, Waterlily. When he succeeded in killing his first rabbit, he brought it to his grandmother, saying, "This is for my sister's meal." Gloku praised him loudly so that others might hear, perhaps flattering him a little and announcing to all who came by as she was preparing the rabbit, "Just see what Little Chief has secured for his sister!" And they said, as was expected of them for the boy's sake, "Of course. That is as a man should do—look after his sister," or "It is good that he has begun so early to be a protective brother. Waterlily

will not have to worry." All of which was calculated to spur the
boy on in the way he was headed.

But he was, after all, far from arrived. He was in fact still timid
in certain respects, and proved it that morning during the Sore
Eyes Moon (March) when Bear Heart, a brother of Black Eagle,
started training Little Chief and his cousins. Early in the morning
the people inside their tipis heard him making his way towards
Gloku's home, where the five little boys slept in a row in the
honor-place, all being grandsons of her and her spouse. They
heard him saying as he came, "All those who consider themselves male should be out by this time. To such it is nothing to be
cold or hungry."

He entered the tipi and squatted in the callers' space, letting in
gusts of bitingly cold air by holding the entrance curtain gathered
in one big grasp. Glancing icily around the tipi until he saw the
boys deep under their fur robes with only their black eyes shining
wide on him, he glared at them for a long moment as if he
despised them. "What? Are they still in bed?" he appeared dis-
gusted. "Up with you, every one of you! Up with you—unless I
have been mistaken in thinking you were males!"

That cut deeply. To be a female was all right if one was born
so, but for a male to be called a woman was intolerable. The boys
sprang out of bed and stood there shivering in a huddle, waiting
for the worst. It came. Stepping outside quickly, Bear Heart
drew a deep breath and then bellowed, "Now, out with you!"
The naked boys, looking very small and slight, filed out, cower-
ing as they passed the massive warrior, and stood dancing on the
frozen ground so as to keep off it as much as they could, their
teeth chattering in unison.

Bear Heart pointed toward the creek. "Run!" he commanded,
and the frightened boys scampered off, with him following
swiftly. They paused on the bank and looked into his face for the
least sign of mercy, but there was none. "Jump!" It was unimag-
inable, but they knew he meant business; they had no choice but
to obey. Screaming and struggling and crying as they struck the
icy cold water, they swam and paddled about as they became used
to it. In a few moments they were laughing and splashing water at
one another and enjoying the surprisingly easy feat after such fear

of it. By the time their trainer ordered them out and sent them home for a quick rubdown in the tipi, they were ready to give defiant little war whoops—as well they might, for they had won their first big victory.

But it was Little Chief, the youngest of the lot, who was too fearful to jump in and had to be pushed by Bear Heart. His terrifying shrieks brought his grandmother running, with Waterlily on her back, and when Waterlily saw what looked like abuse of her brother, she screamed and cried in his defense. On the way back, once again the grandmother got in a bit of kinship teaching: "Your brother needs to be brave, strong, and fearless. He needs to be ready to do great things. He has just won a victory and it is your place to cheer and sing his praises, not cry."

Any of several warriors in Black Eagle's camp might have assumed the task of training the boys, now that they were ready. But when Bear Heart assumed that responsibility it was all to the good, for he was qualified, by his own record as a warrior, to give an all-around training. An outstanding warrior, he had been through everything, and it was a tenet of the tribe that only those who had themselves experienced difficult things were fit to ask them of others.

By this initial and voluntary gesture, he had pledged himself to spare nothing to make the sons of his sisters and women cousins into brave and worthy men. By bothering with their sons, he was in effect honoring the women of his generation, whom he had been taught to respect, protect, and aid. And although his manner this first morning had been austere and frightening, he had assumed it on purpose.

The grandmothers of the boys, being mothers or aunts of Bear Heart, protested weakly, "Is that not too severe for a beginning, son (or nephew)? Remember, they are still children and unused to shocks. Can't you give it to them a little at a time?"

"A little at a time!" he brushed that away in disgust. "Listen. Do you think any foe is going to be so considerate as to give it to them 'a little at a time'? Certainly not! So let them start at once to take what comes as it comes, in whatever dose or severity." This was by no means the first class of boys Bear Heart had trained, and always his method and guiding principle remained the same.

Ordinarily, uncles were very agreeable and companionable relatives who took enormous pains with a nephew, quietly training him by instruction and by practice to become physically fit and to protect himself, and to hunt and to use weapons skillfully. All of Little Chief's uncles were good to him, even Bear Heart, except during his training, but it was Black Eagle who gave him his first riding pony that spring, not long after his harsh experience in the cold stream.

Black Eagle had left orders. "When my nephew comes in I want to see him." And then he went out to sit on the ground with his men guests to smoke and talk. He was so absorbed in the subject being discussed that it was a good while before he realized the boy had been standing silently behind him. Turning, he said, "Ah, you have come, my nephew. See yonder, there is a pony. He has been carefully broken and is gentle enough for you. But ride him cautiously at first, and slowly, until he and you become friends in spirit."

Then he went back to the group. Little Chief knew he had just been given a pony; it was the usual way of presenting a gift. He was already familiar with that. It was not customary to point out a horse and discuss its merits to someone unless it was intended for him. The boy's thanks stuck in his throat. But, after all, what could he express with mere words? And anyway, Black Eagle had finished with his nephew and was satisfied that the boy was happy; he did not have to be told so. That was the lordly way to give—casually.

Already Little Chief knew how to stay on a horse. His elder brothers and cousins, and some uncles who were themselves still boys, used to take him with them on their ponies to race them, even before he could walk. Later he had ridden alone while they led the pony around. He knew the feel of riding. But this was quite different; here was his very own pony. He could ride him anytime, as he wished. And he would water him and feed him and groom him well.

That first day he hardly dismounted once, even to eat. His aunt Dream Woman humored him by taking him his food to eat on horseback. Just as Black Eagle had said, the pony was entirely tractable and willing to go anywhere Little Chief wanted. The boy almost rode him into the biggest tipis, much to the annoyance of the women relatives sitting inside, who begged him to back out, even while they admired the pony to show Little Chief they were not entirely hostile.

Dream Woman, who was his special aunt, promptly produced some elaborate riding things for him—a bridle, a whip, and a blanket, all worked with brilliantly colored quills as fine as any, so that at the coming celebration he could ride with the other little boys and look as fine as the best. For it was the custom for the young to prance their ponies around the circular parade track in front of the tipis and show off their trappings though seeming quite unconscious of them. Dream Woman had intended her brother's son should not want for decorated things—and she was the artist to make them for him.

That was how it happened that Little Chief, who was now always riding, failed to realize when strange activities were afoot at home; that the womenfolk, with the help of neighbors, had hastily set up a small new tipi in back of their lodge, where it was secluded from the people constantly passing in review, bound for someone's tipi down the line. Had he noticed, he would also have seen two strange women who were being well feasted by his grandmother, Gloku. They were midwives engaged for the coming birth of Little Chief's and Waterlily's baby brother or sister.

During an all-day absence of Little Chief the baby was born, a boy. Immediately the mother was made comfortable, given some soothing brew, and left to sleep while the baby was laid in his two fancy portable cradles, one after the other, just for the formality of it, so that when he was old he could honestly say, "I was laid in two beautiful *postan,* gifts from my two aunts." That would be his subtle way of boasting of the kind of family he was from—a family in which the conventions and kinship etiquette were carefully observed.

Rainbow's father promptly named the child. Taking him in his arms at sunrise, he "let the sun look on his face" and proclaimed, while those within hearing stood silent, "The sun shall hear my grandson's name: Ohiya, the Victor." This name he had chosen in memory of an uncle who was said never to have known

defeat in battle.

All day the visitors came in a steady stream bringing presents for mother and child, for this was an important family. Some day there would be feasts in this child's name and those visitors would very likely be honored with return gifts. It was customary in presenting a horse to give the figure of a horse cut out of rawhide and painted in a color to indicate that of the horse. So when someone brought the baby such a figure painted blue, the onlookers told one another, "Just see! Already on his very first day the baby is an owner of a horse, a blue horse," for blue was the term used to indicate an iron gray horse.

Little Chief, riding in for a bite to eat, was baffled at all the activity and excitement. He heard someone speaking of the new baby. He would have to see. So he tiptoed in when all attention was elsewhere outside and stared at the tiny red face for a long minute, with the intention of slipping away again, unseen. But Gloku never missed anything. "Come, grandson, and see your little brother. He has arrived in a belligerent mood, you know. 'Where is that fellow?' he has been asking. 'I want to see him. What does he have that I do not have? Is he so handsome?' Clearly he thinks himself a rival, so you better stay home and defend your rights."

Such silly talk from his usually sensible grandmother! She knew that he knew the baby could not talk, could hardly even see. Little Chief squirmed under the hand on his shoulder, worked himself away and back onto his horse, and called to Gloku, "Grandmother, let him talk; I'm not afraid of him!" And with that he dug strong heels into his pony's flanks for a quick escape, anxious to get free of such womanish nonsense. "When he gets big enough to have fun with, then it will be all right," he said by way of redeeming himself for his indifference.

Not so with Waterlily. The new brother completely went to her head and she claimed him as her personal property and started playing nurse from the very beginning. She posted herself beside the sleeping infant, looking very big and grown-up beside the tiny one. All day she sat fanning his little face with her fat arm to keep him cool and drive away the flies. Her proprietorship was so real that to humor her, people went through the routine of obtaining permission to see the baby.

Nor did this devotion wane as the days passed. All summer she neglected her little tipi and its tiny people to take care of her brother. When he was warm and fretful she was miserable in sympathy. Now and then she even sat holding him on her lap, if an older person was nearby. She did not try to pick him up, because she was told that "no one did so," meaning of course no one her size. "Little babies sometimes get cross and throw themselves backward. It takes a big, strong person to hold them and protect their back. Old Wandering Man who came to sit with your grandfather yesterday was hurt in that way when he was a baby. That is why his back is humped." Waterlily understood this more or less; at least she knew that it would be bad for the baby if she picked him up and tried to walk around with him. Whatever would be bad for him, that she most assuredly did not want, so she was content to sit by and watch him.

Only once she left her post, and with near-disastrous results. At sunrise everyone had gone to pick the wild plums that were everywhere ready and plentiful. Only Waterlily and her grandmother remained, sitting outside by the campfire, where the grandmother had set out some food for the little girl's breakfast and then continued to cut out moccasin soles of stiff rawhide for everyone in her family. "I can at least have these ready in pairs," she was saying, "and when your mother and aunts find time they can decorate the tops and finish the moccasins for those who need them."

As Waterlily sat eating, still drowsy, her grandmother said, "Grandchild, step into your tipi and fetch your father's whetstone for me. This knife is very dull." As Waterlily went, she continued, "Dear me, every day our knives grow duller, while he spends all his time smoking and talking with his cronies. Will they ever get talked out?" She was complaining about her husband, of course. Spouses did not say "my wife" or "my husband" but simply "she" and "he," and everyone understood.

A startled scream from Waterlily brought the grandmother running and panting to the scene, followed by several neighbors who had stayed at home. A huge snake lay coiled about the baby Ohiya, still asleep in the tipi. Not in immediate contact, to be sure, for Teton infants were always bound in small blankets and laced in with a single long strip of skin so that in case of a raid at night they could be snatched up and so carried along like neat packages. It was the juxtaposition of innocent baby and dangerous snake that was unbearable.

But there was nothing to do without risking harm to the child. As the crowd grew, they warned one another in hushed tones, "Stay back! Do not stir! Speak low! If you frighten the snake he might strike the child." In no time at all the whole camp circle and even those who had been out in the wood picking plums were there, standing helpless. And then someone said, "Here comes the snake dreamer. Make way for him."

As the quiet little man passed through the way made for him, the people whispered to one another, "If anyone can help, he can. His spirit helper is the snake. They understand each other; you shall see." Just outside the doorway the man seated himself and filled his pipe and smoked, with his eyes closed. "He is getting in touch," the word went about. Everyone wished he would hurry, but he took his time, maddeningly. At last he stood and addressed them. "There is no cause for alarm here. My friend, my brother, does not know where he is, for he is blind at this time of year. But I tell him he lies wrapped about the body of a sleeping infant, and he hears me. By and by, when my friend, my brother, is ready he will move quietly away. Be patient."

Then he entered the tipi and sat down to smoke again, this time so near that he could have reached out and touched the snake or the snake could have struck at him, but they did neither. "They are in rapport, that's certain," men murmured, in wonder. At last, at very long last, the snake began to move and uncoil himself; deliberately and with awful grace he glided past his friend and brother, so close that he all but brushed the toe of his moccasin, and still the man sat calm, with eyes closed, still smoking. Forcing his way out from under the tipi, the snake went on toward the wood. "I did not wish to embarrass my brother by looking at him as though to hurry him," the quiet little snake dreamer said later.

With tears of relief the women picked up the baby and passed him around. The family feasted the snake dreamer and Rainbow gave him the best horse he owned, while his sister Dream Woman took the snake dreamer's measurements for the handsomest pair of moccasins she was ever to make.

"Do not change your tipi from this place," the man told Rainbow. "It was a mistake, and my friend is too wise to do it a second time. Do not insult him by supposing he would repeat it on purpose. I could not help you in that case." So Rainbow's tipi remained where it stood until the entire camp circle removed to another region.

"Watch this boy," the snake dreamer advised. "You will see that he will be blessed in many ways: with long life, good fortune, and a great degree of supernatural help in time of crisis. Because he has been endangered much, he shall be much blessed." And everyone was happy over the prophecy.

CHAPTER 8

When Teton children could be reasoned with they were then said to have their senses. Waterlily was past six winters and going on her seventh when this could be truly said of her. Before that time, many things that happened were known to her, but not always because she remembered them in sequence. Rather, she knew them from repeated accounts of them. And how she loved those recitals of her early doings and sayings—so much that she came to think she remembered them as they had occurred.

"Mother, what was that I did before I was even two winters old?" she would insist, while Blue Bird pretended to forget the story she especially liked to hear over and over. "Let me think . . . You did so many things, I hardly know . . ." And then, finally, "Oh, yes, for one thing, you once forecast the weather."

"Did I really, Mother?" she would ask, surprised all over again. "What did I say?"

"You said nothing. You were too small to talk yet. But you toddled into our tipi with two sticks for the fire. We did not need a fire, for it was summer, and very warm. We did not ask for fuel."

"Oh! And then?"

"Well, then"—Blue Bird always had to smile into the eager upturned face at this point—"And then you seated yourself by the fireplace and warmed your hands."

Waterlily would laugh merrily. "And what did Grandmother-killed-by-the-tree say to that?" Blue Bird's old grandmother who was killed by a falling limb was of course unknown to Waterlily, but because her way of dying was a familiar story, Waterlily had so named her.

"She said, '*Hina!* This means we are going to have a hard winter, sure! Children do not pretend cold weather for nothing.'"

This was the place for a long, thoughtful pause, always. And then Waterlily asked, much impressed with her power, "And did we have a hard winter, Mother?" She knew the answer very well, but it was good to hear it again. "Very hard. One of the worst our people could remember. There was snow and more snow. Men could not hunt and no buffalo came near, and our food gave out and many people died. A very hard winter indeed; may we never know another like the one you predicted."

"Oh, my!" Waterlily would say with awe, her amazement renewed with each telling. "How did I know that, Mother?" And Blue Bird would say, "Well, how did you?" and they would laugh, and the interview would end very satisfactorily to Waterlily.

She liked to go over her past with Gloku, too. "Grandmother, what did I do when you carried me on your back?"

"You were such a lively little girl—never quiet. You used to take my two braids for reins as if you were on horseback, and pull first this way and then that way until you had my eyelids stretched back so far that it is a wonder I did not fall into a gopher hole with you on my back!" This was very amusing. Waterlily would clap her hands and laugh, and ask, "Did it hurt, Grandmother?" But Gloku would say, "I forget if it hurt. I only remember how you enjoyed yourself."

Then Blue Bird would cut in, defending her mother-in-law,

who was always too indulgent of her grandchildren, Waterlily included. "It was not funny, Waterlily. You were naughty to hurt your grandmother. How would you like your two braids pulled?"

Waterlily would not like it at all. But those had been days when she did not know any better and nothing she did could be held against her. Now, going on seven, she was growing more and more accountable and able to remember past experiences and to be guided by them. And that was because she had her senses at last—her senses and her memory; it was all one.

The autumn day was raw and overcast when Gloku took her dogs and went after fuel, leaving Waterlily and her grandfather in the tipi. "You are a big girl, now, grandchild. Remember to hand water to your grandfather when he is thirsty. That is why your mother wants you to stay with him while I am gone."

The energetic Gloku set her tipi to rights while she said this. She hung all the food high up on the tipi poles, beyond the reach of dogs that might stray in. Then she made her old man comfortable. His sight, which had been failing for years, was now practically gone and he had to have things handed to him that were not close by. So before leaving him alone, Gloku always seated him exactly right, where he could blow the ashes from his pipe into the fire. He was able to fill and light his pipe and to clean it out when he finished, having developed the habit during the last few years by sitting with eyes shut and doing things by feel, as though preparing for total blindness. At least he was already well able to take care of his smoking needs.

The old man sat silently, with thoughts of his past activities. Waterlily threw back the fur rug and set up her play tipi on the ground for a pleasant time with her little dolls. She assigned them different roles and invented simple situations such as came up in the family. She carried on a spirited conversation as though the dolls were talking. After a long time she remembered her duty. "Grandfather! Grandfather! Water!" She held some water out to him. He groped for the dipper, saying, "*Hao,* grandchild," by ways of thanks, and drank noisily.

Soon he was back into his reverie, and Waterlily played on until she felt hungry. Opening out the container of food her grandmother had left for them, she offered some to the old man and then started to eat. But the food did not taste as good as that sweetened cake of pemmican hanging high up on the tipi pole. Suddenly she wanted some of it, so badly that she piled up many rawhide cases full of dried meat until she could reach it by standing on them.

It was of a pemmican base, filled with wild fruits and held together in a hard cake by rich oils derived from bones. A little of it was enough, for it was the richest delicacy there was. But Waterlily ate and ate and could not leave off, until she began to feel miserable in her stomach. She was lying very still when Gloku returned. She could hear her outside feeding and thanking her dogs as she unhitched them.

The old man called out, "Are you back?" He knew she was, but this was their way of saying hello. "Yes," she replied. "I am back." As she entered, he said, "You better see what the child has been up to. For a long time she played very nicely with her dolls. But since we ate our meal, she has been very still, and for a child to be that still is a bad sign. It seemed to me she was moving heavy things about and reaching upward—to judge by her grunting efforts. For a time she was all over the place and then she became very silent. I called to her, but she did not answer. See if something is wrong."

Very soon Gloku discovered the half-eaten pemmican cake and let out a cry of distress that brought her daughters and Waterlily's mother running. "My grandchild has sickened herself! Oh, what is to be done?" Her only concern was for the child; that the pemmican cake was largely a loss was something she had no time to think of. But she did turn on the old man. "And you! Here you sit placid while terrible things go on! You might have called out to the others—our tipis all but touch!" Not a word from him.

Waterlily's aunts and mother tried to force medicine down her throat, but it seemed to Waterlily that the tipi was turning round and round. The tipi poles meeting overhead were a great spider web spinning rapidly; the anxious faces of the women whirled with the web until they were all of a piece, slowly fading into darkness.

Fainting was considered the opening step in the dying process. To give in was to surrender to death. If the one fainting were allowed to recline and lose consciousness, permanent death could ensue. With such beliefs, the women shook the ailing girl and kept her in a sitting position though she toppled this way and that. They continually dashed water in her face. Gloku kept saying as she rubbed Waterlily's cold wrists and temples, "Do not forget, grandchild. Keep remembering, or you will die." Remembering also meant being conscious. But Waterlily was not frightened by the threat of dying; it was not important. "Let me alone. I just want to lie still," she moaned.

The medicine eased her enough that she finally slept normally while her relatives sat around her all night. Early next morning the first person she saw was her stepfather, Rainbow. Never had he spoken directly to her till now; always at a distance had he provided her wants dutifully. Waterlily, closer to his mother and father, felt herself a stranger to her silent stepfather. But now his worried eyes said he was very much affected. "Daughter," he spoke to her, "I have tried in my humble way to provide for you because I do not want any child in my tipi to grow up in want. Yesterday you gave me a great fright, but if you will hurry and get well, then by and by you shall wear a gown and put red paint on your face."

It was not a very exciting promise to Waterlily. What was so extraordinary about wearing a gown, when one had always worn a gown? And red paint? She had worn that, too. But to the adults who understood the significance it was very important, for Rainbow was saying he would arrange and pay for a *hunka* ceremony for Waterlily. To become a *hunka* (child-beloved) was to be elevated to a high station in the tribe, and that was an honor that did not come to everyone.

Rainbow began at once to hunt for elk and to watch the hunting of other men so that he might buy from those who shot an elk the teeth that would be needed to decorate Waterlily's ceremonial gown. People were much impressed and spread the news about. "Have you heard? Rainbow is pledged to a great undertaking. He is making that little daughter of his wife a 'beloved.' Right now he is collecting elk teeth for her gown."

Everyone helped. But it was slow work because each animal

yielded only two teeth that could be used. Moreover they must come only from the female elk. So widespread was the interest that even hunters from other camp circles saved elk teeth for Rainbow and sent or brought them to him from time to time. For these that were proffered he gave suitable presents in return. Only where he asked for teeth outright did he buy them.

When enough elk teeth were on hand, his sister Dream Woman made the gown; and it was something to behold. Many women, especially those who fancied themselves to be inspired artists, as Dream Woman was believed to be though she never said, came in to examine the finished gown and went away marveling at its beauty of material and workmanship. As usual, Dream Woman had dreamed an original design. It was worked into the wide border of embroidery that topped the heavy fringe around the bottom of the skirt and of the loose, open sleeves. The matched teeth, which had been painstakingly polished to a high luster by the grandfather, who was happy to help to that extent, were appliqued in pleasing groups all over the upper half of the gown, above the belt and down over the sleeves. The gown was exactly alike both front and back.

Two whole years were spent in getting ready for the ceremony, and meantime Waterlily was preoccupied with a new baby sister, to the extent that she often forgot for long periods the great event awaiting her. The baby was named Mysterious Hand, and that was in compliment to her aunt Dream Woman, whose hands turned out unvarying beauty "too perfect to be human," as people said. But Mysterious Hand would be the ceremonial name, not to be spoken carelessly. Waterlily's descriptive term for the baby became her nickname, Smiling One.

But at last the great day arrived. At dawn Gloku began to prepare special foods for the *hunka* candidate and fed her as the sun appeared. Then Blue Bird bathed her at the stream and washed and oiled her long hair until it shone. She braided it in two long braids in the usual style and tied on the new hair ties that were part of the special outfit. They were fragrant, for Dream Woman had made colorfully embroidered balls and stuffed them with perfume leaf, and these were attached to the ties.

The new gown and the necklace and belt and bracelet were put on Waterlily, and some long, wide pendants of tiny shells were hung from her ears. Though they were so heavy that they pulled the small lobes down, elongating them, Waterlily knew they must be endured for beauty's sake. Last of all, the new moccasins of solid red quillwork with matching leggings went on. A detail of the dreamed design on the gown was here skillfully repeated, making of the entire costume a charming harmony. And not only the tops but also the soles of the moccasins were covered with quillwork. This seemed extravagant and unnecessary, and Waterlily ventured to say so. "When I walk, I shall quickly break the quills and ruin the soles." Her aunt Dream Woman replied, "But you will not walk." Then she told the girl that child-beloved moccasins for the *hunka* were always decorated so, and that one did not walk to the ceremonial tipi; one was carried.

And now Waterlily was sitting stiffly attired in the rare outfit, so heavy with elegance that she hardly dared move, nor even so much as look sideways because of the ear ornaments that hung well below her collarbone on either side. She was all ready, there in the honor-place of the tipi, but as yet she was not wearing the face paint Rainbow had promised her.

Leaping Fawn and Prairie Flower, her cousins, brought other girls in to admire her. Leaping Fawn thought it needful to explain, "You see, my cousin nearly died, but lived. That is why she is being honored. My uncle promised her this ceremony." That was a perfectly acceptable explanation, for everyone knew that there was always a valid reason for parents to go to such expense—either because of a vow, as in Waterlily's case, or because a child was sickly and there was fear of its death, or something of the sort.

Now and then a child asked, but not often, "Mother, why is my brother a *hunka* and not I?" And then he was told, "Because we prayed for his recovery and promised to feast the people in his name if he should be spared to us, and he was." A feast always accompanied the ceremony, and through it everyone in the community was related to the child being honored. The singling out of a child for the honor was accepted by the other children when they understood. They had always been taught it was shameful to be jealous of a brother or sister. "You are all one," they were told.

"Be happy for each other." Children with normal endowments and sound health did not need any such compensating honor, and the majority lived and died content without its coming to them personally.

Little Chief stayed around home today, as did everyone, for this was an occasion. He watched the ceremonial lodge being erected in the center of the circle and then ran home to wait for the ritual custom called the "pretended search" that was soon to start. Presently he shouted, "Here they come!" and ran telling everyone. But he knew what the searchers would do. He had seen them act out their role on similar occasions, for, like all boys, he often roamed throughout the circle and had watched many family ceremonies of several kinds, of which the *hunka* was one. He knew about the dramatics connected with bringing in the candidates, of the way the four men who were sent out as escorts for the candidate must pretend to lose their way.

That was what they were doing now. They came out of the ceremonial tipi and walked rapidly away, only to stop short, argue, and change their direction. Three times they did this, and only the fourth time did they head straight for Black Eagle's camp. And each time they stopped to confer and decide on another direction, they sang the traditional song that said,

"Just where do they live?
"Just where do they live?"

though they knew all the time.

The men arrived, entered the tipi, and lifted Waterlily gently onto the back of the one who was to carry her. Then the four men left the tipi, with Waterlily riding high and looking a little bewildered. The spectators who jammed the entrance made comments in praise of her costume, but she did not hear them.

Three other children whose parents were also honoring them were borne in the same way by their particular escorts to the ceremonial tipi. There they were seated in the honor-place and an immense curtain was held in front of them while the officials gave them the *hunka* painting: tiny pencil lines of red vermilion down their cheeks to signify their new status. They were now children-beloved. All their lives they would have the right to mark their faces in this manner for important occasions, and people would say of them, "There goes a *hunka!*" and that would be an honor. It would mean "There goes one whose family loved him so much that they gave a great feast and many presents to the people in his name." To have something given away in one's name was the greatest compliment one could have. It was better than to receive.

When the painting was finished and the curtain removed, the spectators saw the four children sitting in a row, each one holding a beautiful ear of blue corn mounted on a stick. This was to symbolize the hospitality to which they were in effect pledging themselves by accepting *hunka* status. They were now of the elect.

It was required of the officiant of every ceremony that he first declare his qualifications. Accordingly, the man who had been engaged to administer the *hunka* rite began by saying, "I have myself known this rite. And have ever striven to live up to its demands; all who hear me know that this is so. I have gladly accepted the obligation of hospitality. No one in need has opened my tipi entrance curtain in vain," and so he "presented his credentials."

Then he sang a very holy song while he waved the *hunka* wand over the heads of the candidates to invoke on them a blessing. The wand was wrapped solid with ornamental quillwork, and long strands of horsetail dyed in bright colors hung from it. At the end of the wand was a pipe.

After the song, the man offered a drink of water to each child and then withdrew it as they were about to take it, saying, "As you go on from here, there may be those about you who are faint and weary. Of such you shall be mindful. And though you would hastily bring water to your lips to quench your own thirst, yet you shall first stop to look about you," and only then he allowed them to drink.

Next he held a piece of food over incense and then cut it in two. He threw one piece in the fire and laid the other on the candidate's tongue, saying, "Whenever you sit down to eat, there may perhaps be someone waiting near, hungering for a swallow of your food. At such a time you shall remember what you have become here. And though you might be lifting meat to your mouth, yet you shall stop midway. You shall forbear to eat your food alone. Only half the morsel shall you eat, and with the other shall you show mercy."

This was all of the ritual; the feasts followed at the homes of the candidates. Rainbow gave some horses away in Waterlily's name and provided much of the food, allowing the other relatives to share in giving it, for that was the way of the people—that all those families who belonged together help each other.

Waterlily did not immediately understand what she had been committed to, but she would learn as time went on. She had been set apart as one of those who must make hospitality their first concern. Until she was a mature woman she would not be expected to carry on independently; till then, her mother and other relatives would carry on in her name. But the *hunka* obligation had been laid on her and it was a compelling thing. Its reward was high in prestige. The hairline stripes of red which she was thereafter privileged to wear were a sign of that.

Immediately after the feast the elaborate costume was laid away and once more Waterlily wore ordinary dress, so there was nothing in her daily appearance to make her different from other children. Nothing further was said about her recent honor. In time she would realize fully that she was of the elect, but the honor was something she must appear to wear casually. Let others speak of it—self-boasting was out.

Waterlily was beginning to take homely things and family doings with more appreciation. These she had always taken for granted, until this grand gesture of her stepfather brought them into focus. And so it was very much to her liking when one of her cousins, the youngest son of Black Eagle, came in one evening with the following report: "I came upon a stray buffalo with a broken leg today, so I shot him and left him in the hollow he rolled into and died."

News of meat was always a cause for rejoicing. For Black Eagle, this particular news was cause for pride and elation, for it was the boy's first real killing. Immediately he invited any of the family members who wished to go, to move out to the scene with him and camp there for the butchering. In short, it was to be a family outing.

At dawn, Rainbow and his sisters, First Woman and Dream Woman, and two or three cousins, all with their families, and of course the grandparents, Gloku and her old man, moved out there, leaving their homes standing in the camp circle and setting up temporary tipis near the ravine where the buffalo was. All the men were experienced butchers. They always cut up the animals they shot and brought the meat home in pieces. It was the Teton custom to skin the animal carefully, since hides were as important as the meat, and then to dissect the flesh according to the muscle structure. Each muscle was removed intact and called by name. The anatomical names of parts of animals were many. As each piece was removed and handed to the waiting women, they set at once to preparing it for drying. The old people took care of the bones, pounding them and then boiling them to derive their rich oils that took the place of butter, which they did not have.

But it was not all work. There was feasting on the side. Nothing seemed so desirable as meat broiled while still fresh. It was the men who took charge here, broiling the whole sides, on a grand scale called "warpath style." Over a huge fire of elm and oak they made a dome of green willows, and when the fire died down to a pile of hot coals, they flung the meat like an immense tent over the dome. It quite well covered the fire and caught all the rising heat. To a people subsisting principally on buffalo meat, the sound of sizzling juices dripping into the fire was delicious to hear; the occasional flare-up from the melting grease whetted all appetites. When the meat was cooked, it was lifted off by means of stout sticks sharpened to a point and was laid level on elm boughs spread on the ground. Then it was cut into juicy strips and passed around. And everyone had a wonderful time, the children making the most of it.

Inveterate givers of food as the Tetons were, it was not enough that Black Eagle's group of relatives were feasting after this windfall in their midst. No, they must share it. So they scanned the surrounding country for people passing in the distance and summoned them by waving a blanket or by calling to them, or some youth on a swift pony was dispatched to bring them in, to partake of the feast.

It was wonderfully pleasant to be out there. When all the meat had been cared for properly, nobody wanted to return to the camp circle just yet, though it was in sight and there was constant going in and coming out by different ones, especially the boys on horseback, who were sent back with meat for those who did not come out.

The fact that the *tinpsila*, wild prairie turnips, were at their best and grew plentifully on the hillsides offered a good excuse to stay; the women wanted to dig them for winter use. Meantime the men hunted desultorily. If one brought in a deer it was all to the good—more broiling of fresh meat. But they were too near the large circle to be hopeful of finding many.

To Waterlily these were memorable days, for this was the time she began to like her mother best and enjoy being with her more than with the other family members. Before, she had turned as readily to her grandmother, aunts, and other relatives as to her mother—it was the way of related families—but now she was learning to appreciate her mother for the rare and sympathetic person she was. The two were beginning to have little heart-to-heart talks on serious matters that were on Waterlily's mind, which her mother seemed to anticipate.

There was that lovely afternoon when they went from the camp for a walk, just Blue Bird and her three children, Waterlily, Ohiya, and Smiling One, who was now past two winters. Beyond the knoll they sat down to rest, and there was nobody and nothing in sight, only country. Blue Bird looked on her children fondly and said, "Now I am truly happy—surrounded by my children." And this she said because here was one of her rare opportunities to love them without limit, and to show them that she did. For in the larger family, where all adults acted parental toward all the children, they tried to be careful not to seem partial to any.

Waterlily said eagerly, "We are happy, too, Mother, having you to ourselves. Mother, let's play that game 'hard times' that we used to play with elder brother."

"Do you remember that, Waterlily?" Blue Bird was surprised.

"You were very little, you know, when your brother Little Chief invented it for the three of us. It was fun, wasn't it?" Then she added, looking far off, "Your brother is too big to play with us any more. He is out there somewhere, riding with the other boys. And that is right. These are the times when he must learn to ride. It is needful that all men ride well. Come now!"

She pulled her wrap over her head and brought her three children under it. They snuggled up to her as she began a running commentary about their "awful plight," and listened to the imagined misery with playful shudders.

Now . . . here we are . . . all alone . . . just us four. On a wide, deserted, strange prairie. And worst of all, we have so little food, and it is not likely we shall find any more . . . Oh dear, isn't it terrible?"

"Terrible! Terrible!" The two older children repeated in a chorus, being well into the spirit of it.

"All we have is this tiny shelter . . . only a makeshift and not at all secure . . . Well, at least it protects us . . . if only the wind would not blow so hard!"

"The wind! The wind!" They shuddered again.

"Come, Ohiya," the mother said, "a little closer in. Waterlily, pull the tent downward and hold it firm, there, back of you . . . Oh, for some anchoring pins! But there is no tree to cut from, alas. The wind grows worse, and colder. It could rip our shelter right off . . . Hold tight! Oh, whatever shall become of us!" The children loved it—it was such fun to be so wretched when it was only play.

Ohiya added his bit of make-believe by crying, "Mother! Look at Smiling One, crawling out from under the tipi!"

"No, no, Smiling One, come back here or you will freeze! All of you, keep close so we can warm one another." They huddled still closer, in a tight knot. And then Ohiya began to moan in great misery. "What is it, my son?" "Mother, I am starving . . . soon I shall be dead. I have eaten nothing for three days and three nights . . ."

His mother was appropriately distressed, as she hastened to offer him food. "Here, son, I have a very little pemmican . . . a mere handful. But at least hold a bit of it in your mouth . . .

don't swallow it . . . swallow the juice only . . . That will sustain
you. It is what warriors sometimes have to do."

"Give, give! Quick!" And Ohiya gasped and rolled his eyes in
agony, according to his notion of correct dying from starvation.
His mother passed out a pinch of the food to each one and took
some herself and they sat holding it in the mouth, swallowing the
juice only.

"I wonder, Ohiya, whether the storm has spent itself . . . it
seems suddenly very quiet. Just peek out and see." She said this to
find out if the children were tired of the game. Far from it. At
least Ohiya wanted to prolong it, for he stuck his head out and
then jerked it back in with teeth chattering noisily. "Ouch! My
ears are nearly frozen off, it is so cold . . . I think we must stay
here some more."

Waterlily said, "Mother, in that case, tell us a story." And so
Blue Bird told them not one story but two and then a third. They
were the same little stories long familiar but always welcome—
about the stupid bear; the deceitful fox; the wily Iktomi, master
of trickery; and about Meadowlark and her babies.

In due time the children, who had wriggled about into more
comfortable position against their mother, were sound asleep,
their heads on her lap. She gazed on them tenderly as she wiped
their flushed faces damp along the hairline, for it was actually a
very warm day. "A lapful of babies—what more should a woman
want?"

She sat very still, her back against a rock, so they might have
their rest, until someone called from beyond the hill telling them
their evening meal was waiting.

On the way back she carried the baby while the two older ones
walked ahead. Suddenly Waterlily turned back to her and said,
"Mother, this was such fun! Can we go walking with you
again—often?"

Waterlily went everywhere with her grandmother, Gloku,
and her aunts and others, and always it was very pleasant, for
they were all most agreeable. But now at last she had found her
preference, her own mother, who could play games and talk
about many things that were perplexing, clearing them away.
She would stay close to her from now on. It was well she decided

this, for very soon she would be needing more guidance through the extraordinary days of adolescence that were not too far off. And then it would be her own mother who would be most understanding and helpful.

CHAPTER 9

Incidents now stood out more distinctly, and lingered, in Waterlily's memory so that she could recall them with nearly the same immediacy as when they actually happened and could feel the same sensations they had first aroused. Three of these were events that had to do with her brother Little Chief, to whom she was especially devoted: when he first struck coup, when he ran away and joined a war party, when he killed his first buffalo. These were deeds that made her very proud of him, as a sister should be.

It was a cold, late spring after a particularly severe winter. No buffalo had been sighted yet and meantime the store of food was fast running out. As usual at such times it was up to the heads of families to go out hunting individually for whatever they could find. Rainbow and a cousin with whom he especially enjoyed hunting decided to go out in search of deer, taking their immediate families with them. With the cousin were his wife and two of her nephews who were old enough to help, and Rainbow's mother went with his family.

They were lucky, for deer hunting proved worthwhile in the locality they had chosen. The men were out all day while the women kept busy taking care of the previous day's kill. But in the evenings they gathered around the common outdoor fire between the two tipis where they cooked and ate together. It was a typical deer-hunting feast, for each individual was able to hold his slender limb bone of a deer in his hand and pry out enough marrow for each mouthful of meat, and that was considered a great luxury. The sharp flavor of fresh sticks, with which they pried, enhanced the taste like a condiment.

It was while they sat after such a meal, wrapped in furry robes, for the nights were chilly, that suddenly a bird began to call from the nearby bushes, interrupting the informal conversation. After this happened twice, the cousin's wife remarked, "That is a *pakoṡka* [whippoorwill], isn't it? I did not know they sang at this time of year." After that, the conversation went on, the bird's calls no longer noticed.

Only Rainbow was disturbed by an idea so he could no longer engage in carefree talk. Instead he waited momentarily for the next call, holding his empty marrow bone poised. At last there it was again. Hurling the bone toward the bushes, he called out, "*Pakoṡka*—where?" The song stopped instantly. The cousin said, laughing, "That finished him! Now we won't be interrupted again." But all night long Rainbow lay awake. "Why didn't the bird fly to another spot and sing again? Could I have actually hit him with so blind an aim?" he wondered. A vague suspicion nagged at him and he could hardly wait for the dawn.

As soon as he could see, he stole out of the tipi and went toward the source of the bird's calls. Just as he had thought, it had not been a bird at all; it had been a man. A Crow scout lay at the edge of the timber with a bone penetrating his temple. It had been a direct hit. Rainbow was a hunter, not a warrior. And he had never killed a man before. Nevertheless, he knew, as all men did, that the formal announcement followed a certain routine. He gave some startling war whoops that brought everyone running out of the tipis in time to hear him say, "I, whom you designate as Rainbow, I this day have killed my enemy in a direct hit!" It was what warriors always shouted.

As the others came, dragging fur robes behind them, he hurried to his tipi, brushing past them, to arouse his son Little Chief. "Stand aside!" he commanded, "Stand aside, for it is my wish that the lad strike first coup." He led the drowsy boy to the scene, teaching him what to do. Accordingly, Little Chief touched the dead man gingerly on the shoulder with his bow. Simple as that act was, it was a tremendous thing for him, though he was not aware of it. Before he was fifteen winters old, he had "killed an enemy." This was an honor that came to very few at so young an age.

Rainbow invited his cousin to strike second coup and the elder of the two nephews to strike third, then he struck fourth—and that was all that counted. The younger nephew stood watching diffidently, satisfied that his brother had been given the honor. Then the two men together cheered for Little Chief in the traditional words of praise, "Little Chief, *Eyahahe!*"

It was indeed something to cheer about. Of course the entire matter was formal, a vicarious honor for a vicarious deed. Yet it was no less meaningful for the boy's record. Blue Bird took Little Chief to one side and whispered to him, "Do not forget this, son. Do not forget that you have a father who is so unselfish as to transfer the honor he has earned to his son. It is because he wants you to get top glory. Such a deed is praiseworthy. You are fortunate to have such a father."

The dead scout was handsome, tall and well-knit; and best of all, his trappings indicated that he had been a person of note back home. That made the deed even more gratifying, for this warfare of the plains was a perpetual tournament between the tribes, wherein they complimented one another by being "worthy foes." There was less pride in vanquishing an ordinary man as opponent. Warriors went so far as to dress in their very best before an open battle. From their youth up they had been reminded to be "a worthy foe." And that was understood not only to mean brave, crafty, strong, but also, just as much, to look the part.

But the victors could not stand there long, admiring the dead man. Here was a scout from an enemy war party. If he did not promptly return, the others would come searching for him. The hunting party was in great danger. Rainbow gave rapid orders: "There is no time to lose. Let the women save only the meat that is dry and light and compact for carrying. Forget the tipis; we have others at home. And you," turning to his cousin and the two boys, "take the women and children and ride quickly away."

Skirting the hills on the west, since apparently the scout had come from the east, they dashed away. When they were beyond the hills, Rainbow stopped and dismounted and the others came to a halt. "Keep straight north along this ravine." He knew the lay of that part of the land well. "Stay out of sight; race your horses to the limit!"

As they galloped away he tied his horse to a stump hidden by tall brush and crawled on his belly all the way to the top of the hill where he could see the abandoned camp. For some time he lay watching, motionless, holding a bunch of sage over his head. His legs were thrust far under a sage brush and he was one with the land. No one could have said that a man lay there.

Sure enough, he saw a war party moving along the high ridge beyond the camp. They stopped; they had seen the camp. On signal they charged it, racing downhill with shrill cries and shooting arrows into the empty tipis. In a moment they were tearing them apart.

Rainbow did not wait for them to find their comrade. When he reached home his horse was white with foam, its flanks working like powerful bellows. Already the whole camp circle was buzzing with the report brought in by his party and his name was being lauded to the skies. He had ingeniously killed an enemy and had saved his party, and without doubt also other hunting parties in that region. Members of the Kit Fox society had already gone out to warn them and bring them in. But best of all, to Rainbow, was the praise for his son. "Little Chief has struck first coup!" was the general cry. "With so auspicious a start, he will surely become a great warrior," old men prophesied of him.

All of this was highly exciting to Waterlily. At the next dance, she knew, the incident would be marked in many ways. Little Chief's aunts and his mother, Blue Bird, would outdo themselves at the give-away in his name. It would all be very wonderful! It was also personally important to Waterlily, in a unique way. Gloku had already explained that she, as the sister of a warrior, was the proper person to carry the scalp in the victory procession; that, she said, was always the prerogative of a hero's sister.

For days on end Waterlily enjoyed a delicious torment in anticipation of her coming role. She would be so proud to carry the decorated pole with the trophy mounted away up there at the top—but could she endure the gaze of so many spectators? She remembered a legend about a sensitive youth who was knocked down physically by the mere concentration of all eyes on him; might that happen to her? It would be too dreadful!

For Waterlily was fast becoming "bashful," as a well-trained young girl was expected to be. At the age of ten winters she was

already reticent and demure from watching the conventional behavior of her cousin Leaping Fawn and the other girls older than
herself, taking her cue from them. Not independently had she
done this, but because she had also been admonished in that
direction. "The loud, bold girl is not approved," Gloku would
say. Waterlily saw that this meant Alila specifically. Alila, for all
her warmth and friendliness, was loud and bold. Instinctively
Waterlily knew enough not to copy her.

At last she confided to Gloku. "Grandmother, I think I am too
young to be in the procession with grownups." Gloku could see
that, much as the girl was elated over the idea, she would be more
comfortable not to claim her right at this time. "Well, perhaps
you are," she soothed her. "But don't worry. There will be other
opportunities, for your brother will be a real warrior some day.
His feet are set in that direction." In the end it was Blue Bird who
carried the trophy in her daughter's place. To have the right was
enough for Waterlily; she could take quiet pride in that.

Rainbow had gone after deer, not enemies, as everyone knew.
Even so, his accidental deed merited the same recognition as a
deed intentionally achieved. A war deed was a war deed, no
matter what.

That early sampling of military glory did things to Little
Chief. He found it hard to wait until he could legitimately join a
war party. "Perhaps in four or five years," his grandfather had
said. It seemed an intolerable time to wait, while doing commonplace things again. So he took matters into his own hands
and got his taste of battle much earlier. Of all things, he joined a
war party that was setting out in anger, determined on reprisal.

Early that following fall, the enemy struck with unbelievable
boldness during a peaceful night. Stealing right into the camp
circle, they wantonly scalped three children and spirited away a
young girl as she lay asleep. In addition they took the best horses,
though the owners had them picketed near their tipis.

The camp circle was in an uproar at dawn, when the losses
were discovered. There was universal wailing for the dead children and the disappearance of the young girl, and their parents
and relatives mutilated themselves recklessly in their grief.
Meantime the warriors were assembling in anger, to start forth

after the offenders. That master warrior, Bear Heart, had already rallied them. "Men," he said to his followers, "This is an insult that must be avenged—with our lives if need be. Are you with me? Then bestir yourselves; I wait."

And while he sat on the grass and smoked in ominous calm, it was Little Chief who broke in on his silence. "Uncle, I am going with you." The boy's eyes were blazing with eagerness, but Bear Heart did not laugh him off. One must not ridicule young ambition, for fear of killing it. He puffed away for some time, and then said: "I have to say no, for a good reason. This is no trip for you, my nephew. This is an angry errand, a determined one. Unless we are victorious, we mean to die on the battlefield. There may be no one to bring you back safely."

The boy said nothing, but his silence was more insistent than pleading. The uncle had to say more. "If this were to be the usual kind of warpath, a mere seeking after adventure for the sport and glory of it, then I would say yes. But let me make you a promise. When next I go on such a warpath, you shall go with me."

"Thank you, uncle." The boy slipped away.

The war party started at noon and traveled all night. The next evening, it being still within Dakota country, the men stopped to rest for a while and sent two young men to fetch water and fuel for cooking a meal. When those two returned, they brought Little Chief in. How he had followed and managed to evade their constant lookout was a puzzle. One of the young men had stumbled on him lying in the brush where he had gone to pick up some wood.

They stood him before Bear Heart, who smoked on as though not seeing him. At last he looked earnestly at the boy. "Ah, my nephew, this was what I did not want, for I needed freedom from personal care. I meant for nothing to impede me seeking revenge. But now I must worry over your safety at the same time. However, you are here now, and you shall go on. We can spare no one to take you back."

As it turned out, Little Chief proved himself very useful to the expedition, though he was not permitted to see the actual fighting. They left him behind, in a hidden spot some distance from the enemy's camp, to take care of the relief horses and the food and extra supplies of the war party.

The return trip was a complete triumph, for there had been reprisal killings of the enemy in hand-to-hand fights. All the stolen horses were recovered and many of the enemy's finest were taken in addition. Best of all, the young girl was rescued unharmed from the lodge of the chief, where she had been taken in adoption in place of a daughter recently dead.

The party rode hard day and night until they were once more in familiar country. There they stopped, being fairly certain of not being followed, and feasted on parts of fresh buffalo meat, from a stray animal killed on the way. For Little Chief it was a thrill merely to sit among the warriors, to hear them recount around the campfire the details of their individual struggles with the enemy. There were many further things he wanted to know, but he hesitated to draw attention to himself, knowing too well that he was there on suffrance only, still an unnecessary burden.

It had all proved to be more wonderful and terrifying than he and his companions back home ever imagined from hearing war tales. For while the battle raged and the cries and shouts of struggle reached him in his retreat, he had been badly scared and the enormity of his step in tagging after this war party had come to him with frightening impact for the first time. It had been so presumptuous of him. However, he felt better when a seasoned warrior, during the talk by the campfire, laid a hand on his shoulder and said, "What would we have done without this fine lad? We owe him much, my friends. For it was he who enabled us to leap from our spent horses to fresh ones, all without slackening speed!" That was somewhat exaggerated, of course. But Little Chief did have everything packed and ready to go, so that when the warriors came, they could start homeward immediately.

He felt better. In fact he began to fancy himself quite a warrior, little knowing what still lay ahead of him—the initiation tests regularly given to a boy who stole out on the warpath as he had done. First they sent him for water at night and expected him to find his way though the dark and dangerous woods to the stream. And when he brought it to them, they rejected it and sent him back for more. "This is not the water I wanted!" they said after tasting it, and spat it out contemptuously. Three times they did this, and only accepted the water he brought the fourth time, though he got it all from the same spot. This last water they passd around, sampling it in turn and exclaiming, "Ah! This is it! Boy, why did you not bring it before?"

Next, when they stopped at noon they sent him on a scouting mission. "Boy, now go about the surrounding hills. See what you can see that we should know." So he ran over the low-lying hills and the ravines and returned with a report that there were deer tracks near a waterhole and that there were evidences of a recent camp beyond one of the hills. The two young men sent to verify these statements returned to say they were both correct; that there had been a campfire very recently put out, with the embers still warm. And for proof of the deer tracks one of the riders brought back the deer, slung over the back of his horse. Little Chief felt his prestige soaring as he heard the men's praises.

But it was not until the warriors had conferred certain awards on him, just before they reached home, that he was completely happy, feeling that he belonged. The awards were the proofs of his success. One was the stick with a little bag attached in which he had brought the water; the other was a cluster of feathers, which the warriors called "the flutterers."

The man who awarded him the water carrier said, "Take this wand as proof of your courage. It shall be your first war standard. To it you will attach trophies you win in the future. Observe that it is of ash. Ash is strong. Though it may bend, it will not readily break. So be like the ash, resilient. The water cup is made from the sheath of a buffalo's heart. It says, 'Be hospitable.' You will notice the wolf tail dangling from the wand. It is the warrior's symbol. A warrior should be friends with the wolf, for he is the chief warrior. He knows the hills and the valleys of the land. He knows where to hide and how to fight. From him you can learn many things. Observe the crow feathers on the wand. The crow is a bird that flies straight and far and does not lose its way. So should a warrior go, unerringly. Take the wand. You have earned your water carrier."

It was his own uncle Bear Heart who next awarded him the

flutterers. They were four long feathers trimmed to their naked quills and tightly bound together at the base with a cord of sinew. The tiny fans left on at the tips were the finest barbs that caught the air and remained in continuous motion. Little Chief had never heard of flutterers before, much less seen one. Boys who sneaked after a war party were rare; and those who passed the test were rarer still. Handing the award to him, Bear Heart said, "Take this, my boy. It is the symbol of scouting. Keep it always, and from it learn to be superhumanly aware. Note that the tips are atremble even on the stillest days when men of duller sense feel no movement of air. So should a true scout be—ever more alert and aware than others." The man spoke with great solemnity.

With such tangible proofs of a successful warpath, Little Chief was no longer afraid to get home. He had felt right along that his people must be worrying about his absence, but now he was sure that they would forgive all. He hoped his father would approve and would say, "It is admirable to sample warfare. It is well to be off to a good start so young. It is a privilege to go under the able tutelage of the great Bear Heart." Rainbow did not say precisely those words, but he was glad that it all turned out as it did. At the victory dance to celebrate the success of the reprisal journey, Little Chief actually walked with warriors, while his relatives, especially his aunts, gave many gifts in his name and cheered him again and again.

When Waterlily was in her twelfth winter the third important honor came to her brother. He killed his first buffalo. That morning a blizzard was raging outside, making the tipis very dark, as though it were still night. Nobody wanted much to get up. Since no work was possible indoors or out, it seemed just as well to sleep the day away.

But then, suddenly, there were excited voices outside, men shouting to one another from tipi to tipi. But what they were saying was incoherent against the noise of the storm, and those in the tipis caught only snatches at first. Gradually, however, it came to light that a herd of buffalo blinded by the storm had walked right into camp and were discovered at dawn roaming aimlessly among the scattered winter tipis, just like domesticated animals.

And what a welcome accident that was! Men hastily organized to drive them onto open ground away from the tipis and to hold them there if possible until the others could get ready for the chase.

"Make haste! Make haste!" the village crier went about shouting. "Of their own accord our brothers, seeing we were in need, have again come to feed us! Bring your sharp knives for the butchering!"

Listening to the commotion, Waterlily was glad she was a girl and could remain cozy in bed. The poor men, who must go out to a chase in weather like this. And then she heard her father, Rainbow, outside the grandparents' tipi, where she slept. In urgent words he began calling Little Chief, who also slept in the tipi, to get up and come outside. "Wake up, my son, wake up! Only women may be excused for lying curled up at a time like this. A male must expect to bang his skull to earth a time or two. Remember your sister and cousins—doubtless they would be cheered by a bowl of hot buffalo soup. So come! Today calls for men!"

Waterlily could hear her brother scrambling to a sitting position and hurriedly putting on his clothes, saying nothing back to his father, only breathing very hard and audibly through his teeth, for it was cold. He was not balking. He knew his father was right. This kind of thing was his destiny. Waterlily lay very still, with face to the wall as tipi etiquette dictated, and with eyes tightly shut for good measure. It was not only bad manners but also a lack of kinship obligation to look at anyone getting up or dressing, especially a brother.

Gloku also got up and sat leaning forward from her sitting space to blow on her fire again and again, coaxing the damp wood to catch, her eyes wrinkled shut against the smoke from the sluggish fire. Between blowings she hurled out complaints in behalf of Little Chief. "But he is only a lad yet. He is too young to take part in a winter chase."

Rainbow ignored his mother's interference, if indeed he heard. Instead he called again, "Hurry! The herd will get out of hand while we crawl about. Let's be on our way!" He could be heard readying his buffalo ponies as he talked.

"Son," Gloku called louder, "At least let the boy stop long enough to drink some soup. I will have it warmed up at once." But Rainbow called back impatiently, "Mother, don't pamper the boy. He is old enough—and he is a male, remember that! Send him out at once!" Little Chief rushed out of the tipi trailing his robe after him. That was the last seen of him until he returned late in the day, bedraggled and chilled to the bone—but with his first buffalo.

Gloku at once cooked the tongue, considered the choicest part, and served it as in a rite to the boy's respect relatives, Waterlily, Leaping Fawn, and Prairie Flower, for whom the boy had, as it were, risked his life. His father was quietly pleased, but his blind grandfather was boisterously proud as he began naming off a list of his cronies whom he wished as guests to eat the boy's first kill. Nor were they slow in coming. Singly or in genial groups they began to arrive, each one carrying his eagle-wing fan (which was standard equipment for old men, both summer and winter) and his long-stemmed pipe and his pouch containing a blend of tobacco and kinnikinnick. For wherever old men foregathered each must play the host in turn by filling his pipe and sending it around. It was the custom from of old that the man on his left lit it and puffed on it leisurely two or three times before handing it to the one on his left. The pipe always traveled clockwise around a circle of friends, the host smoking it last.

The aged guests seated themselves with some delay, deferring to one another with a "You sit there, friend," "No, you," with courteous dignity as became friends. While they drank a great deal of the rich meaty soup, enjoying it noisily, and chewed laboriously such meat as they had teeth for, they praised the boy's achievement highly. It was gratifying to Little Chief to watch them enjoying food he had made possible.

When the old men had eaten their fill and started the pipe around, they fell to recounting their own first hunting experiences while Little Chief listened with eyes shining; he knew what they were talking about. After a little, one of the guests turned to him. "And now, grandchild, let us hear how you got your first buffalo."

Confident because he had something to relate, the boy cleared his throat in preparation and began. "Well, it all began this way. There I was, cozy in bed and very sleepy still, when the old man called out a hint that I was acting like a woman by staying in bed. Of course that brought me instantly into a sitting position."

"Of course," the guests said, "what man would ignore that?"

The boy went on talking, as a man among men who had hunted the buffalo. "Out there in the open I was so blinded by the whipping snow that I did not know where I was. Then I faintly made out the rump of the beasts running ahead. Just as I set an arrow to my bow, a gust of wind jerked my robe off partly. But because it was tied to me around my neck, the robe only flattened out behind me, choking me more and more the harder I rode. The wind cut through my naked body and smacked against my face, making my eyes water till I could not see, for the ice quickly formed on my eyelashes. I tell you, it was hard. But somehow I managed to separate one animal from the herd and as he ran I shot two arrows into him, which made him stumble again and again though he was tough enough to keep going. But I knew I had him, that sooner or later he would fall. So I jumped off to rub my hands in snow, for I had lost all feeling in them. Then I shot again, running up to him as he weaved and staggered. And then he fell dead."

Through this recital the guests sat tense, but as soon as it was ended, they rubbed their palms together as they always did to denote satisfaction, and one or more placed a hand over his mouth in the gesture of wonderment and admiration, exclaiming, "Splendid, grandson. You did well!"

The boy went on. "Soon two men appeared out of the grayness. They were my father here, and one other, and they carried sticks for a fire. While I warmed myself, they threw my robe back on me. It had slipped off when the tie broke. But I was colder with it on than without it, for in that short while the shaggy fur had become packed with snow. It was very bad, I tell you." When Little Chief said that last, he quickly dipped and then turned his head to the side with a jerk by way of emphasis—a mannerism that boys and young men affected.

"I am sure it was," his grandfather agreed in a trembling

voice. Then he turned to his guests and said proudly, "But note, my friends. He got what he went after, his buffalo."

The guests cried in a chorus, "He did indeed!" And one of them, who liked to be ceremonious, added while he held up an index finger, "One!" with a rising inflection as though beginning to count. He meant "One, and then two, then three, and then many more. This is only the beginning." The prophecy pleased the grandfather mightily, so mightily that he said to Gloku, "Put out some more food; let us feast again. It is some time now since we ate." It was not, but Gloku quietly obeyed and the old men ate another lunch before they went home.

Three achievements of her brother—all successful. Waterlily was bursting with pride and wished she dared get up before all the people at the next give-away and take part, to honor him as women honored their brothers for like deeds.

CHAPTER 10

Star Elk had proved so thoroughly inadequate as a husband, during the short while he and Blue Bird lived together, that there was no reason to suppose he might have measured up any better as a father and that he would have brought to Waterlily the honors that came to her through her kindly stepfather, Rainbow. He had arranged the *hunka* for her when she was a child. Then, when she was fifteen years old, he sponsored for her the rare Buffalo Ceremony, which marked her turning point from childhood to adolescence. For both he bore much of the cost, which came high. But it ensured Waterlily lasting prestige such as only the beloved child enjoyed. It was only natural therefore that as she grew more thoughtful and observant she grew more appreciative of him, and that it was something of a personal triumph for her when Rainbow was bidden to the Kit Fox society.

The bid came as a complete surprise. On a beautiful autumn morning the herald, as usual, went around the camp circle proclaiming the news just released from the council tipi in the center; and as usual, everyone strained to catch his words as he came nearer. When he rode past Black Eagle's group of tipis the words were plain, though their meaning was at first obscure. He was saying, "I am few. Four of me have gone south [to death], and I am few. And so on this day I invite you, Gray Eagle, and you, Swift Hawk, and you, Resting Wind, and you, Rainbow, to meet me face to face."

The old and time-honored Kit Fox society was speaking; the herald was its mouthpiece. In such formal and cryptic language had the Kit Fox bidden new members since time immemorial. Of course the entire camp circle buzzed with the news, for this was one of the truly great and rare occasions. There would be generous feasts given by the relatives of the initiates, and there would be much to see. The Kit Foxes would first mourn ceremonially for their deceased members, and then elaborately welcome the new ones chosen to replace them. With spectacular pageantry they would stage their unique dance, which always drew crowds of onlookers. They would wear the distinctive Kit Fox attire and the one-sided haircut peculiar to them. It would be an exciting affair, and everyone, big and little, began at once to plan on it, wishing to look well in gala dress because of the many visitors that would surely be on hand.

The actual time and place of choosing new members was always private, though of course it was expected, eventually, after a member or members had died. The ones bidden were as surprised as everyone else, and quite understandably pleased by the very high compliment, for it was a fact that membership in the proud Kit Fox might in no way be bought or sought. A warrior was bidden who had achieved his four feathers designating four major war deeds; or a man of peace was bidden who was industrious and had some outstanding skill. In addition, every candidate must have a record of consistent hospitality and generosity, which were the qualities that marked a good citizen of the camp circle.

For Rainbow, it was a signal honor, he being the youngest of the four. The other three had long been prominent and articulate in tribal affairs, while he had always been content to remain quiet in the background. It was a surprise not that those three had been chosen now, but that they had been bypassed so long. Of Rainbow, people said, "To be sure, an excellent choice. He is just the type—quick, agile, ready to serve whenever necessary, as a Kit Fox must be."

"That is true. And though he never has much to say, he concerns himself in tribal activities. Look at the feasts he has given, honoring his daughter, who is not his real daughter . . . A good man." Enough could not be said of him. He had general approval and the good wishes of all. No small thing it was to be bidden to the Kit Fox.

The bold heralding of the candidates' names without first warning or sounding them out was the haughty Kit Fox way of daring them to refuse the invitation. Should one do so, it would only mean he was unsure of himself, or of his worthiness, or that the Kit Fox had made a mistake.

But the Kit Fox did not make false choices. It picked its members wisely and could boast that no bid it made was ever turned down. This fact, this record, gave it enormous prestige, comparable to that of the other five ancient societies in the tribe. Spurious societies sprang up from time to time, flourished for a while, and then died out. Only those six had always been, their origin, their institution, lost in mythology.

The executive Chiefs' Society and the advisory Owl Headdress were composed of elderly, venerable worthies who did much sitting and deliberating. The remaining four, known as Badgers, Stout Hearts, Crow-keepers, and Kit Foxes, were military orders ever alert for action. It was not demanded of them, or of any man, to go to war unless he wanted to go. The military orders functioned rather as messengers, scouts, camp police, in short, as guardians of the camp circle and its people. They patrolled and regulated the communal hunt and in every way carried out the orders of the magistrates and council. These four societies went on duty by turns. When, for instance, it was the Kit Fox's turn, the members must be ready for any assignment and any emergency. The rest of the time they were a loosely organized social club and met occasionally for dancing and feasting, free to pursue their individual interests otherwise.

But winter was upon them now, and preparations could not be made hurriedly for the induction. They must wait until spring, when the people would be in the camp circle again. This gave the families of the candidates ample time to get ready to give feasts and generous gifts at the give-away that inevitably followed. The relatives in Black Eagle's camp bestirred themselves to make a creditable showing in honor of Rainbow, for although he was an outsider tied to them only through marriage, he was well liked by all because he was a good relative to all.

Through the constant visiting that always went on, the news had been carried far and wide, and many came from other camp circles to join in the festivities when they took place in midspring. Among those visitors was one who came from High Eagle's people, far to the east and south. The man brought a message for Rainbow that entailed a journey for him immediately. It was fortunate for him that the Kit Foxes had only recently gone off duty. He could go and return before it would be necessary for him to function in his new capacity.

The bearer of the message came to his tipi, upon his invitation, and Blue Bird immediately set food before him. After he had eaten and the two men had smoked the pipe together, he said, "I come from far away to bring my nephew's message. He was very ill all winter but is now well, and this is what he said, 'When I lay at death's door I thought of my friend and longed for his companionship again. Tell him if he can to come to me for a few days' visit; I cannot go to him at this time.'"

"I will go at once, if my friend wants me," Rainbow replied. "Uncle, when you return I will accompany you." The man went away.

"I suppose that is the man you call Palani [Pawnee]," Blue Bird said. Palani was someone definitely placed in her mind from Rainbow's telling about him, but she had never met him.

"Who else?" Rainbow asked. "For him alone would I make a journey at this time. Get ready now, and get the children ready. We shall start very soon."

Blue Bird did not question his decision because she knew what fellowhood meant. A kola was someone special; his wishes and needs could not be ignored, for that was the basis of the relationship. Everyone knew that. Blue Bird knew the story of Rainbow and Palani's meeting. During those restless years following the death of Little Chief's mother, Rainbow sojourned in distant places. There he and Palani met and took an instant liking to each other, and before parting they entered into what was known as fellowhood, a solemn friendship pact that must endure forever. "Fellows" were men of comparable standing and ability who were drawn together by like tastes and by a mutual respect and admiration for each other's character and personal charm. "The best I have is for my fellow" was their code from the time they pledged eternal loyalty. In line with that, one's best horse automatically went to the other whenever they met after a prolonged separation. When possible, they went on the warpath together in order to protect each other. In every phase of life they must act without thought of self, in defense of and to the advantage of the other. One must give one's life to save the other. Fellowhood was a compelling association whose obligations were a pleasure.

Two men who became fellows, *kola,* immediately thereby placed themselves in the limelight, fully cognizant that others watched them, as if saying, "Well, so they think themselves worthy of so high a calling, do they? We shall see how they will measure up!" For men of doubtful stature who became *kola* without counting the cost soon petered out and became the butt of many jokes and the derision of men. It was no wonder that instances of fellowhood were not common, since much thought was needed before taking the step.

The demands on fellows were somewhat greater even than those on natural brothers, loyal and devoted as brothers were supposed to be. And automatically, like brothers, each fellow was son to the other's parents and father to his children. All other relatives were likewise shared. Each was brother-in-law to the other's wife, but with this difference: whereas an informality, marked by joking and taking one another in an offhand manner, was ordinarily permitted between brother- and sister-in-law, men in fellowhood must respect and venerate the other's wife like a sister.

They planned to travel together, for both safety and sociability, the uncle, his wife and their son, and Rainbow and his family and his mother, Gloku, making up the party. Prairie

Flower, whom Waterlily had insisted on inviting, was also going. Her mother, Dream Woman, quickly packed her things, including a fancy gown for dress-up, and she was ready. Leaping Fawn was a dutiful cousin to Waterlily, but, being older by a few years, she was used to friends her own age. Besides, so Waterlily told her mother one day, there was something stiff and formal about Leaping Fawn that kept her a little distant. "Not that she scares you, but it is not so easy to have fun with her as with Prairie Flower." The two girls going on the journey were excited over the prospect. They had never been far from the camp circle before.

It was a leisurely trip. To spare the horses, now that Palani was well again, there was no need of hurrying there. They stopped each day near some stream or pond and made camp in daylight. The men, who were ever on guard, rode out from the party from time to time to see that no enemy war party was about in the stretches of deserted country they must cross, and incidentally they were able to shoot a deer or other animal and supply fresh meat for the cooks when they made camp.

For Rainbow and his family the evenings around the campfire, where all the cooking was done and all the travelers sat together to eat, were especially exciting. Both the uncle and his wife had much to tell that was novel and fascinating about the place they were going. One evening the uncle turned to Rainbow and asked, "When you visited High Eagle's people, the time you and Palani made your pact, was the camp circle on the open prairie perhaps? Well, you will find that it is now permanently located on the bottomland near the Roiled Water [the Missouri]. It is near good water and there is plenty of firewood from the willow copses and the cottonwood trees along the bank. But that is not the only reason. Truth is that they want to be near the stockade where the Long Knife soldiers stay."

Everyone in Rainbow's party was agog, wishing to hear more about the American soldiers, their appearance, their possessions, their habits, and their families. Up there in their home territory, in the northwestern part of Dakota country, the white man was still a rarity. So the uncle was happy to talk and impress his audience. "Listen to this," he said. "Every single day their big-holy-iron booms out the most deafening blast at sun-set. You cannot imagine the sound. Wait till you hear it! People out hunting far off claim they can hear it. I promise you it will hurt your ears until you think your hearing is killed, but you will get used to it in time." That was his description of a cannon salute.

But that was only the start. He told also about "rolling wood," by which he meant wagons. The wheel and its operat-ing principle was especially difficult to explain and the man ended by saying, "Wait and you shall see for yourselves." He said rolling-wood carriers were hitched to mules or horses and that people sat in the carriers to be hauled about. Well, it was understandable that such a queer people would use their own queer vehicles. But when the uncle said that some of the Dako-tas themselves, whose daughters lived within the stockade as wives of the soldiers, also rode about in them, that was too much. Blue Bird turned to the man's wife with an aside. "I am sure no one could ever coax me into one of those rolling-wood things. Have you ridden in one? *Ya!* I would die before I could step back out onto solid ground!"

The woman was talking next, telling of woven goods that lay in thick bolts on the traders' shelves, in all sorts of bright colors and designs and figures. To this Blue Bird said, "And you mean that people go in and buy pieces, any length and any color, as they want?" It was unbelievable. She would have to be shown. "Back home," she told the woman, in quiet tones so as not to disturb the conversation on the men's side of the fire, "we see once in a while a shirt or a gown of that stuff, when visitors come for celebrations, and I have actually owned a piece of red goods, but they remain a curiosity. To think that I am going to see them in plenty, and actually buy what I want of them! I am really eager to get there now!"

The two girls whispered into each other's ear. "What kind will you buy?" "Some red stuff; I want a bright red gown to take home." That was Waterlily. "And you?" "I'd like a gown the color of the sky." That was Prairie Flower. To young girls used only to clothing of skin here was something they could hardly wait for.

But the woman was talking again to Blue Bird. "The traders' stores are full of everything. There are knives and kettles and things all made of *maza* [metal]; and also there are bowls and cups of a stuff like mussel shell"—the things she had to tell! Was there any end to the unheard-of items? The wonder of it all! As if the travelers were going straight into another world—which of course they were.

Rainbow was speaking. "What kind of people are the Long Knives, really? The only one I ever saw at close range I did not like. It was at Two Packs' winter camp up north where I was staying. He showed up one day hungry and ragged." He turned to Blue Bird, "I have told you of this before," then back to his companion, "The man was all hair. And his eyes were the color of clear ice, blue and cold. His hair was yellow as a sunflower on his head and over the lower half of his face. He undressed before everyone and you could see that his arms and neck and chest to the navel were black with hair, matted, ugly! That was as far as he was exposed. No one doubted his whole body was just as hairy. Glum and queer-acting as he was, he interested Two Packs, who planned to adopt him. 'I will have him as a son, for an oddity,' he declared. 'Perhaps in time he will learn our language and then we shall know what he is thinking.' But the fellow sneaked off at dawn one day," Rainbow chuckled, "taking Two Packs' best horse."

Little Chief and the son of the other family had been out tending the horses and Ohiya had tagged along. They had come in sometime during this conversation and were sitting quietly behind their fathers. Suddenly Ohiya asked, "Did they track him down and recover the horse?" Rainbow replied, "What do you think, son? Had he not been received as a guest?" and that seemed to answer Ohiya's question.

Long after the meal they sat talking, so long after that everyone was hungry again and glad of the lunch Blue Bird warmed up and served by the light of the lambent fire. Just when the conversation seemed to die down for the night, the uncle said, between puffs on his pipe, "To go back to your question, What are they like? Well, I would say that many of them seem very stern and hard. They are strangely dull toward those about them. They go along on their way without recognizing fellow humans as they pass, very unmannerly they seem, some of them at least. Of course, I only see a few. And their looks? Well, first of all, let me tell you about their eyes. Many have blue eyes, some have brown, some have yellow, and not a few have black eyes, as black as ours. And their hair? If it is not yellow, it is brown, or black, or a blazing red. Their skins are faded and pale—what of it you can see through the hair, that is. But— here's an odd thing—if they stay in the hot sun all day they do not turn a dark brown as we do, but actually a bright crimson!"

"Oh, unbelievable! Crimson faces!"

"Yes, and arms, too. I once saw several of them swimming in the hot sun, stripped to the waist. They were hairy and red, all right."

Waterlily was aghast, so much so that she forgot she had been taught never to break into the conversation of her elders, especially of men. Her curiosity got the best of her and she asked, "Do their women have hair on their faces, too? And do they get crimson in the sun?"

"I think not," the uncle tried to recall. "I think not. I never saw a woman with a red face, and I believe their faces are free of hair. But we do not see the women close because they stay inside the stockade most of the time."

Blue Bird had listened to the incredible story with very little comment till now. But when she gained the woman's ear she said to her in a low tone, "And their children—what about them?" Her interest always leaned toward children, her own first and then others.

"Ah, wife of my nephew, I was coming to that. And it will surprise and shock you." She spoke with the air of one about to tell something too fabulous to believe. "Listen! those people actually detest their children! You should see them—slapping their little ones' faces and lashing their poor little buttocks to make them cry! Why, almost any time of day if you walk near the stockade you can hear the soldiers' wives screaming at their children. Yes, they thoroughly scold them. I have never seen children treated so . . . Only if a woman is crazy might she turn on her own child, not knowing what she did."

Blue Bird was speechless for a time, but at last she sighed, "It is hard to imagine that. Why do they do it?"

"I suppose," the woman said, "when the children are naughty, that is the quaint way of training them to be good. By talking loudly and fast and by striking them, the people doubtless hope to scare them into good behavior. I know it sounds queer."

"Truly," Blue Bird said, "I can see but one effect, myself. It should only make them act worse, frightened so they cannot think. But I suppose the children are used to it, knowing no other way. Poor things!"

The woman went on from there in a happier vein as she described the fragile beauty of the American soldiers' children. "Their chiseled faces, their flowerlike coloring would make you believe the Maker of Men fashioned each one by hand while studying carefully for the best effect." But Blue Bird found little solace in that. After all, could one's physical beauty compensate for so horrible a lot? She hugged Smiling One close, feeling sick with sympathy for the unknown children. Such were the impressions Rainbow's party got from the things told them.

Next day they traveled only a short while and then made camp for the night, even though their destination was all but in plain sight and the day was young. Visitors should not straightway enter, without first letting it be known that they were about to arrive. The uncle rode on ahead to announce them and particularly to report to Palani that he had brought Rainbow with him and that the meeting of the two *kola* was very near. At once Palani and his *tiyośpaye* got ready to receive them. And meantime, at their camp, Blue Bird unpacked the various articles she had brought for return gifts, knowing that they would be feasted and given presents and many women would be bringing courtesy food to her tipi.

Soon enough, for Palani had remained in readiness daily, he was seen coming out to welcome them and bring them in. He rode a black horse and led a handsome iron gray, and everyone knew that one was for Rainbow. But Rainbow was ready, too. He had kept a sorrel mare with blond tail and mane tied to a stake near his tipi, where she was grazing contentedly, unaware that very shortly she would be changing owners.

In those days, the ordinary run of horses were called "com- mon horse," a term that referred to the small animals derived from wild herds of mustangs that roamed the plains. From tribe to tribe they spread rapidly, by trade or as gifts exchanged during times of truce, but more often by a systematic horse stealing, which was a legitimate part of all intertribal warfare. Almost everyone could and did acquire common horses. The so-called white man's horse, or American horse, was something else, and quite special. It was a larger animal, better in all respects but principally in its looks and power to endure. The American horse was rare. Only very able men here and there managed to acquire them and owned them with pride. Both Palani's iron gray and Rainbow's sorrel were American horses. Between men in fellowhood, nothing common would do.

When Palani approached, Rainbow, who rode out to meet him, dismounted for their greeting, "*Hao, kola!*" ("Greetings, friend!") As they spoke, they incidentally exchanged the ropes by which they had been leading their horses, without saying anything about them, so that when they walked back to the camp, Rainbow was leading the iron gray and Palani the sorrel. On this, their first meeting since ten years before, when they pledged abiding loyalty to each other, they thus quietly carried out the imperative of their code, "The best I have is for my *kola*." It was neatly done.

"We will start at once for the camp circle," Palani said, after greeting his new sister-in-law and the others. At once he began to address Gloku as mother, Rainbow's children as daughters and sons, and Prairie Flower as niece, according to the system of relationships through which all social life was carried on. And when they arrived at Palani's camp, the welcome accorded Rainbow's family was no different from that to lifelong relatives returning home after a long absence. It was, in fact, a homecoming. The wives of the two brothers addressed each other as sisters, and all Palani's relatives also became appropriately related to Rainbow's family. Before long they were all associating together, even the children, as close relatives in a warm, intimate atmosphere. The visitors could not feel strange where everything made them belong.

They were feasted and honored in various ways, and as their acquaintance spread, it seemed as though they did nothing but go from one tipi to another, where they were bidden as guests. Amid all this social whirl, Palani invited his friend to stay long enough to enjoy the Sun Dance celebration in his company. "It is now only a few days off," he said. "And the preparatory events are already under way. I should be sorry to have you leave now." He had a plan, when he said this, that did not show up until later.

Thus it happened that the visitors from White Ghost's camp circle decided to remain. That decision was to have great significance for the young girl Waterlily. A new, wholly exciting, and at the same time baffling experience lay just ahead, which, far more than the ritual of the Buffalo Ceremony, was to change her from a child to a woman.

Unaware of all this, Waterlily found it thrilling enough just to see the great crowds of visitors arriving from faraway places whose names she had never even heard before. They were all Dakotas, but they were not all Tetons. Some spoke the familiar language in strange dialects that made her and her cousin giggle as they imitated them in private. For some were from the Yankton-speaking people across the Roiled Water, and some, a few, were from the Santee-speaking people still farther east. To one hearing their speech for the first time, it was startling to say the least.

"Isn't it funny, cousin?" Prairie Flower asked. "I know what they are saying, and yet it sounds different."

"Yes," Waterlily tried to explain it, "It is as though they were talking beyond a curtain—it comes out all right, but not too plainly."

The young girl felt vicariously honored to see how popular her father, Rainbow, was. Many men had known him before, and now, since he had been recognized by the local Kit Fox members by his one-sided haircut, he was being included in their meetings and activities. Such honors! How glad Waterlily was that they had come.

Each succeeding day was more interesting than the last, and now this—the Omahas were coming. They were coming to sing. Whatever that might mean, as the crier rode by announcing it, Waterlily did not understand. But it sounded intriguing, especially because the entire camp circle buzzed with the news.

"They have already arrived! Yonder you may see them putting up their camp. They are preparing to sing. We all know how they can sing! This is an event. You men who are *men,* you who can give away your best without your pulse quickening, get ready to give as becomes you. According to their custom, the visitors are coming to 'sit down Omaha style.' Be prepared to meet them worthily!" In such phrases the announcer rallied the people.

"It will be a great sight," Palani told his guests. "Up there in the north your people have never seen anything like it. You will enjoy it. You must all go and look on."

If the word "Omaha" and the term "to sit Omaha style" had any vague meaning to Blue Bird, they certainly were completely strange to the girls. Among White Ghost's people, the names of distant tribes in the south and east were only names. But to Rainbow, the erstwhile roamer, the Omahas were known. He had heard tell of their record in war with the southern Tetons, and of their periodic meetings with them under truce, when they came with their families. Certainly they were welcome to the prayerful Sun Dance. Among the Dakotas all traditional enemies were received in friendship for that annual celebration, and the courtesy was reciprocated. There were no instances known of Dakotas' being refused entree to the Sun Dance of another plains tribe.

The following morning was crisp and clear. The air was charged with expectancy. As the Omahas in the distance methodically arranged themselves for their approach, the more far-sighted of the Tetons announced their movements from time to time, not always agreeing in what they saw, however. "Now they are ready." "Now they are moving." "No, not yet; they are still marshaling themselves." "Yes, so they are." "Now! Now they are walking." "Yes, they are walking." "They are definitely on their way."

During all this time the Dakotas too had been arranging

themselves. The men who were *men*, who prided themselves on being able to give their best unflinchingly, "without their pulse quickening," were spanned out in a front rank, holding one or more gift horses by ropes, while the women and children and such men and youths as had not yet attained top status in the tribe followed them in a great crowd. The Dakota group was comparable in size to the Omaha group.

At the instant when it was clear that the Omahas were marching, the Dakotas shouted the usual signal cry, "*Hokahe!*" and started together. Steadily and determinedly the two peoples drew toward each other in ceremony, out on the open prairie. But they did not meet. When they were somewhat more than one hundred paces apart, both sides came to an abrupt halt and stood arrayed facing each other.

There was no denying it; the Omahas presented a magnificent picture. Waterlily and Prairie Flower whispered breathlessly that never had they seen anything like it before. Tall, stalwart, and self-assured in their gorgeous costumes of costly white buckskin heavily fringed and brilliantly ornamented, with war standards high and feathers flying, truly the Omahas were a breathtaking sight. And as they stood motionless there on the lush green grass, under an intensely blue sky with only a few sharply white clouds floating against it, the fresh morning breeze caught their colorful standards and flirted them about gracefully.

And so they stood without a word for a long moment before the Omaha men in front seated themselves on the ground in a long, straight row, facing the Dakotas, who continued to stand throughout the entire ceremony. In a solid background the other Omahas remained standing behind their men. All the Omaha faces were painted red, even the children's.

Immediately then their singers stepped out in the open, in front of the seated men, placed their drum on the ground and gathered about it, and began to sing in clear voices, beating time with ornamented drumsticks. All the Omaha men took up the strain and swelled it, filling the air with indescribably sweet melody. The many and varied songs were extremely well sung. To many of them the women added a descant, something quite apart and yet related to the melody, coming in unexpectedly, in shrill voices at a piercing, high pitch.

Song followed song to regale the Dakotas. Occasionally an Omaha, no doubt one of their best singers, stood up to sing alone. Again the women added their peculiar accompaniment, but more softly so as not to drown out the solo voice. The Dakotas listened entranced and cheered each song at its close, whispering to one another as they applauded, "The Omahas *have* come to sing, indeed!"

Especially to the visitors from the north all this was gripping. There was so much here to tell back home on a winter's evening, when callers would surely come in to hear tales of the south. They must observe every bit of it; they must not let any detail escape them. But the total effect—how could that ever be communicated adequately? For here was something one must see and feel for oneself, all this color and sound and action on this exquisitely beautiful day.

When the last song died away, it was the Dakotas' turn to act. Nor did they hesitate. The ceremonial give-away was fundamental to all plains life. For the Dakotas, it was their particular pride and glory. And now here it was to be elevated to its sublime height, in one concerted act. Not from person to person, as usual, but from tribe to tribe. The men who were *men* were ready to give their horses. Their wives, standing behind them, could hardly be seen for the great packs of other gifts that they proudly bore on their backs.

The Dakotas were all rather shabbily dressed. They had in fact come just as they were, in commonplace daily garb, for that was the custom: the host must be plainly dressed so as not to shame the guest by seeming competition. But the guest was free to be as elaborate as he could afford. It was expected of him.

After the vigorous give-away, when all Dakota gifts were in Omaha hands and the Omaha singers and cheerers had lauded the givers to the skies, then some of the Omahas stepped out into the open and briefly danced the characteristic social dance for which they were known, the Omaha, or Grass, Dance.

Suddenly it was over. The visiting tribe turned about and

betook themselves to their own camp yonder, while the Dakotas broke ranks and walked home in informal groups, on the way discussing and admiring the sing. And as they began to head for their scattered tipis, men shouted to one another, "Tomorrow it will be our turn to sing. We will be wise to prepare at once. Tomorrow at this time we ourselves shall come out to sit 'Omaha style.'"

And so they did. The entire event was repeated in reverse, with the Omahas coming out as hosts and givers and the Dakotas as guests to sing for them. This time it was the Omahas who were simply dressed while the Dakotas wore their finery, which, if anything, was even more impressive than the Omahas', or so it was agreed by the two girl spectators. The taller Dakota men appeared even handsomer, their costumes more stunning, their stride more direct, their carriage more erect and regal. All the men forming the front rank had on their splendid eagle-feather warbonnets, some round, the long plumes drooping gracefully about the shoulders, others with the long feather trailers that gently brushed and bent the grass behind the men as they walked along. For this was the Dakotas' headdress, and it lent a certain majesty to its wearer. Prairie Flower was proud to say, "Every man is a chief."

The Dakota singers took their position in front, and as they sang, their songs after all proved an even match to the Omahas' in beauty and intricacy and style. The visiting tribe was delighted with them, to judge by the cheers and spirited applause after each song. It was always a treat to hear the songs of other tribes, for even though all plains singing might sound monotonously alike to an unaccustomed ear, the character of each tribe's songs and its style of delivery were distinctive enough for neighboring tribes to identify them and enjoy their novelty.

Truly the Omahas had come not only to receive but to give. With the same liberality and readiness of the Dakotas the day before, they gave their gifts, of many kinds and equally high quality. The result of this mass generosity back and forth was an increasing sense of friendship and comaraderie. Now at last the two tribes mingled freely and the visitors were invited to move in and be one with the Dakotas. All enmity was forgotten as they prepared to pray together in the great Sun Dance. "Any Omaha who has made a vow and cares to carry it out at this time is welcome to do so with us," the visitors were told. None was barred from this common prayer because of tribal differences.

For a time it was all Waterlily and her cousin could do to dodge the crowds returning homeward. But at last they were in the clear. Waterlily was thoughtful and disturbed and wished her enthusiastic young cousin would not go on and on talking about everything. For her own thoughts were on a certain member of this Dakota group of singers who had drawn close to their immense drum and led the chorus.

And well she might, for he was at once the youngest and the handsomest of all the singers. His sweet voice continued to sing in her ear and a moving picture of him in action unreeled endlessly before her eyes, and she did not see the people about her. Such ability in leading the singers, all older than himself! Such personal charm—or so it seemed, by the way the others continually looked to him for direction and at the same time laughed and joked with him. Was he born singing and leading? You would think so by the fact he was completely at home in his role and unflustered by the hundreds of eyes on him in admiration. Who was he? What was his name? Where did he come from? The questions surged in Waterlily's brain, piling up on each other until she suddenly grew frightened, thinking she had actually asked them aloud. But Prairie Flower was quite unaware of her in her own excitement.

Here was the first man Waterlily had noticed. Since her turning point in the Buffalo Ceremony she had been eligible to be courted. But until she saw this altogether attractive youth she had taken no notice of men. She had deliberately stayed away from the courting hour, too diffident to go with the other young women when they went out near sunset for food or water, knowing that the young men of the camp, wrapped in their blankets, waited in hiding to catch them alone and declare their intentions.

From the instant he caught her eye, she had found it a struggle to keep from looking at him. And if in glancing about casually he happened to look in her direction, she had quickly looked elsewhere, frowning as though puzzling out something yonder that was not there at all. She was sure her finesse had been perfect. He could not have supposed on any account that he attracted her; that she, a total stranger, was boldly making up to him. No, that would never do. It was contrary to all the rules of maidenly behavior, rules that had never been any effort to keep. Perhaps tomorrow she might meet him again. If so, she would in every way be circumspect. Her cousin, Prairie Flower, who was always with her, must not suspect anything. Nobody must!

She was almost glad to be on her way home to safety. But then her cousin, still a child since she had not had a Buffalo Ceremony, shocked her by a too candid question: "Cousin, you know that youngest singer—the one who kept looking at you—he . . ." Waterlily's interruption was casual-sounding, "I am sure I have no idea what singer you mean." But the question excited her all over again. To think that he too had been unable to keep from looking! And that Prairie Flower had noticed it!

They reached their tipi hot and tired from all they had seen. Waterlily wanted to get where she could think, where no one would upset her. And she felt impatient to find Smiling One digging right in the doorway while a small relative stood by with her first tooth in her hand, waiting to bury it. "Get out of the way," Waterlily said sharply. "Not where people must walk! Bury it to one side of the entrance. Do you want our cousin to sicken and die from people's walking over her tooth?" She said "die" callously. To her, dying was still no more than a word. One so young and so alive could mouth it without apprehension.

Blue Bird came in just then, eager to hear all about the sing, for she had offered to stay home with all the children of the relatives that the parents might have an opportunity to attend. "Daughter," she asked with unusual interest, "Was it wonderful again? Did our tribesmen look and sing as well as the Omahas yesterday? I hope so."

Neither had caught the other's mood. Waterlily was indifferent to the question, unable to see how much it meant to Blue Bird. Blue Bird failed to notice that there was a change in Waterlily, that something was preoccupying her. Never had she been offhand to a question from her mother before. The girl answered absently, "Oh, yes . . . I guess so." And then, seeing her mother expecting more details, she added, "It was about the same . . . it was all, well, fair." Already the "Omaha sitting" to which she had looked forward with high excitement was commonplace, in the light of what might happen tomorrow.

CHAPTER II

The Dakota Sun Dance might vary in minor details from band to band, but in essentials it was all the same—in purpose, in mood, in character. And in importance it was rated higher than any other ceremonial. For there was brought together, into one great religious event, the fulfillment of all the vows that men in their distress had made during the preceding year; there also the corporate prayers for the tribe's well-being were offered, in tears.

Time was, so the ancient ones said, when each man fulfilled his pledge to the Great Spirit singly. Fasting and weeping and singing, and sometimes even scarifying himself, out alone on some distant peak, he did his praying solitarily. But long before Waterlily's time the Sun Dance had become an organized complex, made up of many small rites and elements accompanying the actual dancing while gazing at the sun.

Rainbow's party were about to witness the Sun Dance as Palani's people staged it. And now, some days after the arrival of the Omahas and of tribes coming in groups from many places far and near, they were ordered to move to the site that had been selected for the main ceremony. The traditional specification was observed, "A virgin spot apart, unpolluted by humankind."

No sooner had the crier completed his round, telling the people to get ready, than tipis began to come down and in an unbelievably short while the move began. The destination was not far; it could have been easily reached without the necessity of stopping to rest on the way. But this was a ceremonial move and it was essential to make the four ritual pauses along the way, in honor of the four sacred directions, the Four Winds.

At the new site the people placed their tipis in one vast circle that embraced hosts and visitors together as one. From then on, the events at hand were the subject of all conversation. One heard people saying, "Tomorrow is the day they bring home the tree for the sacred pole." "Already the scouts have located it . . . very

straight and tall it is, they say. The finest in the woods." "Did you know that tonight the holy men will sit in a special tipi and sing prayers the whole night through, asking for a clear day?" "It will be a clear day tomorrow . . . You wait and see." "It never fails; that prayer is always granted." And it was a clear day with a sky unmarred by even one cloud.

The preliminary rites leading up to the Sun Dance itself always followed a certain progression. Already some of them had been finished at the old site. And now one more, perhaps the most significant, was at hand: the getting of the sacred pole. A solemn rite must first be performed in front of it as it stood in the woods, as though it were sentient and understood what was going on.

For some unexplained reason Palani was most insistent that Waterlily and Prairie Flower attend this. He said it more than once to Blue Bird. "Sister-in-law, you must take the girls there. I want them to go." When he was leaving for the center, where the planning committee to which he belonged sat, he called back once again, "Don't fail now!"

Blue Bird was interested in going, anyway. The three hurried to be there on time. Already there was a great crowd milling about looking for a vantage ground from which to see. "It is quite hopeless," Blue Bird said. "We may as well go back. We don't have a chance here." But before the girls said anything either in agreement or in protest, a man came up to them.

"Palani wants me to look out for you and find places for you where you can see. This way," and he wedged through the crowd with Blue Bird and the girls following him, until they stood inside the ring of spectators.

An open space had been cleared around the tree by removing smaller trees and underbrush, so that only the victim-tree remained in solitary splendor, for a little while longer. Here and there the several men's societies sat grouped about their drums, by turns singing their own songs. In the Kit Fox group they saw Rainbow, sitting with his back to them. When all the singing ended, a holy man who had been engaged as officiating priest for all the rituals of the Sun Dance stepped out into the open and a silence fell on the crowd.

He carried a pipe of peace on his arm and wore a buffalo robe with the fur on the outside. On his head was perched a stuffed redheaded woodpecker looking real enough to be alive. The holy man made straight for the bowl of incense at the base of the tree and reached out, feigning to take some of it, and then withdrew his hand. Three times he did this, and only the fourth time he actually took a handful of the incense and sprinkled it on the fire burning nearby.

Almost at once the smoke rose thick and dark and very aromatic. The holy man waited a second and then held the pipe above it, letting the smoke play over it thoroughly. Then he raised the pipe high and performed the Peace Pipe rite. This was called "presenting the pipe." And rightly, for he first offered it ceremonially to the Four Winds—the west, the north, the east, and the south—in that precise order. Then he offered it skyward, and lastly earthward, murmuring appropriate ritual words of supplication. From time to time throughout the entire Sun Dance, this rite, like a *Gloria Patri,* was woven in.

After thus presenting the pipe to all that was holy, the officiant recited the "Apology to the Birds." It was a tremendous thing to dare to take another's home, just as it was a serious thing to cut down a kingly tree. This rite was in recognition of that fact, and a justification. The man held the pipe aloft once more and described a great circle overhead with it while he called out in a moving cry,

"You! You living ones, who wing the hillsides of the clouds,
"Give ear to me!
"You, called the red woodpecker,
"You, the flicker,
"You, the robin,
"You, the crested woodpecker:
"This is your tree; your home.
"Here you raise your young.
"Today a comely youth offers himself in sacrifice,
"And he needs your tree.

"He says, 'I take your tree only that my people may learn of you

" 'The way to raise their young as you raise yours, with tender care.'

"He says, 'Only so that my people may live!' "

And then as he ended and stepped to one side, the groups seated about began chanting together the song called "The Tree's Lament." The tree was speaking:

"Once at midday I stood holy,
"Greeting all people, I stood holy.
"In the midst of all, I stood holy.
"Once at midday I stood holy."

The time had come to cut the tree. This cutting was an honor, too, and was performed by eight beloved young people, four youths and four maidens. When they were summoned to the fore, the youths stepped out of the crowd promptly enough, and then two girls, reluctant from shyness, emerged slowly and took their places. But where were the other two?

The crowd waited restlessly, looking around for them. It was at that moment that someone from behind caught Waterlily and Prairie Flower by their wrists, startling them. It was Palani. "Come girls," he whispered, "it is my wish that you have a part in this."

He had been planning it all the while, as still another way of complimenting his special friend, Rainbow, and was prepared to make the necessary gifts for the privilege of entering his daughter and niece. For them personally it was a conspicuous honor. Those who were caused by their relatives to cut the holy tree in their youth had something to recall with pride all their days. Old people would sit together, eyes blind and ears deaf, perhaps, and skin wrinkled and age bowing them down, and yet their faces would light up for an instant as they said, "Once I too cut the sacred tree!" Those who heard them must show them respect for it—not for the actual deed, but for what invariably accompanied it: the giving of feasts and gifts in their name by loving relatives.

Only those in whose name the tribe benefited were worthy of respect; it was the people's way.

Waterlily could not realize what was happening, much less its implications, so suddenly had the honor been thrust upon her and her cousin. But from habit she managed to retain her maidenly composure, with eyes demurely cast downward. When her turn came, the man in charge taught her what to do and she followed his instructions mechanically. She made as though to strike the tree once, twice, three times, but did not touch it with the light ax put into her hand. Only on the fourth did she actually strike. All eight beloveds did the same, hardly denting the bark, for this was only a token. Afterward, strong men with sharp axes quickly felled the tree. But it was not permitted to touch the ground. Ten men in pairs stood ready to catch it on the crosspoles they held between them. And so they bore it homeward, reverently, as though carrying a bier.

As for the crowds, they quickly decked themselves with leaves. Those on foot carried branches of heavy foliage in front of them, some as tall as they, and many persons managed to break off a stem of leaves from the sacred tree to wear for its beneficent effect. Those on horseback decorated not only themselves but also and even more their horses. Each horse wore a huge collar of leaves and a fillet of the same across the forehead; festoons were intertwined with the bridle and reins and tail, and garlands were wound about the flanks and hoofs, until very little of the horse was visible. The riders carried great shields of leaves held by a string caught onto the left arm. They also wore fillets. The total effect of that much green moving toward the camp circle was grand. "A magnificent spectacle!" people said who watched at home.

By midmorning the affair was ended but still the onlookers continued to swarm about the tree being prepared for erecting. Blue Bird told the girls, whose excitement was beginning to get out of hand, "Let's get out of the crowd. It is time to get home and rest. This has been a full morning and there is much more to follow."

"What will they do now, Aunt?" Prairie Flower continued to

look back, curiously. "The usual thing. They will put up the tree and then quickly build the Sun Dance lodge around it and the screen at the honor-place. Just as at home. You have both seen it before."

"It will be bigger, Mother, much bigger," Waterlily insisted. "I heard one man telling another, 'Never was there a Sun Dance so great as this is going to be. I am told that there will be as many as six or seven groups of dancers this time, from the many people who have come as well as our own people here.' So I know it will be bigger."

"I expect so, but it will be the same—except for size," Blue Bird assured them. They walked on saying no more until they stopped to rest midway, for the distance was considerable to any point in the camp circle from the center of activity.

"I should like to see everything, Mother," Waterlily began. "Somehow everything about this Sun Dance seems new and more important than the Sun Dances at home."

Blue Bird laughed. "You're growing up, Waterlily," she said. "You are thinking and seeing more in what goes on, and that is right." A moment later she added, "I'll promise you both this. When, just before sunset, the candidates are marched in to begin the dancing, we will be there to watch. That is something to see, for me too. It is a moving thing. The heart beats faster at the sight of men coming of their own free will to endure suffering in order to keep their word with the Great Spirit. I can never watch them enter the Sun Dance lodge without weeping."

That promise was to the girls' liking; it was something to look forward to. But all afternoon tension ran so high everywhere that the girls got restless and, in time, too excited to sit quietly in their tipi. And so in the general confusion they stole up to the center to see what was going on, and then immediately hurried back un-missed. In the stream of people coming and going nobody took notice of them. Because it was all so extraordinary, their own daring impressed and delighted them as much as what they saw. Most of their lives until now, both girls had stayed under the watchful eye of their women chaperones and been content.

The girls found the Sun Dance lodge completed and the sa-cred pole set up in the center, reaching far above the lodge. The beautiful tree they had helped to cut that morning now stood humbled, shorn of all ornamental green, a plain, lonesome pole, its nakedness hidden with only a film of red ceremonial paint. At the very top a bundle of things was tied fast, and from it some objects cut from rawhide dangled on a string. Waterlily made out the figures of a buffalo bull and a man. She was later told that they were symbols of things for which men prayed. To those who yearned for outstanding military success and glory, the man figure meant an enemy worsted. To those who would be exceptional hunters, the buffalo figure meant food in plenty for them to bring to their people.

The Sun Dance lodge, so called, was not an enclosure but a great circular arbor supported by posts in a rude colonnade. This was for the onlookers who would overcrowd it, some sitting out in front, some standing behind them. The broad, open central area was for the dancing and for incidental activities. At the base of the pole was the sacred object, a buffalo skull. Opposite the entrance into this area, corresponding to the honor-place of a tipi, there were stalls for the dancers to rest in, and behind them was a screen of willows interlaced tightly. Thus all who had a part in the Sun Dance would be exposed to the sun, only the spectators enjoying a measure of comfort in the shade. Men were putting on the finishing touches. Otherwise the dancing space was empty.

At last the time to begin was at hand. All preliminary rites had been carefully finished and everything was in readiness. Already a crowd was there, and from everywhere more and more people, including Blue Bird and the girls, hurried to the scene.

Shortly before sunset all eyes were on several distant tipis set in a row within the circle of tipis. They were the places of preparation for the different groups of dancers. Any moment now the dancers would be emerging to line up and approach in single file toward their place of suffering, accompanied by their mentors, one for each group. At this moment a lone man--the officiating priest who was to direct this particular Sun Dance, who had painted and dedicated the sacred pole and the buffalo skull, who had only that morning apologized to the birds at the cutting ceremony, and who would perform all the remaining rites—that man now entered the dancing space unattended and quietly sat down to smoke and meditate. The mentors alone managed the dancers.

"Here they come now!" was heard on all sides in the waiting crowds. Waterlily and her cousin, with Blue Bird, were fortunate enough to be standing very close to the entrance, where the men must pass directly in front of them. "This is about the best place," Blue Bird said. "We shall see the dancers very near."

There were several groups of the men, from the several camp circles that had come together. They approached with their mentors always alongside their lines, directing them. But even when they were still far away their voices could be heard in what seemed to be a chant, growing louder as they came nearer. Suddenly Prairie Flower whispered to Blue Bird in surprise, "Aunt, it sounds as though they are crying. Imagine men crying!"

"Oh, but they are," Blue Bird whispered back. "This is their ceremonial wailing. They always do it."

Each man held a huge spray of the broadleafed sage in front of his face and wailed behind it. It sounded tragic, as though they felt genuinely bad and were not simply doing it out of formality as part of the ritual.

All of the men were dressed alike, with no attempt at adornment, for they were concerned only with praying intensely, and not with their appearance. Some were further concerned with the prospect of undergoing physical torture by their own volition, according to their particular vows. From the waist up they were naked; their legs, too, were bare. Only their feet were clothed, in moccasins, but those were not neatly tied about the ankles as was becoming and proper. The wearers simply stood in them. About the loins they wore two very white and pliable deerskins, hitched to a belt and allowed to hang loose like two separate pieces of skin, one in front and one behind, and overlaid down the hips. The skins were left intact, not trimmed square, with the result that they hung unevenly down to the knees.

Each man wore a strip of rabbitskin around wrists and ankles, and a rawhide disk "the size of a newborn baby's head" suspended about the neck by a thong so that it rested over the heart. The disk was painted with blue earth and notched around the rim. A single downy feather, pure white, dangled from its center. Each dancer also wore a wreath of sage about the head, and four highly decorated sticks were pinned into his hair, one straight up, one down, the other two horizontal like the arms of a cross, and this was in deference to the four sacred directions.

Waterlily counted the men as they passed her—forty in all, excluding the mentors. Forty men who in some desperate hour had cried out for supernatural aid, "If you help me, I will dance for you while gazing at the sun!" or, "I will hang by my living flesh from the sacred pole," or, "You shall have so many pieces of my body for a sacrifice."

Such were some of the vows about to be fulfilled. Because the men were dressed uniformly and their faces were hidden behind the sprays of sage it was impossible to distinguish one from another. But at least one could tell which were pledged to hang, for they brought their own ropes of braided thong, painted white and carried in a coiled loop suspended from the left arm.

There was so much to see at once that before Waterlily realized it, the various groups had been arranged in lines facing the sun, now low in the west, and the singers had arrived and were seated around their drum, their fancy drumsticks poised for the first beat. They immediately began to beat time softly. Then suddenly they began to sing and at the same instant they beat loudly and decisively on the drum. With the very first beat, as the dancing began, each dancer inserted a Sun Dance whistle between his lips and blew in sharp, shrill staccatos. The whistles were made from the bone of an eagle's wing, and whatever their individual ornamentation, one thing was the same on all of them: a beautiful downy plume, pure white, was attached to the outer end. The plume moved in rhythm with the drumbeats. With each expulsion of breath the plumes flew straight out and with each slight intake they fell. Forty plumes from forty mouths, operating in relentless unison, were a fascination to watch.

Meanwhile the sun had set imperceptibly and twilight was deepening; then it was night. But the moon, full as always for the Sun Dance, cast an eerie glow that threw everything below into half-shadow. The dancing, so begun, continued at the same pace—the throbbing drum, the incessant whistling, and the singing of the musicians—all night long. And so it would continue with hardly a break until the ceremony was completed.

Blue Bird was all too aware that under cover of night many young men were out for a lark and she must keep an eagle eye on the girls. When two youths came and stood very near, she thought it was time to leave. "It is getting late now; we must go home," she said. "Tomorrow you may watch as much as you like." "May we come by ourselves?" Prairie Flower asked. "Yes, as long as it is daylight you may." With that prospect the girls left willingly enough. It had been quite a day and they were tired.

On the way home Prairie Flower talked eagerly of many things but Waterlily was strangely silent as she turned over a problem in her mind. Finally she said, "Mother, when we stood there in the dark I heard two young women arguing whether or not to take water to one of the dancers tonight. Isn't that against the rules?"

Blue Bird admitted that it was. "But sometimes an engaged girl thinks she cannot bear it for her sweetheart to suffer so much, especially if he has undergone torture, and feels she must get a little water to him at any cost. It is rather early to think of that yet, though . . . It is not approved, of course, but the mentors generally manage not to be looking." And then, sensing Waterlily's disturbance, she hastened to add, "It very seldom happens, I think."

"Oh, but that spoils it for me," Waterlily said. "I like to think the dancers keep all the rules . . . What's the use of rules then?" "It spoils it for me, too, cousin," Prairie Flower said. And they talked of it further, the idealistic young girls a bit disillusioned, the mother more tolerant, as they went home to bed.

Several times throughout the next day the girls went to look on and then returned, and each time the scene was changed somewhat, for more elements were introduced as they fell due. People came and went constantly, and at night those with young children were obliged to remain home. But the dance went right on, nor did it want for spectators at any time. The ever changing crowd watched, and assisted with their presence. They spoke only when necessary, and then in hushed tones and briefly. Jok-

ing and laughter were entirely displaced with reverence, for this
was a prayer.

At the evening meal, as the two friends sat talking, Palani
spoke thus: "*Kola,* I wonder if you have noticed one of the dancers; a mere boy he is. There is quite a story about him." Waterlily
and Prairie Flower were also eating in the tipi, and they listened
quietly to the men's talk.

Palani gave the high points of the story. "The father of this boy
had been ailing all year, it seems, and finally died at dawn one day.
Thereupon the boy ran away to the hills and prayed and wailed all
day, "Great Spirit, you alone have the power to give my father
back to me. Give him back, and you shall have one hundred
pieces of my living flesh." At sundown he returned home and
found his father just coming back to life. And so because he
bargained with the Great Spirit for what he wanted most, his
father's life, he is now here to pay that vow. Sometime today, I
understand, he is to give one hundred pieces of flesh for a sacrifice."

The two men agreed that the boy's vow had been a reckless
one, the vow of impetuous youth. "A maturer man," Rainbow
said, "would first consider, even in his despair, whether he would
be able to keep his promise to the full."

"Such a vow," Palani observed, "is not unheard of, certainly.
You and I know of men who have given comparable sacrifices.
But in every case, at least as far as I know, they were fighting men,
men who had tried and proved themselves many times over.
They were seasoned warriors, with great fortitude, who nev-
ertheless knew from many battle wounds how it would hurt."

"Yes, you are right." Palani said. "I do not know the boy or his
real name, but everybody calls him Lowanla, the Singer. And,
you know, he has a beautiful voice, a remarkable skill as a singer.
If he were not dancing now, he would most certainly be leading
the singers. He is in great demand as a leader."

Prairie Flower at least had the good sense to keep still. But as
soon as the girls were alone, she said, with more eagerness than
tact, "Cousin, do you suppose that is the one who sang at the
Omaha sitting?" Waterlily affected indifference. "The dancers

are all so alike; how can we tell which one is youngest or oldest? And they are all skinny from hunger, and with those fillets falling low on their foreheads and their hair hanging over their faces and their heads uptilted toward the sun—how can we tell one from another? Me, I think they all look terrible." "But they aren't trying to look handsome," Prairie Flower defended them, a little amazed at her cousin's unexpected hardness.

When she said nothing more, Waterlily spoke more like herself, "I often wonder why people taking part in a ceremony always leave their hair hanging loose." This was in an effort to change the subject. Prairie Flower took to wondering, too, and soon forgot her original question: Was this Lowanla the same as the singer at the Omaha sitting? Waterlily had neatly sidetracked her cousin. But her own thoughts continued chaotic and dubious, and she felt unaccountably irritated at the girl, though she knew she had meant no harm.

After the morning meal at sunrise—everybody rose early— Blue Bird and the girls went to the center again. The affair was moving steadily toward the climax now; this was the final day. Tomorrow at dawn it would all be over. They found the scene changed and with more variety. During the night more new elements had been introduced and the tortures begun.

The vows of various dancers involving serious physical mutilation had been carried out and their women relatives were wailing for them in low tones. The whole enclosure was filled with suffering. There was something to see wherever you looked. Yesterday it had been more placid and slower paced. Only the dancing while gazing at the sun had gone on, with an occasional rite out to the side, like an ear piercing and naming of some important baby, or the healing rites, when all who were suffering some ailment were called out and placed near the pole to let the sun's curative rays rest on them with accompanying prayer.

But today! Yonder stood a dancer fastened to four posts (which had not been there before), by means of ropes tied to wooden pins skewered through incisions in his body, two on the chest and two below the shoulderblades. And as he continued to dance he threw himself violently away from one post to another in a frantic effort to tear himself free. That man had vowed to "stand corraled." Near him was his favorite horse, tied to one of the posts. He stood quiet and patient, and was fasting too. All day he would go without food and water, in sympathy with his owner. Only after sundown would he be led away to water and grass. But he was not injured; after all, he had made no vow.

Some of the men were not scarified, for they had only promised to dance fasting and gazing at the sun. Not all Sun Dancers had to undergo torture but only those so pledged. No man could compel another to be cut or pierced, nor could anyone try, even out of pity, to dissuade another from keeping a vow once made, however drastic it might be. To promise something to the Great Spirit and then fail to fulfill it was a fearsome thing.

Certain men who were attached to the sacred pole itself, by cuts on the chest, danced on, intermittently jerking away, sometimes pulling back so far that their flesh stood out as though its elasticity were unlimited. When finally one broke away, tearing out the flesh, he fell headlong, amid the cries of anguish from the women spectators, as attendants rushed in to help him to his couch in front of the willow screen. When he had recovered sufficiently, he staggered to his feet and got back in line to dance some more.

But the worst sight of all was that of a man who actually hung from the pole by means of a white-painted thong rope pinned into his back muscles slightly above the waist. It was hard to believe that the weight of his body should not put enough strain on the flesh to tear it out immediately, and yet it was so. With his feet he "danced" in time with the others and all the while he continued to pole himself away as far as possible with the staff in his hand. His feet were less than the width of three fingers above the ground, just enough to make futile his struggles to get a toehold to brace himself. To watch him trying was sheer agony.

Would he ever work himself free? Or would he give up and die hanging? Suddenly a woman broke from the crowd and screamed out in despair while she hurled out a red stick. "I can bear it no longer for my brother to suffer! There goes a horse for the needy!" A few old people in shabby dress and several small boys scrambled for the stick as it fell, knowing that whoever got it got the horse.

So she would ransom her brother; she would buy him back from paying his vow in full, that while the poor were being benefited in his name his suffering might be shortened, justifiably. His mentor hurried to him and cut away the quivering flesh, whereupon he fell limp to the ground and was borne off to rest.

It was all horrible—and fascinating—but the individual sufferers were like sideshows while the main event swept on relentlessly, the singing, whistling, and drumming continuing always at the same tempo. All day long the mentors maneuvered their groups with such skill that they faced the sun constantly as long as it was in the sky. At sunrise they faced east, at sundown, west, having swung around with a movement so smooth that the spectators were unaware of it.

The Sun Dance priest, as intercessor, stayed within the enclosure all the time, but he had nothing to do with the dancers or the sufferers. Unnoticed and free, he moved about quietly. Sometimes you realized that he was sitting near the painted buffalo skull, and at another time at the base of the sacred pole or off to one side; always alone, speaking to no one, he smoked his pipe now and then in deep meditation. But his presence was essential; it validated the religious rites. His time to pontificate would mark the climax and the close.

It was midafternoon when, in a scene more dramatic and unusual than the others, the youthful Lowanla made his sacrifice. Pitying his tender age, the mentors had agreed to postpone his ordeal until the last so that afterward he would not have to dance so long.

An elderly man walked into the dancing groups and tapped the youth on the shoulder from behind and led him away. There in the open space between the pole and the entrance he made him sit down. Then he began to speak. Few could catch the import of his words against the singing, but everyone knew that he was giving his credentials, in the customary way. He was no doubt saying, in effect, "I should not presume to cut the living flesh of another man. I should not feel myself fit to have a part in so great an offering but that I myself know what it is; on my body I carry one hundred scars." Such a statement was a prerequisite in such instances. Never was it allowed for one who had not himself endured hardship to require it of another.

The old man rubbed cold water over Lowanla's shoulders and down his arms. Then, using a strong cactus spike, he pricked the skin and pulled it out while with the sharp knife he quickly snipped off a tiny piece and laid it on the hide spread out to receive it. Starting near the neck and alternating from one side to the other, he made a line of cuts along the shoulders. Blood trickled down in parallel streams, but the youth only bit his lip and frowned and did not flinch nor utter a sound.

The grieving people watched in silence, knowing that this was something that must be done and that any protesting in his behalf would be out of order. But after the man had taken ten pieces from each side, with eighty to go, two elderly women who were the youth's aunts rushed out, frantically tearing away their gowns and baring their shoulders as they went, and demanded that the remaining cuts be made on them instead. This was extraordinary. Nothing like it had ever been known before. Perhaps it should not be permitted, since there was no precedent for it. A man must and did keep his own pledge by himself. But even then Lowanla had fallen backward in a faint. The several mentors went into a hurried conference and decided, "We will allow it this once. The boy is still so tender. It is right that his aunts should come to his rescue. It is admirable of sisters to honor a brother by being good to his child. We will allow it this time."

The aunts were very brave. Haughtily they looked on as the man cut their flesh, leaving a line of tiny wounds evenly spaced and extending well down their arms, fifteen on each side. The two women had given sixty pieces and would have given more, but that at that instant the cutting was interrupted when Lowanla's two elder sisters came up and quietly offered to give the remaining twenty. So the man took ten from each, and the one hundred pieces, so recklessly pledged, were paid. The cutter tied them into a small bundle, painted the bundle red, and delivered it to the intercessor, who sat at a distance. After seeming to reject it three times, as a ritualistic gesture, he accepted it the fourth time and buried it at the foot of the sacred pole, where all sacrificial elements belonged.

Lowanla had made Sun Dance history. Never before had one so young made so extravagant a pledge. Never before had one been rescued in this manner—by women relatives coming boldly in to assume part of his agony. The camp circle was in an uproar over it. "Surely," the people said, "This day will never be forgotten. For on this day we have seen the loftiest expression of kinship affection."

It happened that Waterlily was at home taking care of Smiling One and Ohiya at the time and did not see what had taken place. But since everyone was discussing it, she knew of it almost at once, and at the early evening meal around the outdoor fire she heard all the details.

The sun was still high; it was all right for her and Prairie Flower to go up alone to look on until dusk. Arriving, they found that they could not penetrate the crowds under the arbor and that the only space was in back of the screen against which the dancers rested when they broke away from their torture. They pushed aside the leaves that covered the screen and looked in between the willow uprights.

The dancers were facing due west now, for the sun was on its way to setting very soon. They looked ready to drop but they still danced on, determined to see it through. Suddenly Prairie Flower grasped Waterlily by the arm. "Look there, cousin," she said very excitedly. "Isn't that the young man everyone is talking about? It must be—see the fresh wounds on his shoulders!"

It was indeed. Watching him dancing, the girls were choked up with both pity and admiration. "Isn't he wonderful?" they asked each other. "Think how much he must love his father, else he would not have vowed a vow too big for him, forgetting himself." "How reckless, how daring!"

His appearance shocked them. Could this be that carefree and personable singer at the Omaha sitting only a few days ago? Surely he knew what was ahead, even then, and yet how cool he had been as he led the singers, even exchanging jokes with them. And now look at him—so gaunt and weary! It was plain he had not eaten for days; everyone knew that the candidates for the Sun Dance fasted a good while even before the actual dancing— five or six, or maybe ten days. "How hungry he must be now!" Prairie Flower cried. "Yes," said Waterlily, "Hungry—and thirsty. Oh, the poor thing!" She almost wept for him.

As the sun momentarily rested on the horizon, just before commencing to go under, all the dancers extended their arms toward it and moved open palms from side to side while holding their arms stiff, the usual gesture to attract the attention of someone in the distance. This was a final entreaty, or perhaps a farewell, as much as to say, "We have done our best."

At that moment both girls saw the tiny shape of a woman attached to the little finger of the young Lowanla's left hand. Some of the other dancers had similar tokens of rawhide representing their private desires. It could be that Lowanla had been imploring for the recovery of some sick woman relative—a sister, say—and then again it might be that he was praying for a charm to capture an elusive girl. Men prayed for all manner of things in their hearts.

The girls said nothing of the figurine, each hoping the other had not seen it. And for a while they stood there, whispering of this and that. Though nothing interested them in the least, they tried to be very casual as they looked over the scene. Suddenly the whole exciting affair went dead.

"Let's go now, while it is still light," Waterlily suggested. On the way she confessed, "I'm tired of visiting. I hope we go home right after this is over."

"Me too," her cousin agreed, and added tactlessly, "Sometimes I wish I hadn't come, when I ache to see my mother. I'll be glad when we start back." Then she remembered she had come on Waterlily's invitation and had honestly enjoyed everything. So she hastened to add, "But I am glad I came. We have seen so many new things to tell about. I think the best part was our visit in the stockade where the American soldiers live. What did you like best?" For Palani had taken the two girls to visit the trading post and watch the soldiers drill on horseback. The tour had been full of surprises.

As they neared their tipi, Waterlily remarked, "I am tired of

the Sun Dance and the crowds. After all we are young yet. It is
the old people who think so highly of it. I'll be glad to stay home

tonight."

"Me too."

They occupied a tipi with their grandmother and the two
children Smiling One and Ohiya. Only Little Chief slept in his
parents' tipi and came in occasionally for meals, being gone
somewhere with other young men on horseback most of the
time. The girls hardly saw him. The children were sound asleep
but Gloku was still out, no doubt sitting in a friend's tipi for a
while. She was an insatiable visitor and made friends without
trying.

The sounds of the dancing reached them and the two girls lay
awake listening for a time. The insistent drumming and the endless staccatos of the dancers' whistles were clear enough at night,
but the singing was remote. "Just think," Waterlily observed,
"even while we sleep and dream that goes on without stopping . . . and each whistle means the tired dancers are still blow-
ing and those white plumes are still shooting out and then falling,
as if they were alive." Prairie Flower was not so impressed with
the dancers' endurance, being too sleepy to comment.

"Wouldn't you imagine they'd give up from weariness?"
Waterlily asked after a while.

"It is because they are praying," Prairie Flower explained
vaguely, yawning. A moment later she was asleep.

Waterlily lay very still but wide awake. At last she sat up and as
quietly as possible began putting on the moccasins she had pulled
off a short time before, fearful all the while that her grandmother
might return and ask her what she was doing. But there was no
sound of her approach though the girl strained to hear. She
would be coughing a little as she came; she always did, from
habit.

All reasoning stopped for Waterlily. Mechanically she located
the tiny tin bucket that Palani had bought for her at the trader's
because she admired it so much, and now she poured water into it
and fitted the lid on tight.

She stole outside, holding the bucket under her wrap, and
stood studying the stars and the moon absently. There was still

time for retreat. She stood immobile, as though her feet were pegged to the ground. If her grandmother came now and saw her standing there, she would suppose Waterlily had been waiting for her. But there was no sound of her returning. Waterlily began to walk away from her tipi, experimentally, a step or two at a time. And then first thing she knew she was running—straight toward the center, unaware of the people who passed her, for many people were about, coming and going.

She stopped behind the screen in the rear of the lodge where she and Prairie Flower had watched earlier. Some young women were there, waiting. When the dancers came to their sagebrush couches to rest, the women quickly passed small bowls of water to their sweethearts, who as quickly received them, half knowing they would be offered. How skillfully it was done! Waterlily coveted the young women's coolness; would that she could be so cool.

After sunset the rest periods allowed by the mentors came at reasonable intervals though they did not last long. Soon enough the mentors called their men into line again. It seemed as though they had hardly stopped dancing, especially since the singing went on all the time.

The young women left immediately and Waterlily remained there all alone. And now the dancers were seating themselves again, but in the half-shadow she could hardly tell one from another at first. Compared with the young women who had expertly given a drink to waiting hands, she felt very insignificant and naïve. And she felt ashamed, too, knowing she had no right to be here, that no one was expecting her. Nevertheless, she crept along the base of the screen, occasionally pushing the elm leaves apart and peering into the stalls to find the youth named Lowanla. If only she could see the marks along his shoulders! If only the drying leaves did not crackle loud as thunder each time she touched them! After nearly three days in the hot sun they had curled around the edges and were brittle. It frightened her so that she had to wait a moment to regain her courage. There! That was he! She was sure of it. The shape and pose of his head was unmistakable.

Now was the moment; it was now or not at all. Working the

willow uprights wide enough apart with sudden strength in her fragile fingers, she managed to force the little bucket inside.

Then with a stick she began pushing it cautiously along, bit by bit, until it sat almost touching the dancer's left hand, flat on the ground behind him as he braced himself in a sitting position.

Suddenly he moved and brought his hand back down again, squarely on the water. But he did not take it. He only stared at it for what seemed ages. Then, unexpectedly and with amazing agility for one who had known torture that day, he sprang back against the screen and tore away the leaves savagely to see who had brought a secret drink to him.

But Waterlily was already running as hard as she could toward her tipi, her wrap pulled up over her head to hide her face. He could not have pursued her if he would. It was not allowed for a Sun Dancer to leave the scene on a whim; he must stay and see it to the end. And the screen was too firm for a man to break through, even if it had been allowed. Even so, Waterlily ran every step of the way as though wild beasts were at her heels.

Expecting the worst, she stole into her tipi. Miraculously, Gloku was still out. So she crawled in next to Prairie Flower, who slept innocently on, and lay down, utterly exhausted in body and spirit. Her heart pounded in her ears and jarred her frame, and even the ground, it seemed. Shortly after, the grandmother came in and prepared for bed. Then, as was her custom, she made a quick bed check, asking, "Is everybody asleep?" The silence she took for an answer in the affirmative. Satisfied that all was well with her grandchildren, Gloku lay down and was promptly asleep too.

"Why did I? Oh, why did I?" the question repeated itself in Waterlily's mind, over and over again. She could not find any answer. But she made a vow: "Even if I should live to be a very old woman, never, never will I tell anyone what I did tonight! Never!" She felt very bad and was very tired. She was all mixed up inside. Even the terrible pity that drove her to such an astonishing performance no longer seemed to explain it satisfactorily. And suddenly she felt she never wanted to see that singer Lowanla again.

It had been a long, full day, confusing and wearying. Gradually the sense of guilt was overpowered by physical need and she slept. Before dawn everyone was up, hurrying about to be on hand for the closing rite. Gloku woke the girls and they went drowsily along beside her. "Come, nobody should miss this who is old enough to understand," she told them, but they scarcely heard.

The Sun Dance lodge stood wilted and silent, a little shabby, like any deserted stage. All movement had ceased. The last relay of singers had withdrawn. Only the dancers, having kept their long vigil and survived their ordeal, were there, sitting far back on their sagebrush couches, in separate stalls. Numb and forspent, they looked devoid of any strength or will ever to stir again.

The spectators' circular arbor was still as death. The throng waited in a universal hush for what was about to follow. Indeed, the very world itself was hushed with expectancy in the predawn air so fresh and bracing. In the west the night was dying. The lacy, fading moon hung low against the dark sky. But the east was aglow with the promise that just below the horizon the sun was waiting to begin its daily ritual.

This was the intercessor's moment. Out of the shadow he emerged and walked swiftly to the sacred pole. He stood by it for a moment or two and then, with startling suddenness, he flung wide his arms and clasped them about the pole with all his might while his limp body hung inert from it, his head almost straight upside down, nearly touching the ground.

Breaking his many hours of complete silence, he lifted up his voice and wailed as he hung thus. He wailed a great corporate petition—that all the needs and hopes of the people, for which the dancers had paid in full by fasting and vigil, even by physical pain, might be granted. He wailed with an importunacy that would not be denied.

This was the unspeakably holy moment, the climactic event towards which the whole colorful drama had been moving since the first simple preliminary rites days ago. It was the holiest moment in the life of the people, for it had to do with their very existence. Here and there were those with desperate needs and they softly wept with the priest.

At last he stopped and sat down at the foot of the pole, beside the buffalo skull, to wait for the sun. Meanwhile he filled his pipe and smoked leisurely, his eyes on the east. The people, too, gazed toward the east, that they might see the first sight of the miracle. And as they waited, the dazzling, powerful sun began to appear, unhurried but sure, in its own time. Instantly it sought and touched with blessing everyone there, young and old, rich and poor alike, wrapping them in new life and warmth.

When it was well up, and not before, the crowd dispersed and began to thin out. Avoiding common talk, the people radiated from the Sun Dance lodge toward their own tipis, confident, because they had faithfully kept all vows, that for the ensuing year misfortune would skirt their borders. Last to leave were the dancers and their mentors and the priest, each man going alone and without ceremony. The lodge, with its sacred pole pointing skyward far above it, would remain until demolished by the elements. None would presume to take the wood for secular use, for it was holy.

Everything had been done with punctilious care and order, and, especially, with one mind and one heart. Therein lay the power of the Dakota Sun Dance. "Surely, surely now the people will live."

CHAPTER 12

After the thoroughly gratifying visit of the two men in fellowhood, Rainbow brought his family home. They came laden with many pieces of woven goods, flannels and calicoes, in brilliant reds, blues, yellows and greens, and these were the special desire of all the women and girls. They brought various other manufactured articles, and these, too, were avidly admired by their people. When, as was customary, her friends brought courtesy foods to Blue Bird and she gave them return gifts, those gifts were novel indeed: dress-length material, or a bowl of china or metal, a dipper, a kettle, or perhaps an ingeniously made water keg.

The red flannel was particularly prized and used in ceremony.

Where a piece of deerskin touched up with soft red earth paint had answered before, and well enough, now flannel strips were tied to a stick and planted wherever people prayed, and these were left to flutter there until they rotted. In rites involving a buffalo skull, streamers or neat bows on the horns were a new adornment as well as a symbol of consecration of it, a novel touch indeed, combining ancient custom and new material.

Seeing the new, fine things that were brought back, many families of White Ghost's village, who had been content to stay there for all time, now began planning trips to the settlements along the Roiled Water, where, as Rainbow and the others said, the traders' stores were crammed with treasures carried upstream by the fireboats that plied the river. And then in a short while such things as knives and axes and utensils of metal, not to say firearms, were familiar articles.

But the introduction of white man's goods, exciting as it was, could not overshadow a recent scandal in the camp circle that was creating a great to-do as the travelers returned. A young woman from a good family had eloped with a philanderer who, after keeping her with him in the hills for several days, had left her to return home. That was a tragedy for her, for her reputation would always suffer because of it. There was no real forgiving such a step.

Blue Bird, who was concerned that Waterlily should never make that kind of mistake, took the occasion to talk to her, using the unhappy young woman as an object lesson. As they walked along to the river to wash, Blue Bird said, "My daughter, you are growing into a very attractive young woman. I want you to see what happens to a girl who is not careful of herself. She did not think in time, and now she must pay for her carelessness.

"I want you to remember certain things: When a man talks to you, do not commit yourself at once. Do not be hasty to consent, no matter how charming you think he is. He may be only playing at courtship. Many do, to try a woman out. If she is too easy, they do not want her for life, knowing they cannot trust her.

"Above all, remember this: *he* must see you and decide he is interested—not you, him. If by your actions you force him to notice you, you take a big risk. Forced attention is not lasting; in time he will resent your having tricked him. Even if you are greatly attracted to a man, you must not go after him. That is a man's part; a woman's is to be pursued."

It was a good thing that it was twilight. Waterlily was hot with shame and dared not speak lest her voice betray her embarrassment. Maybe she had tried, just a little, to attract that singer at the Omaha sitting. Maybe he would not have noticed her at all if she had not been so conscious of him. Maybe he saw her look at him first, from the corner of his eye.

"Let a man show he wants to know you; it is unbecoming for you to seek him out or get in his way, and it is never safe. For if you do, you will pay for it." The same thing over and over, in almost the same words. But there was no need of that. Waterlily knew all too well. Hadn't she sent water secretly into the Sun Dance, for a strange boy whose very features she could hardly recall now? What if her mother knew that!

"Never let a man take you anywhere alone, either with sweet words or by force. Some rough men will try that last. But only if a girl is foolish enough to get in their way. Remember this: your purity is without price; guard it well. Then your husband will be happy to think, 'I am of all men most fortunate, for I have married a virgin.' Men do not like a discarded woman any more than you like a discarded gown."

Blue Bird admonished her daughter with deep earnestness, for she remembered well her own foolish risk in eloping with Star Elk when she was very young. Only because he took her straight home as his wife did he save her from lasting shame and censure. She had that one reason to feel kindly toward him, or at least grateful.

Waterlily could not sleep from thinking things over in the light of her mother's words. She decided that she would forget everything relating to that youthful singer. After all, he didn't try to find her. He might at least have ridden past her tipi or gone where he could capture her attention. Yet he had disappeared completely, though Rainbow's family had remained with Palani several days after the festivities and he had had time.

She was able to examine herself sanely at last. Yes, she had been a little fool; she had been false all the while her mother believed her to be so docile and exemplary, and that was very bad. Well, starting tomorrow, why not be what her mother thought her to be? After all, she had done nothing really wrong, had she? It would be quite simple to act maidenly from now on. She would never allow herself to be so enchanted again, by anyone.

She guessed she would never marry. Of all the local boys, the handsomest were her relatives, anyway. She would be a perpetual virgin—a true one, like White Dawn, not a sham, like Night Walker. Then, as she grew older, everyone would respect her character. She knew what people said, in a snide way, of Night Walker, and what they thought of White Dawn.

She had always admired the exquisite White Dawn. Though no longer young, she was still beautiful and commanding. Unlike Night Walker, who was continually announcing herself a virgin, White Dawn needed no reason to talk of her status; she was one with it. In her family group, which was large and influential, she was actually its central figure. She was respected and nearly worshiped there, and looked to for her wise judgments in all knotty family problems. It was said of her—Rainbow had once said it in Waterlily's hearing—"There's a real woman, one whom no man could besmirch with false accusations. Let anyone try!" She was poised and happy and kindly, too. Many men had tried to marry her in her youth, as everyone knew, but this was the life she had chosen. It was her vocation and she was content.

Was Waterlily so worthy? Yes. After all, what had she done but give water to a thirsty man? She too could be a perpetual virgin and then she too would have first right at all Virgins' Fires, rituals at which women swore oaths to their purity, publicly daring men who knew otherwise to expose pretenders. And always the planners of ceremonials would beseech her to carry the sacred pipe ahead of the religious processions, that her indisputable purity might add a blessing to them. She too would be able to move with ease and serenity, and to look any man in the face without flinching. Yes, she could still do all that. And so she would remain all her life—a perpetual virgin, carrying the sacred pipe, wearing a spotless gown.

As it turned out, it was her elder cousin, Leaping Fawn, who became a perpetual virgin. From the beginning she had been a serious-minded, dependable girl. In courtship she was always too wary to become involved in even a simple conversation with a would-be suitor, lest by ingenious twisting of her words he might extract from her a consent to marry him. If a girl unwittingly said yes to some commonplace question, a certain type of man took it arbitrarily for an answer to a proposal of marriage.

Most suitors could tell well enough when a girl was only acting hard to get and when she really wanted to be let alone. Since Leaping Fawn wanted to be let alone, she considered it beneath her to engage in finessing, in scheming and designing more or less plausible excuses to be available. From the beginning she avoided men who wanted to court her. In all respects she had the makings of a contented lifelong virgin.

And so it was a deathblow to her when some stupid fellow confused another girl with Leaping Fawn because they happened to wear similarly ornamented wraps, and released the boast that the elder niece of Rainbow had consented to marry him. The story was on everyone's tongue. Some women, who admired Leaping Fawn's sweet and dependable ways, were genuinely dismayed at this gossip about her. Others, who were nervous over their own flirtatious daughters, were glad enough to hear it. "Well, she is a woman, isn't she? Women are weak sometimes. Why not she?" they said insinuatingly, eager to interpret the story in its worst light. "No longer may she pose as a pure girl. She must have been out with him or he would not have said that about her."

Leaping Fawn was completely crushed by all the talk and wept in secret until Blue Bird, as her aunt, offered to arrange a Virgin's Fire for her—if she wanted it. "Oh, yes, Aunt," Leaping Fawn sat up eagerly at the suggestion. She had been stabbed by her two mothers' silence, as though they believed the story. But they were only dubious and would not speak at once either to defend or to accuse her. They seemed to be saying, "Maybe, after all, our training was not enough. Maybe the young man's claim is sound. The best of girls sometimes make a slip. Mothers can only tell them; they cannot follow them everywhere. We must wait for Leaping Fawn to speak." Did they have so little confidence in her? That was what hurt Leaping Fawn.

But now, as soon as Blue Bird told them what Leaping Fawn had decided, they went into action, much relieved that she dared to hold the ceremony to clear her name. An exclusive feast was planned, with only virgins as guests. When all was ready, the old grandfather proudly walked around the camp circle bidding them to come. A little grandson of his led him about, holding onto the further end of his cane.

"Here ye! Hear ye! There is to be a Virgin's Fire," he proclaimed. "My grandchild is calling in her peers. All true virgins, come ye and feast together with her in the open. So shall you vindicate yourselves again from the idle tongue of covetous men. Come! She whom we call Leaping Fawn is about to kindle her Fire."

The Virgin's Fire was not a religious practice but a social event, and it was held irregularly, as the need arose, to protect the reputation of the unmarried girl from unfounded rumors. Except for the formality of handling the tokens of purity, which lasted but a moment, there was no set procedure.

From many quarters the rightful guests set out, dressed in their best and looking festive indeed. Most of them were girls and young unmarried women. Only a very few were elderly, for perpetual virgins were a rarity, since it was the normal and accepted thing for women to marry. They began drifting toward Leaping Fawn's home. They alone would feast, but many married people came to look on and brought their children along. Behind them, watching from a distance but no less attentively, were the curious men of courting age. These stationed themselves as an unofficial jury to decide the claims of purity implicit in taking part.

The fire, kindled by Leaping Fawn as was proper, was burning beside a huge rock painted red. Next to it were an arrow and a knife stuck into the ground and standing vertical. The guests first reached into a hole in the ground and next grasped the arrow lightly near the base with forefinger and thumb and stroked it gently upward. They did the same with the knife, all the while resting the left hand on the rock. That was the formality. After that they took their places in a circle and chatted informally until everyone was through and ready for Leaping Fawn's entrance. It was said that touching the arrow meant "If I am unworthy, may I be shot with one like this!" and the knife, "If any man accuses me falsely, may he be stabbed!" The fire, the rock, and the hole in the ground were the elemental witnesses to this act.

While Waterlily and Prairie Flower sat waiting after they had gone through with the formality, they observed the girls still crowding about for their turn. There was nothing solemn or timid about them, though they were never hilarious in public. They whispered and jostled one another, joking in mock deference—"You go first!" "No; you!" "But I am afraid! I might be challenged!"—only pretending to hold back because they were sure of themselves. Among them was one strikingly handsome girl, very tall and slim and gowned even more elaborately than the others, but who acted diffident and nervous. Waterlily remarked on this to her cousin, who observed it, too.

In due time all the virgins were seated and all talking stopped. The high point was here. Leaping Fawn stepped quickly from her tipi and walked directly to her Fire. There she stood motionless for one lingering moment while all eyes rested on her. She was allowing ample time for the one who had tarnished her reputation to step forward and challenge her. But he was not even there, having already seen his mistake. At last Leaping Fawn bent reed-like over the symbols of chastity and almost caressed the arrow and the knife as she stroked them, so sure of herself was she.

Then she joined her guests, and amid laughter and pleasant chatter they feasted on the special foods prepared for them. Suddenly all conversation stopped abruptly, and while Waterlily looked around to see what was the matter, a young man grabbed the beautiful strange girl and pulled her out of the circle, saying, "You have no rights here. Come away." The confusion obscured what happened next. Waterlily was afraid to see. But when again she dared look, the girl was sitting back of the circle with her wrap pulled over her head in shame and the man was gone. The virgins resumed their talking and feasting but did not allude to their disgraced member. When they got up and left the scene she went also, losing herself as best she could among them.

It was frightening to Waterlily and Prairie Flower. "Poor girl!" Waterlily said. "And she was so beautiful, too. I am sorry for her." Prairie Flower was not so sure. "Well, she asked for it," she said callously, unable to sympathize one whit. "She will never be able to live this down. People will talk about her the way they talk about Night Walker, won't they?"

White Dawn was chief guest and as always she gave strength and dignity to the ancient ceremony. But Night Walker was conspicuously absent, on the plea that she was called to another camp circle. No one was fooled by that. Eyebrows were raised and cynical smiles suppressed.

This proved to be Waterlily's only participation in a Virgin's Fire, for she was no longer eligible when next someone found it needful to defend her honor. But as an onlooker she had no cause for shame, since she was married properly, and according to the highest form. Waterlily was bought.

Not long after Leaping Fawn's successful vindication, Gloku, the beloved grandmother, died after a short illness and was mourned by the entire community. Surely it would not be enough simply to lay her body away and distribute her belongings and give away some horses in her name. She deserved something more, for she had been a potent personality, known for her good works through which she won everyone's heart. She had comforted the bereaved regardless of their station, and many had come to her for advice. Now that she was gone, hardly anyone but could remember that at some time or other she had reached him by her hospitality. Such a public benefactor left a void. Realizing this, the family could not let her go so completely and irrevocably at once. They must hold her back a while longer. They would keep her ghost.

Ghostkeeping was a long, sustained, laborious ceremony. Until the family was ready to give the ghost feast, accompanied by the redistribution of property at the close of the period, the ghost bundle must be guarded with relentless care in accordance with a ritual that might not be neglected even once. A slipshod ghostkeeping was worse than none. It brought nothing but dishonor to the dead and discredit on the family. For this reason, unless there was a woman relative who felt herself equal to the duty of custodian, it was better not attempted. And that duty was a grueling one.

While the woman lay dying, friends and relatives, and even strangers who had partaken of her many public feasts, waited anxiously around her tipi. They waited in quiet groups on the grass, intending to do her honor by helping with the initial wailing when she should die. The end came at dawn when, without gaining consciousness, she breathed her last. Immediately, as if on signal, a universal keening rent the air, lasting a long time. Just when it seemed to end, others arrived and began to wail. No one was expected to restrain himself; there was no virtue in control of grief over death as there was in control of all other emotions.

When things had quieted down at last, and while close women relatives dressed the body to lay it out in a special tipi, the blind husband of the dead woman called his children to him. He smoked in silence and they waited, knowing he had something to say. In his own good time he spoke to Rainbow. "Son, doubtless you are remembering how your mother loved you. How she gave full devotion to you, and to your two wives, and especially to your children, and spared nothing of herself or her means that they might be creditably reared. Now then, if you entertain any plans for honoring your mother, this is the time to say . . ."

Rainbow sat as though he had not heard. He smoked for some time before he spoke: "Father, you are right. I am remembering everything my mother did for me. And I am thinking this: my mother shall not be gone from me all in a day. She shall linger here a while yet, residing in her own tipi."

The old man almost smiled in satisfaction. "*Haye! Haye!* Thanks be! Thanks be! That you should say that! It is what I was hoping. Your mother deserves nothing less."

Then he turned toward the sisters of Rainbow, "My daughters, it is easy enough to give things away. Property comes and goes and comes again. And it matters not that it goes, since it cannot endure but must decay, even were one to hold onto it with both hands. Who then would balance things that will not last, against one's parent? I know you are all equal to parting with your possessions to honor your mother. Yet there is a far more difficult part to ghostkeeping.

"Which of you is ready and able to take the part of custodian? For that is the heart of the matter. Think carefully, my daughters.

Remember your daily obligations. Could you assume more duty? For it is better not to keep a ghost than to keep it poorly."

But before either woman could reply, it was Leaping Fawn who broke in. "Grandfather, some will say I am too young. But I want to keep my grandmother. I want to guard her ghost against abuse from any quarter, night and day, until she leaves us forever."

If ever a young girl gave promise that she could do this work, it was the dependable Leaping Fawn. Nevertheless, she was of courting age. Guarding a ghost was a settled woman's role. After all, it was only natural for girls to be courted and to marry. During the year Leaping Fawn could fall in love and be distracted from her duty. Then people would laugh at the family. "Weren't they foolish, entrusting an adult role to a mere girl? Now the ceremony is a failure, without a proper custodian." It would be a travesty indeed, for which the adults and not Leaping Fawn would be blamed.

But she had spoken out loud. The Great Spirit had heard. There was no recanting now. Dream Woman, realizing this, said: "She wants to do it and has said so audibly. Let her. I will stand by her, as will her aunt." She knew Blue Bird would never fail her niece.

At once White Hand, the holy man in league with the ghosts and known as a ghost dreamer, was engaged to cut a lock from the dead woman's hair. This was a solemn rite and must be done in private, before only the immediate family.

The women and girls sat on the right side of the tipi and the men on the left. The dead woman lay in their midst, with feet toward the entryway. While they waited for the ghost dreamer, the old widower remained outside, wailing and singing a dirge. The little children walked in and out and nobody sent them away. "Is grandmother sleeping so long?" one small boy asked, and his mother whispered in his ear, "No. She is not sleeping. She is dead." "Oh," said the child, and dismissed the matter, satisfied with the answer. "Dead" was a meaningless word to him now. He would grow up hearing and seeing it and in time would understand it.

At last the old man entered with the ghost dreamer, who

walked directly to the head and sat down. The old man, after feeling the ground, found his wife's feet and sat holding them.

They were encased in handsome moccasins, worked all over, like a bride's or a child-beloved's. Sitting there, he addressed the dead: "My true, my special friend, harken! Your only son, your two daughters, your grandchildren, and me, you have left behind to go away from us. But we cannot let you go. We will hold you here yet a while at least.

"Harken! Your granddaughter, a mere child still, has taken upon herself the great task on your behalf. She says, 'I will supply food on behalf of my grandmother.' Pity her, for she makes herself worthy of pity." By "pity" was meant loving compassion, in the kinship sense.

"Harken! In this our undertaking may the heart of the entire camp circle be kindly disposed toward us. May a ring of sympathy narrow down to a point here.

"And now, pity me, too, for I am worthy of your pity . . . That is all." He let go of the feet and never touched the body again.

The ghost dreamer separated a lock of hair from the dead woman's head and cut it off close to the scalp with a very sharp blade. He wrapped it in a small piece of skin painted blue, loosely so that the hair could be seen. Then he hung it on the center rear pole above the reach of children. Those who came in to look at the dead lowered their voices to a low whisper and moved reverently, always. But when they saw a "ghost" present in the room, they did so even more. When the body was taken away for burial, the ghost dreamer "buried" the hair in its loose wrapping inside a larger bundle that contained in addition certain essential articles. They were four pipes, four knives, four awls, and four disks of abalone shell like enormous buttons, such as holy men wore at the throat by a string around the neck.

Indoors every night and during overcast days, this bundle hung from a low tripod set up in the honor-place, behind the altar. (The altar was a small square where the earth had been pulverized and its four corners were marked with tobacco bundles on sticks. Over the ground was scattered scarlet down that remained in motion all the time.) On sunny days the bundle was hung on a taller tripod outside the tipi. By it everyone knew this was a ghost lodge, and if they had to walk past it they maintained silence and went by reverently.

In a sense the ghost was both resident and hostess. Acting for it was Leaping Fawn, who lived on the women's side of the tipi while her grandfather lived on the opposite side, which was for men. They were the caretakers for the ghost. Sometimes Dream Woman or Blue Bird spent the night with Leaping Fawn. During the day either her sister, Prairie Flower, or her cousin Waterlily sat with her for a time.

Every day Leaping Fawn must fill the ghost's hospitality bowl with the best food possible and set it below the tripod on which the bundle was hanging, whether it was inside or outside the tipi. Anyone who wished was at liberty to come there quietly, eat the food, and go away again. The bowl must never stand empty; that was one of Leaping Fawn's responsibilities, although she did not have to cook the food. The women of the *tiyošpaye* saw to that.

Sometimes men came to sit with the blind old widower. They smoked with him and talked in low tones, of commonplace matters sometimes, to entertain him. Even so, the etiquette in a ghost lodge was regulated by the presence of the ghost. All talk, conduct, and even thought must be controlled with reference to that. It was wrong to indulge in gaiety, to laugh loudly, to lose control of one's temper, or to talk slanderously of someone. It was wrong to act in an indifferent, essentially selfish manner. A constant awareness of the place and a subordination of self to it was required of all.

There were rules for carrying the bundle from one resting place to the other, and those rules were inviolable. Leaping Fawn observed them loyally from first to last, until as time went on the original skeptics began to marvel at her constancy.

But there was more to Leaping Fawn's duties than merely moving the ghost bundle according to rule and keeping the hospitality bowl filled at all times. With her two mothers, her aunt Blue Bird, and the other women relatives she worked in all her spare time, turning out many pieces of fancywork for the redistribution feast to come. Outsiders who had themselves successfully kept a ghost in the past were eligible to bring gifts and add them to the rapidly growing pile being accumulated. They were proud to help, because implicit in their right to do so was an honor to be prized.

But the privilege of helping was not restricted. Anyone who revered the dead woman and wanted to help also did so, coming into the ghost lodge and quietly leaving a suitable gift on the pile. It was all very gratifying. The old man called his children's attention to it. "See? This is what I prayed for when I said, 'May the heart of the entire circle be kindly disposed toward us; may a ring of sympathy narrow down to a point here.' It is as I prayed, and I am thankful."

Thus it became a camp-circle affair, because everybody had been touched by the dead woman's kindness and longed to reciprocate it in some way. Surely, judging from the countless proffered gifts, this redistribution was going to be the greatest that the people had ever seen. Everyone looked forward to it. Many went further by bringing more than one gift. If they brought one in the beginning of the period, they brought another, and another, as suitable articles came into their possession during the year through the constant flow of exchange.

Yet, sacrosanct as a ghost lodge was, camp moves must still be made for the common weal, and at such times the ghost must travel with the people. So it was that whenever the camp circle had to be moved to a new site, a fine horse belonging to Black Eagle, which he had dedicated to this burden, carried the ghost lodge and its contents. It was led by Leaping Fawn or some other woman relative, who walked or rode ahead of it. When the new site was reached, the first tipi that went up was the ghost lodge, where a new altar was at once prepared and the tripods set up. The hospitality bowl was filled and stood ready for the next guest.

Whoever sat down there to eat behaved as one should in a holy place, and when he finished he stole away, carrying away good thoughts about the remarkable woman whose deeds persisted even after her death. And thus did a feeling of goodwill spread throughout the circle. Yet just because the food was always ready and available to them, people did not hasten there to eat it. A nice restraint was becoming. Many of the guests were old people, who could always be counted upon to crave a good meal. But even they, if they took the food once or so during the period, thought that was enough. It was a holy feast. Only an unreasonable person, a fool, would be seen eating there often.

Time did not stand still in the *tiyospaye;* the daily life did not differ from the normal. That would be both unnecessary and impossible. Only the ghost lodge remained set apart. Secular life went on around it still, though nothing very boisterous was considered proper for any but small children, who naturally did not understand. It would be silly to restrain them. Visitors came and went, and the kindred families also came and went on their own business, such as it was. Courtship and marriage, birth and death, warpath and hunting, home-keeping and child-rearing— such things never altered. It was even permissible for the members of a *tiyospaye* keeping a ghost to look on at community events, though of their own accord grownups generally preferred to limit themselves there, too, or not attend at all.

Underneath all that went on, the *tiyospaye* never lost sight of that final event for which they were all responsible. They wanted to do things creditably, to give the best feast possible and to distribute many presents and fine horses. Thus they would truly honor their loved one and could let her go from their midst for good, without regrets, at the end of the ghostkeeping period.

CHAPTER 13

Gloku's death had occurred in late summer. All winter long Leaping Fawn had kept steadily to her task. Young as she was, she had sustained it like a stable, mature woman and for this she won the admiration of all. And now it was spring. The annual Sun Dance was only a little more than a moon cycle away.

Since the families were ready for the final ceremony, it was decided to hold it just before the move to the Sun Dance site, during those preliminary days that were always spent in greeting new arrivals and holding family ceremonies and rites all around the circle. It was Rainbow's idea. When he talked with his brother-in-law Black Eagle about it, he said, "It does not seem right for my niece to carry an adult burden any longer. So why not cut the mourning period a little short? Are we not ready even now to hold the ghost feast and redistribution? Why prolong the time?"

Black Eagle was in accord with that. "You are very right; we are well prepared. I have known of cases wherein families required two whole winters. Fortunately, ours is a big family and all the relatives are loyal and helpful. Then, too, we have countless friends who have helped." Both men agreed that it was largely the dead woman's own knack of friendship that had brought that response in her behalf.

The relatives all bestirred themselves and the plans were going well, when the two very handsome American horses that Black Eagle intended to give away in his mother-in-law's name, as a final, impressive honor to her, were found dead. The boys who tended the horses came in with the report. Some vicious or jealous person had stabbed them in the night.

It was useless to blame it on Crows or Mandans or other lurking enemies. They would never injure Dakota horses; they wanted them alive too much. No, this was the work of a spiteful tribesman.

Black Eagle felt his loss keenly. He had named those two extra-fine animals to be the chief gifts at the distribution. He had meant to start off by giving them away in his mother-in-law's name. It was to have been his last princely gesture to her. "If only I could know who did this," he said to his friends sitting with him. "If I could learn that it was not a responsible man of standing, but a natural fool, then I should be consoled. I should say, 'well, after all, he did not know any better; it was the same as an accident.' And then I could overlook it."

"Why don't you consult a diviner, my friend?" one man suggested. Black Eagle thought that a good idea; he might act on it later. But first he must find two horses at least as good, to give away. That was his immediate problem. It did not free him that through no fault of his own, the ones he had set aside for his mother-in-law to give away posthumously had been lost. He was still obligated.

This problem was preoccupying him while the womenfolk were toiling feverishly to get things ready and the ghost dreamer

White Hand, who had been in charge since the start, was fasting and purifying himself in the sweatbath for his final duties. And then, at high noon, while all this was going on, Waterlily was bought.

Two strange women approached from the opposite side of the circle, each leading a very handsome horse laden with presents. The women were attractively gowned and they walked with purpose, heading directly for Black Eagle's group. They tied the horses outside Rainbow's tipi and then withdrew, saying nothing to anyone. All who saw them knew what it meant. Nor did it take long to learn who the women were. The go-between they had sent on ahead had found visiting relatives on the way and had stopped to see them. Belatedly he reached Rainbow's tipi with the necessary facts.

"Far to the south of here, Bear Soldier's people move regularly about the Black Hills region. From there comes a man of renown called Good Hunter to attend our festivities. He brings two of his three wives. And it is they who offer gifts for your daughter, that she may become the wife of their son, Sacred Horse."

He explained that Good Hunter was an uncanny marksman. Because of that, he was a very influential, well-provisioned man. He was able not only to take care of his three wives and their families, but also to maintain a large retinue of kinsmen besides. The son Sacred Horse was a child-beloved, and all three mothers set great store by him. His every whim they strove to satisfy. Their chief aim in life was to see him happy. Consequently, when he had chanced to say, that morning, that at last he had seen the girl he wanted, they quickly set out to bring fine presents for her, hoping to take her back to him when he returned from riding with his friends.

It was considered a high compliment to have such an offer. Old women sometimes recalled with obvious pride, "I was bought." But Waterlily was only stunned to have this happen to her, and without warning. She did not want to marry just now, and this was not the way she fancied it would be—without any romance. And worst of all, she had no idea what sort this Sacred Horse might be. He might be quite ugly, mean, stupid, stingy, or old; he might have mannerisms that would disgust her. Why, he might not really want her. Maybe he was joking when he spoke of her. His mothers need not have taken matters into their own hands. Maybe when he found out what they had done he would call the whole thing off—and would not people laugh at her!

Waterlily had long since forgotten she was going to be a perpetual virgin. Life was getting more exciting all the time. If she and some of her girl friends went to the woodgathering place at sunset, just for the fun of skillfully dodging the eager young men who would try to court them, it was she who had to dodge the largest number of suitors, for she was a popular girl. Last night, now. Some who tried to speak with her had been total strangers, visitors from far away. Could this Sacred Horse be one of them? It quite bewildered her—so many unanswered questions! So many eyes upon her suddenly!

She was worried on another score, too. Ought she to accept so that her devoted brother Little Chief could have those handsome horses? That would be one big way of showing her high regard for him. "Well, for him I would, I should." At the same time she wished there were some other equally impressive gesture she could make that would not be so final and decisive for her.

She sat thinking in the tipi while the gift horses waited outside for her answer. And then Prairie Flower came in and told her, "What do you think cousin Ohiya said? He said he wished you would marry so he could have the bay!" Waterlily smiled wanly. Then Prairie Flower added, "But Little Chief overheard him and gave him a real going-over. 'What are you saying? We can get our own horses if we are men. Our sister does not have to marry against her will for our sake!' You should see the little boy hanging his head in shame." Waterlily smiled more brightly. That at least was settled; she need not marry to please her brother. She found her voice and began to talk naturally with Prairie Flower.

And so the horses stood untouched still. But later in the afternoon, Waterlily heard something else that made her start worrying over again. In the tipi of Dream Woman, her two aunts were talking as she approached. "Are they not handsome? They look as fine as those other horses," Dream Woman observed.

And her sister, First Woman, the outspoken one, said, "Yes—
and it is too bad that our niece seems disinclined to marry the
stranger. Those two horses might well have been the answer. He
is having a hard time in finding replacement horses as good as the
ones he lost. He is very particular and critical. He seeks only the
best." She was of course referring to her husband, Black Eagle.
The married usually referred to one another in that impersonal
manner.

Dream Woman spoke up, "We do not yet know how our niece
will decide, of course. But if she says no, we must accept it. That
is as it should be. Some families, who set greater store by things
than by kinship, might force their girls to marry. But ours is not
that kind. In our family, Father says, no girl need marry unless
she wishes. And he is right."

Waterlily turned away in confusion. Never before had she
heard her aunts discussing either herself or her mother. Always
they had been loyalty itself. But now, quite accidentally, they
revealed that they rather wished the horses offered for her could
be part of the give-away—if only she would see fit to accept.

"Well, why not?" Waterlily asked herself, recalling vividly
how her grandmother had always treated her, with what love and
tenderness. "From the first she cared for me at all times as one of
her very own grandchildren. How good, unselfish, and long-
suffering she invariably was!" Suddenly Waterlily was seized
with a great obligation to honor the dead woman, a personal
obligation. But was it also a kinship obligation? She would go to
her mother to learn if she had a duty here which the tribe would
expect her to fulfill. Blue Bird was the one to advise her; she had
always done so, dispassionately, and had always been right.

The girl entered the tipi where her mother was at work and
sank down beside her with a deep sigh. Blue Bird was very busy
sorting out moccasins and tying the mates together face to face
by their strings. These many moccasins she and the other women
had made in wholesale fashion, without bothering to match
them up at the time. Waterlily started to help. They must match
in size and texture as well as in ornamentation. The mother and
daughter worked intently in silence for a time.

Waterlily wished her mother would say something. At last she herself broke the silence. "Mother, my cousin tells me that she heard my elder brother say he did not want those horses . . . he did not want me to marry unless I wished to. He thinks that highly of my happiness. He said men should get their own horses and not depend on the marriage of a *hakata*." (Waterlily used the general term for a respect relative of one's own generation.)

Blue Bird smiled, a little sadly, as she said, "That is just like him. He has always been good to you, ever since he came to our tipi and began taking care of you. If he had been your real brother, he could not have been more devoted." Waterlily went on to repeat Prairie Flower's account of how Little Chief had reprimanded Ohiya for coveting the bay horse. Again Blue Bird smiled—but not as if the matter could be settled that simply.

Waterlily had to go all the way now. "Mother, tell me straight. Do you think I should agree to this marriage so that the horses can be used in the redistribution rites?" There, it was out. She held her breath for the answer. Surely her mother must say, "Certainly not, my child. We don't do things that way in this *tiyośpaye*. You do not have to marry unless you wish to!"

But Blue Bird remained silent for many moments. Then she spoke, choosing her words carefully. "Daughter, it is in the nature of things that women marry . . . And some men, who seemed so appealing before marriage, turn out badly, and some, whose fine traits do not show up before marriage, turn out well . . . It is like guessing in the moccasin game. One does not know till later."

Waterlily worked very rapidly, with a concentration out of all proportion to the simple task, and said nothing. Her mother spoke again: "As if from the dead, you and I and our old grandmother Killed-by-Tree came back here because this was where I was born. Our kinsman, my cousin and your uncle, made us welcome at once. He provided for us. His relatives through marriage had never seen us before, yet they did not act distant, but warmly took us into their life. Your new grandmother lavished as much love and compassion on you as on her own grandchildren. And she took constant care of you and kept you happy. I can truly say that you grew up on her back. For your ceremonies she always gave of her best, in your name. Thus she bought a great deal of social prestige for you.

"Now your uncle is worried because he cannot find horses good enough to replace the ones killed. He does not want just any horses. He wants the best, worthy of his mother-in-law.

"You are now of woman's stature and have come to woman's estate. You are no longer a child. You know how these kinship matters run. If you are able to do your own thinking, you will see what a good relative would want to do . . . but that you have to decide."

So that was it. Blue Bird had first implied the crisscross of kinship obligations that held the people together, impelling them to sacrifice for one another. Then she washed her hands of the matter. Now it was up to Waterlily, having those facts before her, to make up her own mind.

Suddenly she felt elated, carried away with the nobility of kinship loyalty, until nothing else seemed important. Yes, she would marry the stranger. After all, she must marry sometime. And so she would be helping her uncle to honor his mother-in-law. He wanted to honor her—and that was noble of him. And he had always been good to Waterlily and Blue Bird. And the grandmother had loved and taken care of Waterlily from the beginning of their relationship. Waterlily was completely involved; she could not step aside. By enabling her uncle to use the horses for the give-away, she would be reciprocating the kindness and loyalty of both Black Eagle and the grandmother. To do this, she must sacrifice herself. The network of deserved loyalties seemed endless. It left her dizzy. But she knew now where she stood and saw clearly what she must do.

Going swiftly to the lodge of Black Eagle, she stood partway in the entrance and looked in. "Uncle, have the horses watered—for my grandmother."

The men who sat with him spoke their approval. "How she loved her grandmother!" But Black Eagle said, "Thank you, my niece. But be very sure it is what you really want to do."

"I *am* sure, uncle."

Her aunt First Woman was plainly relieved. "How fitting! It shows what my niece thinks of her grandmother's memory."

When she said that, she had no idea how a chance remark of hers, overheard by Waterlily, had started the chain of reasoning that ended in her decision.

So it was settled. Some of the men of the *tiyośpaye* untied the horses and led them away. Almost at once the news of acceptance was known round the circle. But Waterlily made one condition. "I will marry only after my grandmother's ghostkeeping rites are finished. Till then, she comes first." When that was reported to the family of Sacred Horse, they found it reasonable. After all, they would not be leaving until the Sun Dance was over, anyway. And then they would have a pretty new daughter-in-law to take with them on their journey southward. They were content to wait.

Very soon the girl friends of Waterlily began coming to see her, to find out how she felt about being bought. They were curious, sympathetic and romantic: Did Waterlily like the idea? If not, what a shame she felt she must accept! If so, how exciting to be sought out, and bought! They did not know whether they would care themselves to be bought. It was a great honor—in retrospect; older women admired the bought woman. Young girls were dubious.

"But don't you know the boy even by sight? Haven't you ever seen him, if only at a distance?" It was the inquisitive Alila who was most forthright, avid to know all the details.

"No," Waterlily said, "and that was what bothered me so at first, but now I don't mind very much. After all," she went on, "it has happened before. I am not the only woman to be bought by a stranger. All I want is for my grandmother to be properly honored at the redistribution. Never mind about me." She spoke this a bit tragically, enjoying her martyrdom for kinship's sake in the zealous spirit often peculiar to young relatives.

"But really you are a bit worried, aren't you? To be marrying someone you might not even like?" one girl asked earnestly.

Alila, who always took things lightly, came up with a solution. "Look, there *is* a way, you know. Why, you don't have to go clear through with it. Just go to his home and let the family make a fuss over you. Accept that as if you liked the whole idea. But then," she was very emphatic here, "but then, just before bedtime, you can run away. If you don't like the man, who could blame you for that? I knew of a girl once . . ."

It was true that the rejection of a husband in a purchase mar- riage was not unheard of. To be sure, it was not in the noblest tradition to repudiate a promise, but it was condoned under certain circumstances. If a girl had been persuaded to accept, against her inclinations, because someone in her family wanted the gift horse, and if, before the marriage was consummated, she ran away, unable to accept the man, then the marriage was annulled. In such a case, the gifts were returned or not, depending on the character of the disappointed wife-buyer, who might or might not be too proud to recover them.

But Waterlily knew that Alila's airy solution was not for her. The gifts had already been publicly accepted—because she had given her word. It would not be right to recant now. "A woman who once gives her word and then withdraws it is not honorable," as Blue Bird's old grandmother had once told Blue Bird. The saying was often repeated to girls of marriageable age.

The day for the final ghostkeeping rites arrived. First there was the symbolic feast, which would be private, with only four girl guests partaking of the dead woman's last food. They had been selected by the old widower: Leaping Fawn, Waterlily, Prairie Flower, and Smiling One. However, that morning Smiling One was not feeling well, and Soft Little Breeze, another grandchild of the dead woman, was chosen in her place, though she was only six years old.

When Dream Woman and Blue Bird had finished dressing the girls it was First Woman who, with unaccustomed gentleness, spread their faces and the center part of their hair with an even film of red paint. Then she gave Leaping Fawn and Waterlily their rightful markings as child-beloveds. This was the third time Waterlily had worn them for occasions of great importance.

As soon as Leaping Fawn was ready, she was called out to hand over the ghost bundle. She entered the ghost lodge and brought it out to the man waiting at the entrance. It was by this time so large and heavy that she could hardly carry it, even with the broad shoulder strap that took some of the weight from her arms. All year long, whenever something exceptionally rare and beautiful and worthy was given by friends, it had been wrapped into the bundle, until the accreted load was the size of two very large pillows. With her surrender of the bundle, Leaping Fawn was finished with her self-appointed duty. At no time had she relaxed her vigil or neglected her exacting task. And now that it was out of her hands forever, she felt a little sad. The end of anything is a little sad. Already the ghost lodge without its unseen resident seemed very empty.

At the right instant, a woman who had herself kept a ghost (which fact qualified her) came for the girls, bearing in her hand a bowl of powdered incense. They followed her out and stopped at the outer end of the "Path of Beauty," which extended about twenty paces from the ceremonial tipi. It had been made earlier, a carpeting of white deer and calf skins, with symbolic painting, laid end to end. Along either side, in matched patterns to please the eye, were placed such things as decorated pipes, awls, knives, tobacco bags, and moccasins, examples of the best in all-over work with quills of bright hues. The Path of Beauty was all new and very colorful.

While the girls stood waiting for the signal to walk, the crowd of visitors craned to see them. In slender white doeskin gowns long enough to brush the grass, they appeared very tall and slim. Their shiny black hair hung in two braids in front, adding to their appearance of height. The waists of their gowns were heavy with solid work extending to the ends of the loose open sleeves bordered with fringe. All their accessories were in harmony; the artistry of Dream Woman was never more evident. "Guests should wear their best, to honor their hostess." The rule was here observed extravagantly.

Spaced somewhat apart, they began walking slowly over the Path of Beauty, the escort going before them and sprinkling their way with the sweet-smelling contents of her bowl. Here and there in the crowd, women exclaimed in low voices at their striking appearance. Nor did the significant markings on the faces of Leaping Fawn and Waterlily escape them. "What pretty girls this *tiyośpaye* is raising!" "Did you ever see more perfect workmanship than there is on those gowns?" "See! The two tallest girls are beloved—note the *hunka* markings." Such admiring comments were heard all about.

But this was a mournful hour for the family. To the visitors, it was as though they had come to witness a second dying of the good woman. Surely it was no time for levity; one ought not to look about for something to be amused at. All the same, it was needful to suppress an occasional smile over Soft Little Breeze. Last in line, she had taken much too literally the order to walk v-e-r-y slowly, until at times she was nearly stationary. Even so, she advanced with an exaggerated dignity that was comical, though she had to abandon it now and then to regain her position whenever the gap between her and Prairie Flower grew too wide. Then, with a hop and a skip, she would move forward, giving a swift kick to her too-long skirt (which had been made for Smiling One) if it tangled about her feet. Undaunted, Soft Little Breeze managed to enter the ceremonial tipi without tripping. Everyone was glad when she made it.

Inside, White Hand, the ghost dreamer, was in full command. He caused the four girls to be seated in the honor-place back of the altar, which had been decorated with quivering red down scattered over it. The constant motion of the down was a symbol of life, of spirit. There a large blue square of calfskin lay spread out, and each girl held a corner of it. In the middle of it was the holy food, a cake of pemmican.

The only spectators were the girls' parents, their grandfather, who followed by ear only, and several outsiders whose previous record as faithful ghostkeepers was their right of entry. White Hand presented the pipe and, as the girls entered, he unwrapped the ghost bundle and hung the hair again on the pole in the center rear. There it hung as at the beginning, pitiful and alone, bereft of all the material things it had been accumulating all year—only to give away, as an expression of the precept "Be generous, for you cannot take material things beyond the grave."

White Hand invoked the Earth, the universal Mother, the final source of all food, and thus of hospitality, in the following prayer:

Thou Earth, our Mother, esteemed by mankind,
Thou Earth, our Mother, compassionate toward
all that move—
On this day, this perfect day of cloudless sky,
On this day, have thou compassion on me, too,
That I may live, a long life, a good life.
I believe it may be so; I have faith in thee; I rely on thee,
And so I attempt this rite.
Thou Earth, our Mother, esteemed by mankind!
Thou Earth, our Mother, esteemed by the Sun!

Thus he chanted the prayer, in behalf of the four guests. Next he took the cake of pemmican, which had been made with prescribed ingredients, and broke off a piece. He held it over the fire to incense it. As he laid it on Leaping Fawn's tongue, he said to her: "This food I deliver to you. This food, mixed with perfume leaf and redolent with incense, you shall hold in your mouth. And thereby you shall know that, in future, no matter who it is enters your tipi and sits him down, he shall be your concern. And for him you shall break in two what you might have eaten alone. So shall you share." In fact, the extending of hospitality was sometimes referred to as a "sweet-smelling deed."

To each of the others he gave the food, with these words. The ghost feast was calculated to touch impressionable girls. Overcome by the low weeping of their elders and the solemnity of the words, like a parting admonition from the dead grandmother's ghost, they felt that nothing on earth could be more important than the continuance of her spirit of hospitality. And now the responsibility would fall on them. Should her good deeds die with her? Never—if they could help it.

The ritual was over. Outside, the spectators, seated on the grass, were served a general feast of good food in superabundance. The women had come properly prepared, with a sack or other container for the food they could not consume there. It was the custom to do this; it was rude to leave anything that had been served. Guests must take it home for future enjoyment.

The redistribution followed. The average guest received some small gift, perhaps only a knife case or a pair of moccasins, but the special gifts were given for special reasons. The two fine horses made possible by Waterlily were given to White Hand in recognition of his devoted services all year.

The finest articles, which had been added to the ghost bundle from time to time, went to guests who had themselves once kept a ghost. And the symbolic articles, which were wrapped in with the hair at the beginning, were specially awarded, as was the custom. The four knives went to the four outside women who had come to assist in the preparations and had laid the Path of Beauty. The four awls were given to the four girls who, at the private feast, had eaten the ghost's perfumed food. They were a symbol of the womanly arts that the girls were expected to acquire.

The four pipes would be carried thereafter by White Hand and three other holy men selected by him; and the disks of abalone shell, known as "holy men's property" and permitted only to dreamers, would be worn by them. Sometime during the day, unnoticed, those four holy men took the "ghost" away. But where and how they buried it was their secret for all time. They were under religious compulsion never to reveal it.

Unlike the usual give-aways, always loud with praises and cheering, a redistribution was solemn and slow. In a sense it was no different in quality from the regular give-away custom of honoring one another with single gifts. But here in the re-distribution it was epitomized, heightened, and crystallized in one magnified act of giving. The gifts given to friends were the things given by friends throughout the year to be added to the pile of goods the related families were amassing. In the re-distribution, then, property was once more leveled. The blessing lay not so much in giving or getting as in having a part in this, the dramatizing of corporate generosity.

That evening, after the last guests had left, the many relatives gathered around a common outdoor fire, weary but happy once more. They were grateful that all their friends had rallied to their undertaking. They were satisfied that they had done their utmost for their dead. Each with his own thoughts, they sat in quiet until the old man spoke a kind of valediction to close the year-long effort.

"Now at last it is enough; now at last we are satisfied.

"Now let her good spirit go freely hence to the land where
spirits abide.

"We have caused it to linger with us for a spell; we have de-
tained our loved one some seasons longer amid honor and
reverence.

"We have enabled her to prolong yet a little longer that hospitality which was her chief delight.

"She has set one last example of generosity for the people.

"Now let her go in peace."

The great encampment of a Sun Dance, so impressive and so
full of life and activity during the days of celebration, always
became a dismal sight at the close. The visiting groups began
early to dismantle their camps and continued to do so, each at its
own pace, all day long. As more and more departed, they left
wide gaps in the circle—skeletal camps with only poles, posts,
stakes, and the willow withes used in the construction of temporary shelters to take care of the overflow, all standing at crazy
angles. Instead of the cheery open fireplaces that nightly glowed
with welcome, only a continuous ring of ashes and dead embers
remained.

By evening only the large section occupied by White Ghost's
camp circle stood intact. They had been the hosts; this was the
center of their territory. At their own convenience they, too,
would break camp and be on their way—but not until all the
guests had departed. The last group to leave was that from the
Black Hills region, and when they left, they took Waterlily with
them.

Whatever her feelings, she was quietly ready when the two
mothers of Sacred Horse came for her. Her womenfolk kissed
her tenderly, while the men took her hand in farewell. Blue Bird
held her to her breast for a moment and kissed her—but there
were no tears. Tears should be controlled, except at a death. It
was a bad omen if someone broke down over a mere parting. It
meant that death would come to one or the other of those taking
leave of each other before they could meet again.

When they were well on their way, Sacred Horse rode up and
took the rope by which his mothers were leading the horse

Waterlily rode. They surrendered it without comment. Only then did Waterlily recognize him. She had, after all, seen him before. Of course! He was that very well dressed young man at the courting hour the evening before the wife-buyers came with gifts.

Waterlily recalled that Alila had cried impulsively, "Will you look at that stranger! I hope he is headed my way!" And the other girls had said, "Why Alila, you shouldn't say such things. It is not becoming," but perhaps they were all hoping the same thing. At any rate, it was toward Waterlily that he had walked, smiling and silent. But she had eluded him, as was the way of Dakota girls who had been properly trained, acting on the advice of their sex: "If he really likes you, he will try again and again—let that be the proof. Do not consent to him at once."

Perhaps he would have tried again and again, but his indulgent mothers had got ahead of him. Anyway, here he was, riding beside Waterlily. She said nothing, and he did not try to make her talk. Thus they traveled, walking their horses so slowly that after a while they lost sight of the others ahead. It seemed as if they were all alone in the whole world, so vast and empty was the land. They would travel alone all the way home. As she thought of her own people, Waterlily felt so homesick that she pulled her wrap over her head and cried softly as she rode. After all, she was still only eighteen winters old and had never been alone with total strangers before. She could not adjust herself to the new situation without a few tears. But Sacred Horse must not see them. He must think she was just bashful of him.

Suddenly he spoke, almost stern in his haste, "Here, hold these," and thrust the reins of both horses roughly toward her. It startled her so that while she fumbled for them, her blanket slipped down. She quickly raised it over her head again.

Already he was running off to one side, crouching low and setting an arrow to his bow as he ran. Near a cluster of wild plum bushes up the ravine he fell on one knee and let the arrow fly. Then he went around the bushes. The next instant he came back with a young deer slung over his shoulder. While he worked at tying it fast on his horse, he remarked casually, "There! Now we can have some fresh meat to broil our first evening."

Waterlily said nothing, though she was no longer crying. She did not even feel lonesome, so busy she was admiring the expert way he had gotten the deer. But she continued to hide her face, not wanting the tear traces down her cheeks to show.

They rode on again in silence. After they had climbed the ridge and were going along over the uplands, he said, as though he were talking to a third person about her, "You know, she must be some relation to the deer; she cried because I killed it." It was an indirect compliment, for in myth and belief the deer was the embodiment of feminine allure.

Waterlily laughed outright and he laughed with her. And then she began to feel more cheerful. It seemed to her that everything was going to be all right. He had been very kind and considerate of her, and very patient. She thought she would like him.

CHAPTER 14

For a Dakota bride, the major problem was not that of adjusting to her new status as wife, which was private and personal, but adjusting to her husband's family and relatives, which was a social matter. Waterlily, as the outsider, must integrate herself correctly into the *tiyośpaye* headed by her father-in-law, Good Hunter. She must make this adjustment smoothly and correctly, or her kinship training at home would be in question. Dakota kinship rules, especially where relatives of marriage were concerned, were very exact and exacting. Her first step was to learn by subtle observation who was what to her, and then she must proceed to conduct herself properly in each case, as prescribed by kinship law. But this was not too complicated, after all. Anyone with ordinary intelligence, who had been brought up within the framework of the system, understood all its intricacies. Nevertheless, a relentless watchfulness was needed, especially at first.

So, with this matter constantly on her mind, she was not very homesick. There was too much in her new life to demand her attention. Then, too, she lived on the knowledge back in her mind that her parents would be coming on a long visit. Before leaving, her husband's real mother had invited them for an indefinite stay, and they had promised to come along with the first sizable party of travelers heading south. She could wait for that. Meantime she would get fully acquainted with her many new relatives of marriage; she would watch her kinship manners toward them all, so that they would know she was well bred—that her people had taught her that most important of lessons, the one regarding her duties toward her relatives. This new responsibility to represent her people kept her very quiet and observant, and she preferred to be a little inconspicuous at all times. That was safer than to be too enthusiastic and perhaps say or do the wrong things.

For the first time she understood what made her uncle, the husband of Dream Woman and father of Leaping Fawn and Prairie Flower, such a reticent man in their midst. Always he seemed to hold back a little, though he was agreeable and alert to be helpful, and though everyone liked him. It was because he was an outsider. In the *tiyošpaye* of Black Eagle, all were his relatives of marriage. He was like a perpetual visitor. He could never quite relax as he might have at home. Right now Waterlily found herself having to act like that uncle.

This *tiyošpaye* was the largest she had ever known. Good Hunter had a tremendous following of his own relatives, and his wives had theirs, too, though not so large. Together, they added up to a goodly number of people. It would not be easy to place so many individuals correctly. But once acquainted, she would see where she fitted into the whole group, and then she would be more at ease—she hoped.

No doubt it was to help a bride among her husband's people, or a groom among his wife's, that newlyweds regularly were left by themselves, until the one from outside got his or her bearings. At any rate, Waterlily found it a very helpful custom. The relatives did not make demands on her, or make her conspicuous and uncomfortable by focusing special attention on her or obliging her to talk, unless she wished. The delicacy of her husband's people in this respect comforted her.

Gradually, from each person's behavior toward her she inferred their relationship to her. For instance, on the first morning after her arrival, when she went outside to adjust the windflaps of her tipi to the prevailing wind, she heard giggling and whispering calculated for her ears. "Hey! Watch out, there! That's a rope across the path. Don't trip over that log! Look out for the post!"

She pretended not to hear, but from the corner of her eye she could see three boys in their middle teens watching her and grinning good-naturedly. Lying in the next tipi, whose bottom was rolled up all around and propped for ventilation, they were having fun trying to rattle her. Nobody needed to tell her who they were. They were either brothers or cousins of her husband, which put them in a joking relationship to her. What they were doing would be extremely rude for others, but it was their privilege to plague a brother's or a cousin's wife in that way, giving her a chance to reciprocate in kind if she liked. A bit of good-natured rudeness was allowable between them. The boys were implying: Too bad! Our brother (or cousin) has married a late sleeper (an indolent person) who walks about not yet fully awake. We must warn her.

They hoped Waterlily would joke back when she knew who they were. This was their preliminary skirmish, to introduce themselves and to find out whether she was the type to enjoy the joking privilege. It was all in fun—to get a rise out of her, if possible.

Waterlily found another brother-in-law one warm evening. As she sat leaning against her tipi on the shady side in late afternoon, a toddler of two came toward her. He had a present for her, a bit of leaf. In offering it, he lost his balance and tumbled in front of her. Waterlily caught him and sat him down on her lap. Thereupon one of her mothers-in-law, who was cooking at the outdoor fire and till then had seemed not to see her there, called out to the child, "That's right! Embrace her and make love to her. When you are big, perhaps she will leave Sacred Horse and elope with you. She is far too beautiful for him, anyway!" So Waterlily learned that it was a little brother-in-law that she held on her lap.

Thus went the business of getting the numerous relatives placed. Before the next moon she had a fair notion of her duties toward them all. Aside from those in joking relationship to her, all the others were formal relatives. Her father-in-law and his three wives were expected to be scrupulously formal, for they were avoidance relatives. They must be distantly helpful and respectful, and their respect must consist in not getting in her way or demanding her attention on them. Her reciprocal role was the same.

In spite of this rule, the eldest mother-in-law, Taluta, the senior wife, who was Sacred Horse's real mother, occasionally overstepped by talking directly and in a chummy way to Waterlily. This surprised the girl, for she had never before met a woman so independent of the avoidance taboo. And indeed some friends of the mother-in-law openly criticized her for it. "But it is too much liberty that you take, the way you talk so freely with your son's wife." To which she replied, "What of it? I can't let that rule stop me. She is only a child, after all, and far from her own people because we carried her off. She must be homesick at times. If I can cheer her up, what is so bad in that?"

So the two sat together often, talking of pleasantly trivial matters, the elder woman doing most of the talking and seeming more like a mother than a mother-in-law. This went on until Waterlily was emboldened in due time to talk more freely. One day she expressed her interest in the size of Good Hunter's tipi. He needed one extraordinarily large, to shelter his three families, though by now the two children of the senior wife, Echo and her brother Sacred Horse, were married and had their own lodges close by.

"Yes, it is large," her mother-in-law told Waterlily. "Thirty-six of the very largest bullhides went into this tent. And it took a good while to cut and piece it together. Women came to help and we held feasts every day for them. Your father-in-law selected the poles from the Black Hills, and his sons and nephews cut and brought them in. His old uncle, who understands such work, spent many days in removing the bark and shaving the wood down to make the poles smooth and of the right shape. They had to lie unused a long time before they were weathered enough."

Waterlily volunteered, "Our tipi had nineteen poles. My uncle's had twenty-three. His was bigger than ours because he always had a great deal of company, being head of our *tiyošpaye*."

The mother-in-law, Taluta, went on to say that the tipis of

Good Hunter all required thirty-four poles, excluding the two outside that controlled the windflaps, and that it took men to raise the poles and hoist the tent; women alone could not erect a tipi this size.

From the first Waterlily had been struck by the way it was laced up the center back with wooden pins, as well as up the front above the entryway. Now she understood why the heavy tent came in two pieces, each half raised separately. It would break one hoisting pole if it were whole. The interior was very spacious, for a tipi. Once when it stood vacant, Waterlily paced it off and found it to be sixteen of her steps across.

Each wife had her own compartment, which she shared with her small children, while the senior wife occupied the hostess's space on the righthand side nearest the entrance. Good Hunter had his own space, and the older children had theirs. Three young sons of the second wife shared one, and six girls occupied two spaces, one of the girls being a cousin living with them. Also present were a grandparent or two. And generally an uncle and his wife, or some other couple who were close relatives, stayed there also. There were spaces for them all. Often, too, some traveler or outsider sought shelter for a night, having no other place to stop. It was Good Hunter's boast that no wayfarer was ever turned away and no visitor, even a casual caller, was allowed to leave without first eating a meal.

The honor-place, with a decorated curtain across the entire rear, was kept in order, and fancy bags and things were placed there, enhancing the background against which special guests sat to be entertained. Everyone kept to his own place, and there was a certain dignity and quiet order in the tipi, even though so many lived in it much of the time.

All the wives—two being sisters and one their cousin—were equally responsible for the cooking. Whoever of them was not working at some task that had to be finished started the next meal, as a matter of course. Likewise, all the women were equally responsible for all the children, being mothers to them all. Indeed, until an outsider was well acquainted, he could not tell which woman was the real mother of any child, except the nursing baby.

Waterlily was, of course, familiar with the idea of plural wives, though there happened to be none in her uncle's *tiyospaye* back home. This was her first opportunity to know such a case intimately and she found it a harmonious household. All the wives cheerfully shared the burdens of the family. They took turns in their husband's affections, and if he seemed to favor one of them overmuch for a time, the others joked about it and let it pass.

But even though the wives were coequal in a sense, it was the senior wife, Taluta, who had precedence. As she told Waterlily with some confidence, "He bought *me*." Later on, her younger sister had been given to him by her parents "that she might be with her elder sister, to help her and to enjoy her protection." It was customary to do this, especially if the young unmarried girl was motherless and needed the protection and counsel of her sister. Still later, the cousin, an even younger woman, had been added to the household on the same plea.

Waterlily had known of several prominent men who had more than one wife, and that great leaders, medicine men, hunters, and such influential men could afford to provide for more than one wife and one family at the same time. She had heard, too, of a holy man among the Santees in the far east who had nine wives! Her father, Rainbow, had been there and seen them; otherwise Waterlily would have thought it was only a myth. Well, here was her father-in-law with three wives, three families in one, and everything ran smoothly. She said so, as politely as she knew how.

The senior wife laughed. "If you had come two years earlier, you might have had four mothers-in-law," she said, explaining that the fourth, a complete outsider, was such a troublemaker that Good Hunter had sent her back to her family in a distant band.

Taluta, the senior wife, the bought wife, was so sure of her position that she was a bit dictatorial at times, if it seemed necessary. But she was kind, and mothered everyone in the family in her crisp way. A big person at heart as well as in body, she concerned herself impartially over the welfare of her husband, the two co-wives, and their several children, as well as her own.

Never petty, she was a just and good manager of their household economy.

When it came time to give a wedding feast for Waterlily and Sacred Horse, she was in full command and made it one of the best and most generous occasions that camp circle had known. "Come and take my daughter-in-law's hand," she invited special ones, and when they shook hands with the girl in greeting, she gave them fine presents, honoring Waterlily.

A day came when Good Hunter decided to make a cache and store away their surplus food against the leaner days that never failed to come, sooner or later. Then it was that the senior wife showed her full capacity to organize and direct the entire family in the work. Waterlily was much impressed by her executive powers—what must be done was so clear in the woman's mind.

It was partly from fear that Good Hunter wanted to hide much food away somewhere at this time. Unlike Waterlily's own camp circle, so remote and complacent, these people were worried. There was incessant talk about the white men and what their presence would do to the food supply. "They are coming in greater and greater numbers all the time, and they threaten our herds. They wantonly kill off our friends (the buffalo) and leave them spoiling on the plains. What manner of men are they, to be so wasteful? Are they children? Do they not yet have their senses? If this keeps on, we shall all starve!" So talked the men, some saying one thing, some another, but all of it adding up to that, and more. To those of lesser vision, it seemed impossible that all the vast herds roaming the plains would be killed off, or that there could be men capable of slaughtering the noble creatures just for a pastime. Yet that was the fear that haunted the camp council.

Good Hunter, who expected the worst, called his *tiyospaye* together. "My relatives," he told them, "this that we hear all around is a bad thing. But a wise man defends—or tries to defend—himself. If he fails, he has at least tried. Now, therefore, I am planning to make a cache in the ancient manner and store away all the meat I can bring together. I advise you to join me. Bring other foods, too, such as fruits of the earth, and store them away. Then at least for a time we shall eat, ere we die."

He turned to the women, including his wives and his daughters-in-law (all the women sat grouped together at this conference, as at all public meetings), and continued: "Each man will get in all the food he can. His wife will prepare every bit that is over and above her daily needs, cutting the meat as thin as possible for drying and treading. When it is ready, she will pack it well into as many cases as need be. We shall have room in the cache for every family to store its food. The cases will be laid in storage according to each woman's own things, plainly indicated by the designs on her containers. Some day, when food is low, she will have it to feed her family and to offer to visitors in courtesy."

Immediately the hunters went out to bring in all the meat possible, and the women worked till sundown every night, cutting it into the proper shape. Certain of the elderly men, who knew the art, meantime went out to an isolated spot under the pines, far from the camp circle, to get the cache ready. They dug a round hole straight down to the length of a tall man's arm and wide enough in diameter to admit a man. From that depth they began to widen it as they worked down. They pulled up the loose dirt in bullhides as the diggers sent it up. Those on top carried the loads on their backs and dumped the dirt in the tall underbrush, so that no one could see it and speculate on the possibility of a storage cave nearby. When finished, the cache was a clean, roomy chamber far underground, its shape resembling an immense jar set into the earth.

The women worked fast, preparing the meat for processing. After it was cut into sheets, it was hung on horizontal poles to dry for a day or so in the sun and wind. Then it was ready for treading. A carpet of fresh leaves was spread on the grass, on which the sheets of meat were laid flat. More leaves were put over the meat, and finally a clean hide was thrown over the whole. Then the treading began.

Some lively boys around fifteen or sixteen years of age were put through the sweatbath and were given new moccasins to wear. From then on, all day long, they stamped and beat down the meat under the hide. Sometimes they worked together, stepping in strict time; sometimes they took turns, one or another pausing to eat and to rest. But always the treading must be vigorous and continuous; and if momentarily the boys seemed to slow down, old grandfathers, now helpless in all else but their tongues, sat by, singing their praises to keep them going, or cajoling, and finally ridiculing them good-naturedly.

"*Ecaaa!*" they pretended to sneer, "Why, when we were boys, treading meat . . ." and they boasted of their boundless energy at that time. "When I was your age . . . Alas, where is the stamina of youth today?" And the boys, trying to vindicate their generation, strove all the harder in their efforts to disprove the charge that boys weren't what boys used to be. When it was deemed enough, the treaders were not sorry. It had been hard work in the hot sun.

Daily this was repeated, each woman entering what meat she had ready. The purpose of treading was twofold: it flattened out such kinks as the meat was drying into, and it pressed out whatever moisture still remained after the meat was exposed outside. After the treading, the meat was hung up again, to dry through and through. Day after day it was kept hanging out till sunset.

This treading and drying was done with each new quantity until the senior wife pronounced it thoroughly conditioned for underground storage. By then it had been blanched to a grayish shade from the dark color it was when it underwent treading. The countless steps pressing upon the meat had so completely broken up the fibers that now it was soft and pliable, as ordinary jerked meat was not. With such tenderizing, the meat would "eat better" when it was cooked. The whole enterprise was an exacting task, with benefits far in the future.

Each woman packed away her own meat in parfleches, flat envelope containers of rawhide. When the four sides were folded and tied up, the container was oblong in shape, possibly as long as a woman's arm and half as wide as the length. The sides were painted with bright colors in fragments of a bold, distinctive design which, when the case was folded, came together into one complete and harmonious pattern. Such containers for dried meat came in pairs exactly alike and were kept tied together. If a woman had more than one pair, they were all painted the same. The purpose was for identification, like a brand. When meat was cached, any woman could find hers by her own design. The pairs were tied loosely together so that it was possible to open one of the cases without the other's getting in the way. When carried on a packhorse, one hung on either side of its body.

To store the packs of food, one man let himself down into the cache by means of a pole. Standing in the center of it, he received from the men above him the pairs of cases belonging to each family, in turn, and laid them around close to the wall. He continued in a spiral, leaving room between the cases so that if one family was compelled to open the cache before the others, they could pull out their own cases easily and the ones remaining would simply settle downward. When the man finished putting all the cases in place, he was helped up and out.

The sod on top had been lifted out intact in large pieces. After bracing the opening underneath as seemed sufficient, the men replaced that sod, mending the sutures with dirt and sprinkling grass and leaves and pebbles so that a passerby would have great difficulty realizing what it was if he should happen onto that very spot, so out of the way—though it might happen. They took that chance.

Throughout this work, the women kept together and apart from the men. Waterlily saw her husband from a distance during the day and they might speak in passing or converse if they had to work at something together. But it was customary for men and women to keep with their own kind in public. The married did not demand one another's exclusive attention. Always aware of the presence of other people, they adjusted to them also. Waterlily asked for no more attention from her husband than did other women from theirs, nor would she have wanted it publicly; rather, it would have embarrassed her.

Only within their own tipi did they come together; there they ate and slept. But they did not talk freely together even there. Waterlily was quiet unless her husband spoke to her. He sometimes worried—perhaps it was wrong to have bought her. Perhaps her heart was not in this marriage . . .

But she shared his life in all ways without demur. She was an industrious homemaker and her little tipi, which her mothers-in-law had standing ready for her when she arrived, was always as neat as could be. It was pretty, too—of white skins, well proportioned, and therefore firm of stance. When the shape was right, a tipi stood firm, pulled groundward evenly. Otherwise it was never entirely wind and storm proof. The bridal tipi was decorated with fancy tassels and other ornaments on the sides, and it was clean and bright inside. Waterlily dreaded winter, when it would be necessary to build an indoor fire whose rising smoke must in time darken the upper half. As yet it gleamed in the sun and she was proud of it. Most of the time so far it had not been necessary for her to build even an outdoor fire for cooking. A while before mealtime came around, if she was still at work on something, food would be standing inside, ready cooked, for her to serve her husband and herself. The many relatives of marriage saw to that, vieing with one another to show her every courtesy. It was well that they did so, for Waterlily was tired after a day of heavy work.

That was the pleasant penalty of having an exceptionally skillful hunter for a husband. The work of caring for the meat and treating the skins seemed endless. But she did not think to neglect any of it. Her mother had talked to her often about industry, and she had heard the derisive comments of other women about lazy wives. Because she, Waterlily, went at her home tasks so systematically, her husband's people praised her to their friends. "My daughter-in-law is indeed a fine woman—a good worker and with much skill in womanly crafts. She made this for me," and the senior wife of Good Hunter exhibited a foot neatly encased in a moccasin of much embellishment, the work of Waterlily. But this took place only where Waterlily did not hear or see her.

In her presence, little of her work or industry was alluded to, except to complain to her that she was overdoing and ought to rest. It was their subtle way of praising her—by not showing surprise or too obvious gratification, as if she were more of a success than they had hoped. That would be like saying they had not thought her *tiyospaye* could turn out such a fine girl.

Busy and well treated, Waterlily was getting nicely acclimated to her new environment. And then, suddenly, she grew homesick. It all started one day when, coming round a tipi, she saw that her father-in-law was placidly dressing his wives' hair, in turn. He was sitting at right angles to the middle wife and had first unbrained the hair on that side, combed it all out gently, oiled it till it shone, and was now braiding it again. All his wives had very long hair. He was proud of that, because it was a mark of good looks. And as he worked, he chatted pleasantly with the wife.

This was a semi-intimate scene indicating the best of relations between the married. Waterlily instantly recalled that Rainbow used to dress Blue Bird's hair just like that. It seemed very long ago and remote, that childhood life of hers when they had sat so. It was a mark of tender affection and the only bit of demonstrativeness between husband and wife that any outsider was permitted to see, for such things as kissing or embracing, even in fun, were definitely not done in public.

Only once in a while a man might indulge himself by performing this simple office for his wife. It was always done calmly and casually, but it was not routine. No affectionate act was ever demanded or taken for granted. A wife did not pout when her husband neglected to dress her hair or pay her any other such attention, and a man was sometimes too busy or preoccupied to enjoy it. Such marks of fondness were not meant to be done like a daily chore. There would be no satisfaction in that for either man or wife.

Waterlily, watching at a distance, felt a sharp yearning for her own parents. In place of her father in-law she seemed to see Rainbow talking quietly about matter-of-fact things to Blue Bird, all the time working carefully with her hair, enjoying the feel of the long strands through his fingers. The thought struck her, "Will my husband ever do my hair?" She knew that some men never dressed a wife's hair, being temperamentally not so inclined, though they might think highly of her.

She was sure she would not want him to—not until they were very old, maybe. But now he would be crazy if he attempted it, and she would feel silly enough to die! Newlyweds did not indulge in any such domestic display. They were properly reserved with reference both to each other and to whoever might see them.

Waterlily did not want her own hair dressed—but how that scene yonder filled her with longing for her home! It was now the third moon since she had come here to live, and still there was no sign of her family. She was impatient to see them, and at the same time worried lest they strike out by themselves over the wild stretch of no man's land between their camp circle and this. What if they had started alone and their tipi was raided on the way and—oh no! She dared not let her imagination run on. She knew what raids were and what they could do. Her mother had lost her parents that way, and she herself was once in a party that barely escaped one, only because of Rainbow's alertness—the time her brother Little Chief struck first coup.

And then, when her hidden concern over her people was at its peak, travelers brought word that Rainbow had had to postpone his visit because his aged father was ailing and likely to die soon. Waterlily realized how Rainbow must feel. She loved her grandfather dearly, too. How she longed to be there herself, now that he was so ill. If he were to die, with her so far away, she thought she could not bear it. Her tears began dropping on the fancywork she was doing.

"Don't cry, sister," the wife of her husband's cousin who sat with her said. (The wives of brothers or cousins were sisters in social kinship.) "Don't cry. You are saddened by news of your grandfather, I know. But as my father always said, tears are for shedding only over the dead. He was right—what else is worth crying about? Only death, because it is forever. But your grandfather is only sick; he may recover. So be happy, sister. No one has died."

She went on again, after a little, "Or perhaps you have felt some forewarning to make you anxious, something that unsteadies your spirit, such as a twitching on your face, below your eyes and down your cheeks, where tears are to flow? Or is your body all alive and expectant, as if invisible hands were about to touch you—something like that? Or perhaps you have heard a ringing in your ear?"

Waterlily recalled that on the previous evening, when she stood alone with her left ear turned in the direction of her home, there had been a loud ring as if from far away. It had come directly at her and seemed to penetrate her being.

"There! That's *it!* That's the disturbing news you have just received." The sister was delighted with her own diagnosis. "But don't you see," she said, "your lips haven't quickened where your mother has kissed you, your arms have not felt oversensitive where you have held your little brother and sister, nor your shoulders where other relatives have embraced you. Why, even your eyes are free of crying signs. See there?" the sister had fully convinced herself. Then she tried in her clumsy way to rationalize. "But even though your grandfather should die, it will be best for him. You say he is old and blind and alone. Don't you know, people like that yearn to die. So do not feel so bad . . . anyway, we all must die . . ."

But that day was the turning point. Before that, Waterlily had been absorbed with the problem of getting acquainted with the very large company of new relatives. Now, having succeeded, she was still not happy, even though they were all friendly and respectful. Something was definitely wrong. Nor was it because of Sacred Horse. Though she still felt they did not know each other well, he was very kind and gentle with her, and a good provider. She had much that many a girl would wish for. What ailed her, anyway?

Suddenly she had the answer. It was that she lacked home-people, relatives of birth. Everyone here was a relative of marriage. They were *his* home-people; *he* was free to be himself in their presence in a way that she was not. This was to be expected, of course. All her life she had seen avoidance respect and thought it entirely proper. But being so recently placed in this new situation where she must live in its formal atmosphere exclusively, she found the strain becoming too hard for one so young and so far from home.

She needed family relatives such as Sacred Horse was enjoying in his own *tiyóspaye.* She needed an environment charged with parental affection, where she could indulge her moods and could be herself without constraint. Parents, uncles, aunts, and grandparents humored you, even spoiled you a little. Before them you could be outspoken, impudent, and perhaps say or do silly things, with the assurance that they would understand. Waterlily needed her menfolk, too, her brothers and cousins ready at all times to protect her and give her social backing. Without them, a woman felt insecure against—she did not know what. But she felt as if here she stood vulnerable and alone.

The environment of the family of marriage obligated one to play an adult, responsible role at all times without slack. The kinship laws so ordered it. Life in the *tiyoṡpaye* of Sacred Horse was, for Waterlily, like wearing ceremonial dress all the time, and how she longed for homely, easy clothes in which to drop her dignity now and then!

Few persons were individualist enough to kick over the kinship traces as the senior wife did to make her son's young wife feel at home. Waterlily was grateful to her for that. But it was not enough. She dared not break rules, too, and behave like a careless child toward her husband's mother. However informal the older woman was, her son's wife was still her daughter-*in-law*. "If only I had one person in this camp circle that was a family relative, so I could relax in her presence just once! Among all these people," Waterlily sighed, "everyone is an in-law to me."

As if in answer, unbelievable as it seemed to her, a man and his wife came one day to visit Waterlily, calling her "daughter." The woman embraced her with motherly tenderness. "My daughter," she explained, "we learned only last night, on our return home, who it was that has become the wife of Sacred Horse. You are in good hands, daughter, for this is an able and upright family where you will always be treated well. And indeed they should be proud of you. I am sure they are." The woman had brought Waterlily courtesy food and gifts. "Your brother Red Leaf it was who told us about you," she said.

Red Leaf? My brother? Waterlily tried to think where she had heard that name. All at once it came back to her. Why, Red Leaf was the little boy with whom her brother Ohiya played during a tribal reunion some years ago, before the trip to Palani's camp circle. She remembered how the two boys took an instant liking to each other and how Ohiya in his eager fashion had made a friendship pact with his playmate. How he had come in breathless and solemn to announce to the family, "We have gone into fellowhood." Blue Bird and Rainbow had accepted the news a little doubtfully, reminding Ohiya that such a friendship was for grown men who understood the heavy obligations and were prepared to face them always. "Maybe when you are men you will not be sure that is what you want," Blue Bird said gently. But that did not deter Ohiya, his sister recalled, smiling. Such a little thing—children imitating adults. And yet here it was working out to her advantage, for here were people she could call father and mother.

Waterlily remembered that Rainbow had said to Blue Bird, "It seems like playing with a sacred matter, doesn't it?" But Red Leaf's parents had taken the matter seriously and approved it so much that there had been an exchange of presents. And then the two fellows were separated and were seemingly destined never to meet again, at least as playmates.

"Daughter"—the woman did all the talking, or nearly all—"we would have claimed you sooner but we have been in the Black Hills where your father has a white man friend. 'Lean White Man' he calls him, and a good name it is, too. For he is very thin and long and weak-looking. But so active! The way he can work would surprise you. Whenever he goes far away, toward the sunrise, we camp near his cabin to guard it for him. And when he returns he brings us very fine presents, like these dishes of metal I have brought you."

Waterlily could hardly believe that a Dakota and a white man could be friends. "And this white man, my mother," she said, "are you sure he is really good, in his heart, toward my father? How may my father know, since he cannot understand his language?"

"Oh, but your father does," the woman was very complacent. "Say something for her."

"Well," and he cleared his throat in preparation, "well, he calls me 'injun'—that means Dakota in his language. I say, 'Got tobacco?' when I want a smoke. It isn't hard. And too, my friend talks some Dakota, so we get along. Oh, he is my friend, all right!"

The wife cut in, "He gave your father many fine things to

bring home. I have for you a piece of red blanket [flannel], too. He gave him knives and spoons, and blue as well as red cloth, and even a holy-iron [gun] to shoot with."

When the new-found parents of Waterlily prepared to leave, after eating the good meal she had served them, the woman said, "Daughter, we live exactly opposite—across the common. Return home whenever you feel like it and spend the day with your own relatives." She indicated the direction with a quick upward thrust of her chin, her hands being full of return gifts from Waterlily. "Do you see the tallest tipi, the one with its upper half painted blue? Well, that's not it. But the second one on the left, the next tallest, that's it." It was the habit of the people to eliminate other, similar objects until they isolated the one they wished to point out: not that, nor that, nor that yonder—but the other.

The father added his invitation. "Come soon and often, my daughter. You have mothers and aunts who will prepare foods you like. You have fathers and uncles, and brothers, sisters, and cousins—and you have especially your own little brother Red Leaf. You have sons, daughters, nieces, and nephews—and many grandparents. They are all eager for a sight of you."

When they had walked off a few paces, the woman turned and said, "Why, I nearly forgot! You even have a grandchild now. Your eldest sister's son became the father of a baby girl only yesterday, so come and see your granddaughter!"

They cut across the common, walking one behind the other, with the man leading. Watching them go, Waterlily felt relief. From now on things were going to be easier. Here were people with whom she could be herself, without stopping to consider her dignity. Kinship came in halves—the family of birth and the family of marriage. In the one, a person was permitted to play the child occasionally; in the other, he must strictly play the adult, as a matter of self-respect, once having accepted an adult role. Waterlily had been cramped, in a one-sided society; now, with its complement, she was going to manage all right. It was best to have many contacts; having both kinds of relatives kept life in balance.

The fact that these new parents were nothing like her own father and mother made no difference. They were older and not nearly so handsome as were Rainbow and Blue Bird, but she did not think to draw comparisons. It was what they symbolized, what they offered Waterlily, that mattered. Being a respected daughter-in-law was all right. The deference continually shown her was pleasant; the challenge to reciprocate that deference as smoothly and correctly offered no problem. She had been too well trained in all the intricacies of kinship courtesy and behavior to make mistakes. But now she could cast aside that formal role occasionally and be somebody's child, and she was glad of that. Now, if only Blue Bird and Rainbow would arrive for that long visit and renew their relationship with these kindly local parents of hers, life would be perfect, she thought.

And then she remembered what it was that was preventing their coming immediately. She thought of her poor sick old grandfather and was sad again. But not quite so sad.

CHAPTER 15

The average Dakota woman did not indulge in confessions or confidences with other women, or in minute analyses regarding her married life. She did not share any intimate secrets of that life, or her reactions to it, whether pleasant or unpleasant. She could live and die with her own secrets, and she did so. Her one concern was to maintain her dignity. She would not make it possible for other women to ridicule her or accuse her of a lack of reticence on that point.

However agreeable or upsetting her marriage might be, she managed a calm exterior, a convincing matter-of-factness about it, that prevented others—including her husband—from guessing her feelings. If her married life was obnoxious to her, she simply walked out of it without a word as to why. If pressed, she might say, "It was not agreeable to me . . . That being so . . . ," and her reason was clear and sufficient. There was no economic need for her to endure in silence. She knew that her brothers and male cousins were ready to provide for her, and her own relatives to take her back into their midst. She did not have to hang on just to be supported by a husband.

Nor was there any need to flaunt her married state. Why should she, since there was no particular triumph where the premise was "man in pursuit, woman overcome." Thus presumably she had not landed him; he had landed her. Let the man gloat, if gloating there was to be. A woman who acted important because she was married was something of a fool and incurred ridicule rather than aroused admiration or envy. Almost any woman could marry *somebody,* and marriage for women was the rule. There was no particular distinction in it that one married woman should play it up.

Back of it all was the kinship reason for a wife's reticence. No matter with whom she exchanged confidences, whatever she told about her husband's intimacy with her would eventually reach his women relatives, particularly his sisters and cousins, and they would bitterly resent his being publicly discussed in an undignified light. They could not forgive a stupid wife who thus made their brother or cousin appear ridiculous or worse. It was the kinship duty of these womenfolk of his to uphold his honor and to defend him in all phases of his life. And since every woman had brothers and cousins to defend, they all held the same attitude in this matter. Thus kinship once again wielded a controlling force here, in muzzling all idle talk about marital intimacy involving specific personalities.

Growing up in a milieu where these ideas and habits obtained, Waterlily could not help but reflect them in her own marriage. Nor had it been enough that she absorbed them from her surroundings unconsciously. Her mother must hammer them in, also, with perhaps too positive strokes. "When you marry, my daughter, remember that your children are more important than you. Always the new life comes first. Your duty to your children must be in accordance to this rule.

"Next, it is your duty to honor and respect your husband and to keep your life with him a secret always. A woman who talks about her relations with her husband is disloyal to her mate and a reproach to herself. Accept your new life as a mature woman, even while you are gentle and yielding. Do not behave in a childish manner toward your husband. You are his helpmeet, not his baby. Be grown up.

"Watch your actions and attitude toward your husband's relatives. If you make crude mistakes, they will think you ignorant of kinship manners and will be sorry their son married you. Be respectful; honor them by 'avoiding' them. And in all your dealings with relatives of marriage hold back a little at first. Keep your reserve at all times. Be composed. Be wise."

Waterlily had followed her mother's advice almost without qualification. It was her privilege and duty to be bashful and prudent in adjusting to her new situation as wife and relative-in-law. That was proper for the young bride, even though it was bound to take time to feel at home with her husband and to break down her habitual silence. The husband who understood this and was willing to wait patiently, and who did not try to draw her out prematurely by tricks, was indeed a wise man. It paid him in the end.

All the same, it was beginning to dawn on Sacred Horse that his wife was being unduly slow, unduly quiet. He could not tell what she was thinking, even while her behavior was all that he could ask. Misgivings began to assail him—could it be that she was a naturally glum person? Or that she regretted her marriage to him? Did he not please her as she pleased him? Would she never snap out of it and feel fully at home with him?

Finally he went to consult his cousin, a man of more years and more experience than himself. "I am troubled, my cousin. She hardly ever speaks unless I start the conversation. She talks along well enough then, but what troubles me is that she never begins and she always stops first. She seems afraid to talk freely. Why, you'd be surprised at the mute life we live together." Then, hopelessly, he added, "If it is always going to be so, how can we have a good life?"

In giving advice, men usually thought a while first. But at last the cousin said, "It is always harder for a newlywed couple to get used to each other within the man's *tiyošpaye*. You made your first mistake in not staying for a while with her family, where she would have only you to adjust to. Then, when she knew you well, she would be better able to meet the problem of in-laws by itself. I say this out of my own experience. At first I stayed with my wife's *tiyošpaye,* where I was the one to act in a bashful manner, not she. It was easy enough for me to stay out of the way, and she was still surrounded by her familiar relatives. That made it easier for us to start our life together. It did not take her long to get used to me, since I alone was a stranger."

He made another observation. "If your wife is still reserved toward you, do not be alarmed. Consider that she was bought. A woman who hastily jumps into marriage by eloping must needs go all out to get acquainted with her husband. She can hardly affect bashfulness after her bold step. One who marries by mutual agreement needs only to meet her husband halfway. But the one who is bought—well, a man must expect to go all the way. He must do all his wooing after marriage.

"But don't you worry, my cousin. You are still a boy and have no knowledge of woman's nature. When there is a child, it will all work out. Shy women always find their tongue fast enough then. Just let a babe lie helpless in their arms crying for nourishment, and then, without a thought as to who might be looking, they forget themselves, driven by their single desire to soothe it. Then they pour out a steady flow of tender words into the infant's ear— and soon they have the habit of talking. Just wait and see."

All that Sacred Horse had told his cousin about Waterlily was true. He could count on the fingers of one hand the times so far that she had talked spontaneously and at any encouraging length. And those rare times were very precious to him. Memorable was the day he killed an antelope and brought it home already skinned. After unloading it outside the tipi, he came in, ate the food she had ready for him, and then lay down flat on his back, on the opposite side of the tipi from her.

"Ah, it is good to stretch out," he groaned contentedly while he watched her from the corner of his eye. She only smiled a little flicker of a smile as she lowered her eyes on her work and said nothing. He tried again. "Now, if someone were to remove my damp moccasins, wipe my throbbing feet, and paint the soles of them with red ceremonial paint, that would be perfect! After a wearying day to be made a beloved in that way!"

He saw her start to smile, with a spark of interest in her eyes— and then quickly bite her lip and look down, a silent little woman in her woman's space. He had not really expected her to paint his feet—not yet. That was another custom for seasoned couples who had learned to esteem one another from a long mutual kindliness through the years. It was no routine requirement for a wife, any more than dressing a wife's hair was routine for a husband. A man did not ask for his feet to be soothed and honored. It was an unsolicited and spontaneous sign of wifely affection and appreciation.

Sacred Horse knew that they were both too young in years and too new in their marriage for that. He only said it as a joke, because it would be for them such an incongruous performance. After a long interval he broke the silence. "I don't suppose you know what that is. One sees it so seldom and it is for couples much older than we." He gave up then and rolled over toward the tipi wall for a nap. She'd never talk, he guessed.

But for once Waterlily did talk, softly reminiscing: "I do know what it is. My mother has done it. One time I especially remember, she did it after a long, hard day when hunting was very poor and everyone was anxious. We were all miserable with hunger. Both Smiling One and Ohiya were crying for food and my mother was very unhappy. But she called us in and said: 'Children, probably your father will have to return without any meat again today. All the animals have vanished together, by agreement it seems. We may have to fill up on more mashed *tinpsila* [prairie turnips] again tonight. He will get home worn out after trying hard to find food for us. So what do you say we paint his feet and put pretty new moccasins on him?'

"We forgot our hunger and got busy. Everyone helped. Mother got the water ready while Ohiya went over the prairie, gathering fresh sage plants, the soft, fragrant kind with tender, velvety leaves, for her to wipe my father's feet dry and cool them at the same time. I took down the paint bag from the tipi pole where it always hung and opened it as carefully as I could because the paint was in powder form. I spread it out so that it would be ready to use. My little sister, Smiling One—she was only three then—sat holding the new moccasins. When it came time, she surrendered them one at a time, so very solemnly that it was funny." Waterlily laughed indulgently, forgetting herself.

"When my father came in he staggered from loss of sleep. He

was limp from fatigue. When we painted his feet, he said nothing, only he moaned a little. But we knew he was happy. And he had brought meat at last, too. He had walked to the big hills on the horizon to find it and had carried a large deer on his back all the way home! But what pleased him most was that even before we knew he was bringing food to us, we had been planning to make him our beloved by putting red paint ceremonially on him. I remember too . . ." But there she stopped short. The long speech had so astonished her, suddenly, that she could not go on. It was at such times, when in a nostalgic mood, that she could forget her new status momentarily and talk freely and charmingly.

"I have to see to the meat." So, murmuring an excuse for leaving abruptly, she slipped outside. Sacred Horse went to sleep, hopeful of some headway. He woke only when she peered in at the entrance and asked, "What have you done with the hide?"

"I left it at twin oak," he said. "I thought you ought to rest this once from dressing hides day after day. It is too much for you. We can afford to lose one skin now and then."

"You ought not to have done that. You ought always to bring in everything that can be of use. It is no hardship dressing hides. I am used to it. Besides, we always need good buckskin for clothing and other things."

Her words were a rebuke. But under them also was happiness that he had contrived to spare her. All the same, she could not leave the precious hide out there. While he slept on, she bridled her pony and rode swiftly out, without speaking of her intention to anyone. When Sacred Horse got up and missed her, he hurried out to the twin oak, guessing that was where she had gone.

She had pulled down the slippery hide from the high fork (where the oak became twins) into which Sacred Horse had flung it. But she was having difficulty in holding it in place while she tied it to her pony. Green hides were always a slimy dead weight. This one kept sliding off, as fast as she had it in place. Just when she was ready to give up, her husband came to her aid.

By the time they were ready to go back it was dusk. The ride homeward was cool and pleasant. After a little while they raced their ponies. Sacred Horse held his in check at first to give her a head start so as not to leave her too far behind. He need not have done that. Soon it was not altogether easy for him to gain on her. How that girl could ride! He had had no idea. Her long, black hair, which had come unbraided during her struggles with the hide, trailed behind her in a level sweep. Her pretty young face was tilted up and she was actually laughing, free as the wind, when he came up beside her.

They slowed down and walked their ponies the rest of the way. Twilight had by then deepened into dark night, lit only by some very bright stars that seemed just beyond reach. She talked a great deal now, mostly about her home and her childhood. She always talked more easily after dark, Sacred Horse thought to himself. Then she was very nice to be with.

It was several days after this that Sacred Horse came in one afternoon and found Waterlily all ready to go someplace. Her hair was oiled to a gloss and neatly braided, and a fresh line of vermilion marked the part. Some of the red was over her face, too. She was wearing a pretty gown, one of several that her talented aunt, Dream Woman, had made for her. Outside the entrance were three kettles of food hot off the open-air fire.

"Well, what's all this for?" Sacred Horse asked genially, sitting down outside the tipi to eat. "Are we giving a feast?"

"No," Waterlily said, "it is only something I prepared for our mother across the circle. She is giving a feast for the new grandchild's ear piercing tomorrow."

"I don't know how to get these kettles over there," she added. "I thought you might think of some way."

He said nothing. But after watering his horses, he brought back a strong pole of ash and ran it through the bails of the kettles. When Waterlily was ready, she grasped one end and he the other, and thus they walked along, sharing the weight evenly, the kettles hanging between them on the pole.

The mother was delighted; even though there was plenty of food already, part of which had come from their local relatives, this that Waterlily had done was so right, socially, that it made the mother very proud. In the shrill, high voice in which women exulted, she exclaimed in cries of delighted surprise, "*Hinun! Hinun! Hinun!* Do come and see what my daughter has done! She honors the grandchild to be named tomorrow!" Then she ran to the tipi a few paces off where the infant lay asleep, and looked in at the entrance, informing it for the benefit of the adults within hearing, "See what your grandmother has done for you! She brings food for your feast! Oh, you lucky baby, to have such a pretty young grandmother who cares so much for you!"

Everyone was impressed with Waterlily's gesture. "How well she does in kinship, for one so young!" they said. "Fortunate is the man whose wife does things well!"

And indeed, Waterlily's initiating a deed like this so early was remarkable. Yet it was the sort of thing her people did and she knew nothing else. Blue Bird, for instance, was forever carrying courtesy food to this or that one, or inviting visitors to eat at her tipi, or helping friends and kinsmen about to give a feast, by contributing food and other gifts, or comforting the bereaved with a meal and words of condolence—every act a kinship responsibility but also a social pleasure. The daughter had only done what she knew her mother would do in her place, and it was admirably right.

Waterlily had been over here often, since she first met her social parents. By happy coincidence they were already social parents of Sacred Horse, too, so that together, husband and wife, Sacred Horse and Waterlily, were son and daughter to Red Leaf's parents. This made a very congenial group, free of restraints and of the need for formal behavior. Both Sacred Horse and Waterlily could be perfectly natural and relaxed before their social parents. It was a fortuitous situation, and not usual.

Basking in the homelike atmosphere, Waterlily was soon joking and laughing gaily when the four sat inside the tipi that evening. She even forgot that her husband, a comparative stranger yet, was present, and her usual diffidence vanished. He watched her with concealed delight. So this was her nature when she was completely at ease—how charming she was that way! Why, there were instances when she even argued with him, and once she actually flashed a bit of petulance his way, like a spoiled child. She had spirit; she was human, all right. However had she managed to keep passive and overly polite all this time? Now, if she would only forget to crawl back into her shell like a turtle, where she could not be reached, when they were away from here again and alone together. It occurred to him then that this was the place for them to come often. This might well be the short cut to the end of her bridal shyness. Maybe, after all, he would not have to wait until there was a child, for her to lose herself . . .

And so they sat that evening, content and happy, with no suspicion of the sinister threat hanging over the whole camp circle that very night, soon to fall upon it, scattering its frightened people to the four winds. They sat visiting until a casual caller, who dropped in later on, gave them a hint of the approaching horror. And even then no one recognized it.

The dog barked a warning and a man outside called, "Do you sit there?" "Yes, come in," said Red Leaf's father. (Men replied to men, women to women.) The woman of the tipi was saying, "Let me see . . . oh yes, there is plenty of stew left. (Tilting her kettle to look) He never wants much, late at night—just a snack . . ." while the husband was saying, "That's Yankton, the camp circle crier, you know. He is our friend. He always drops in to see us at this time." Husband and wife spoke simultaneously. Waterlily caught both remarks.

She and Sacred Horse had been sitting side by side in the honor-place. But now the men and women formed two distinct groups, according to sex. People always tended to do this unconsciously. Waterlily eased over toward the mother and Sacred Horse toward the father. Yankton joined the men on the left side of the tipi.

All the conversation was interesting, for Yankton was an entertaining talker, and in addition he had a prodigious memory for details. Having just come from the council tipi, the forum and center of all discussions and activities, he knew all the latest news.

Presently he was talking about the beautiful blankets, woven in many colored bands, which the two sons of Buffalo Boy had recently brought home from the Arapaho country. They were much in demand as wraps and were especially adaptable for summer because they were lighter in weight than skin robes. These that the boys had brought home were the talk of the whole camp and every woman thought covetously of them.

Yankton explained that Arapaho scouts had found them in

great bundles where they had been dropped by an army passing over the territory southwest of them. "When the blankets were brought into the Arapaho camp, there was a mad scramble for them, you may be sure," Yankton said, "And no wonder, for they are very fine."

"How many did Buffalo Boy's sons bring back?" Red Leaf's mother asked.

"Twenty-odd, I imagine. 'We could have got even more,' the boys said, 'but a bad sickness was raging and men, women, and children were dying fast all around. We did not want to die there, so we hurried away.'"

"And they were right," the father commented quietly. "Home is the place to die—unless it be the battlefield."

The two women shuddered, uttering the woman's expletive of fear and horror, "Yaaa!" And then the mother asked, "What kind of sickness? Did they say?"

"Yes, they said it was many-sores [smallpox]. Something like the sickness that killed off whole families over a generation ago, in some camp circles."

The mother shuddered again, "Yaaa! It does seem that there are coming to be worse and worse sicknesses in the land. Time was when such things were unknown."

But, womanlike, her mind was really on the blankets all the while. She said, "How I wish my grandchild might be wrapped in one of those new robes at her ear-piercing rites! Just long enough, during the feast, when the naming takes place. Then I should want the baby to give the blanket away to the old man who pierces her ears. It would be a worthy gift for her first give-away. I have wanted her ears pierced," she mused. "'My grand-children shall all wear ear ornaments, as children-beloved,' I have often said aloud. 'None shall go through life with slippery-smooth ear lobes, like a stray, without relatives to honor him.'"

Waterlily asked, "But is the old man really going to cut a hole in the baby's ear? Poor little thing, to be shedding blood and crying from the pain. I could not bear it for her to cry, even though it means an honor."

The father commented, "My daughter is right. I could not bear it either. Bloodshed is bad enough for adults, even when they cause it for themselves. No, the child will not actually be pierced. She will not have to cry. The ear piercer will simply hold the blade to her ear lobes in token. Later, when she is a little bigger, we shall keep clamping tighter and tighter about them some of that soft metal that my friend Lean White Man gave me before I left." He meant lead. A band of lead with sharpened ends was used to force a hole for earrings in that manner.

At the mention of the white man, Waterlily remarked in a low voice intended only for her mother, "I have seen only a very few white men in all my life. Where I lived there were none. The few I saw were when we visited in the camp circle of my father's fellowhood friend Palani. Oh, how their cold blue eyes frightened me!"

The father overheard her. "Daughter, you cannot tell about white men, any more than you can tell about Dakotas. Singly, here and there, white men are very good. Take Lean White Man, now. There's a friend for you! I have none better, no, not even among the Dakotas—and that's a strong statement, since they are my relatives."

His wife cut in, taunting him, "I suppose you and he are in fellowhood! I suppose you would die to save him—would he die to save you?" But to this he turned a deaf ear. Elderly couples often bandied words in this vein, neither taking the other seriously. Yet the habit had its uses, too, in that it tended to help them keep each other in check. If the husband was going to far, his wife cut in and set him right, and vice versa. Everyone understood this habit of the long-time married and often found it amusing.

Over such trifles they all sat talking pleasantly, until someone spoke of the murder that had taken place the day before. Dakotas killing one another was a peculiarly dreadful thing. When one did so, it threw the entire camp circle into a state of horror and apprehension.

The reason for the recent killing was understandable in a way, yet nobody could say it was a worthy one. The village harlot, nicknamed "Everywhere," had promised faithfully to marry two different men, Red Lake and Cedar. When she finally married Red Lake, Cedar was so angry that he swore to get them both. But he had killed only the husband; the woman was still in hiding somewhere. "And so, having killed his rival, he then swore to kill Everywhere, too," Yankton was saying.

"I hope he finds her soon!" the woman of the tipi murmured viciously. "It is her kind that bring trouble to good men and women and set a wrong example for our girls." Waterlily was thinking of Night Walker, a comparable character back home, who was the object of derision and the despair of women.

"Well, so Red Lake is dead, and all because of a brazen woman," the father remarked. To this Yankton asked in surprise, "Why, my friend, have you not heard the rest? Cedar too is now dead. A cousin of Red Lake has slain him in reprisal. It happened late today. I supposed everyone knew by now."

"That is even worse," the father said. "Ah, well, at least it is all over. The score has been quickly evened up. Cedar had it coming for killing a man. Whatever the provocation, it is never great enough to justify a Dakota's taking the life of a fellow Dakota. Since he cannot return what he has taken, he can only exchange his own for it. And that Cedar has now done."

Yankton agreed. "Indeed so. It is now cleared, as they have decided at the council tipi."

Nobody spoke for a while, too amazed at the enormity of the thing to comment further. And then the man of the tipi sighed a long, deep sigh and began filling his pipe with the tobacco and kinnikinnick blend, dexterously from habit, without watching what he was doing. Only his hands were concerned; his mind was on far-off things. Looking straight ahead, he soliloquized thus: "So it is all settled and done with. Let it be; it is enough. Now two lives have been destroyed, the one for the other. Let us forget the nasty business and try again. It ought never to happen among men of the universal kinship of humans. Let us have peace once more."

Sometime during the evening the boy Red Leaf had returned, entering unobtrusively, and had settled down back of his understanding mother. And she, seemingly unaware of his arrival, had nevertheless slipped some food before him, and then let him be. There, comfortable in the protecting shadow that she cast, he ate quietly. Mothers had a way with their adolescent boys that was just right. They never drew attention to them or embarrassed them in any way. When Red Leaf had finished, he had maneu- vered himself toward the men's group and was listening there back of his father.

At last he spoke up: "Yes, but will it end there?" A puzzled look was on his face. "What if now a cousin of Cedar were to kill the cousin of Red Lake? And what if a kinsman of the cousin of Red Lake were to kill the cousin of Cedar—what I mean is, since everyone has kinsmen to avenge them, they could continue kill- ing each other, back and forth, until everyone was dead."

"Oh, son! What dreadful things to say!" His mother pre- tended to be greatly horrified.

"But there is some truth in what the boy says," Yankton spoke up. "Of course it likely would never get entirely out of hand. Fortunately, there are always bound to be mild-tempered men, poor haters, who can never get angry enough to kill. We could rely on them to stop it at some point. But a chain of killings, at least for a time, is not impossible. No doubt it was to prevent such a thing that our forefathers devised the ordeals for trying murderers, in ancient times. Thereby they put the matter up to the Great Spirit for judgment. And since humans may not dis- pute the *Wakan* [Holy], the result of the ordeal was accepted as final."

The two men recalled the kinds of ordeals, one in which the guilty man was called on to ride a wild horse without falling off, and one in which he had to jump high hurdles without knocking them down. Either form was used, at the magistrates' discretion. It was not a trial to determine if the man was actually guilty; that was already admitted and generally known. Rather it was a judg- ment on him. If he was intended to die, he failed in the ordeal; if he was meant to live, he miraculously survived it.

"My friend, there is still that other way to deal with a mur- derer, which, to my mind, is the noblest of all because it brings the best results," Yankton remarked. "I wonder if you are famil- iar with the kinship appeal."

"Yes, my friend, I am. Though I have never witnessed it, I

have heard those who have, speak of it with high respect," the
father answered. "But tell the children here. I think our people

have never devised anything loftier than that."

So Yankton described how he once saw the kinship appeal
used to settle a score. The enraged young relatives of the slain
man debated the kind of punishment they ought to mete out to
the slayer, who was still at large. As they debated, their eldest
relative, a man of great influence in the entire tribe, sat listening as
though in accord with them. After they had all talked themselves
out, he began to speak. With consummate skill he gave them the
impression that he was going along with them all the way.

"My kindred—cousins, brothers, sons, and nephews all—
today we have been made to weep without shame, men though
we are. Someone has dared to do us an injury in slaying our
young relative. Has he not thereby grossly insulted our family
pride and our honor? Our kinsman was young; he too loved life.
He was not ready to die—yet he is dead. Should we not vow that
his slayer too shall die? And should we not go out forthwith and
kill him? Very well, then, why do we sit talking here? Why not
give the murderer his due at once?"

He smoked quietly after this, calm and steady. In due time he
resumed speaking. But now he had changed his tack. "And yet
(he repeated it), and yet, my kindred, there is a better way. That
the fire of hate may not burn on in his heart or in ours, we shall
take that better way. Go now to your homes. Look over your
possessions and bring here the thing you most prize—a horse,
say, or weapons, or wearing apparel, or a blanket. Easy ways and
empty words may do for others. We are men of another make, so
let us take the harder way, the better way. If but few are able to do
that, then let us be of that few.

"The gifts you bring shall go to the murderer, for a token of
our sincerity and our purpose. Though he has hurt us, we shall
make him something to us [a relative], in place of the one who is
not here. Was the dead your brother? Then this man shall be your
brother. Or your uncle? Or your cousin? As for me, the dead was
my nephew. Therefore his slayer shall be my nephew. And from
now on he shall be one of us. We shall regard him as though he
were our dead kinsman returned to us."

Yankton and his host smoked a while. Then he said, "My friend, that was a tremendous proposal, would you not say?"

"Indeed it was," his host agreed. "And what assurance of leadership that elder kinsman must have had, to dare suggest such a thing. For it required of each man to undergo inner battle with himself and to master his pride and anger first. That is not easy. I take it they all did so?"

"Yes, they accepted what their elder kinsman said, because they saw that it was right. They saw it was easy enough to fight violence with violence. Killing was the work of a moment. But to take the murderer as a relative, after what he had done, and to live in sincerity and creative goodwill with him, day in and day out to the end of life—that was something else. You may well imagine how proud must have been the spirit of the slain youth, to see his relatives doing the harder thing!

"Now, on the appointed day, the slayer was brought to the council tipi. He was brave. He did not try to run away. He knew he had killed a man and was ready to pay with his life. Even so, not knowing his exact fate, he entered with his eyes averted, steeling himself for the worst. He did not try to infer the decision from the councilmen's faces. He did not want them to pity him. He would not have men say, supposing him to be afraid, 'Poor fellow! Like some hunted animal, he tried to detect mercy in men's eyes.'

"The spokesman said, offering him the pipe of peace, 'Smoke, with these your new kinsmen seated here. For they have chosen to take you to themselves in place of one who is not here.' Hearing these words, the man was visibly unnerved and he began to tremble. 'It is their desire that henceforth you shall go in and out among them without fear. By these presents which they have brought here for you, they would have you know that whatever love and compassion they had for him is now yours, forever.' As he said these words, tears began to course down the slayer's cheeks. You see, he had been neatly trapped by loving kinship. And you may be sure that he proved himself an even better kinsman than many who had right of birth, because the price of his redemption had come so high."

Then Yankton added, "I know this well. I was one of the

youngest and most enraged cousins of the slain man. But I learned then that there is no more powerful agent for ensuring goodwill and smothering the flame of hate than the kinship of humans."

Waterlily and Sacred Horse and the rest sat very still after this. It was too tremendous; there were no words for it. The men smoked mechanically on, in silence, and the women sat with lowered heads, waiting for someone else to speak first. Finally and in a most everyday manner that broke the spell, the woman of the tipi threw some light sticks on the fire and when it flared up she once more tilted her black three-legged pot to the light and peered in. "Let me see . . . Yes, there is some food remaining. I'll just heat it up quickly. These chilly autumn evenings it is good to swallow something hot before going to bed." And as she busied herself in a practical way, everyone shifted a little and came back to the present.

They ate the food while talking of inconsequential matters, until a woman's shrill cry broke out somewhere. "Alas, someone else has died," Yankton's words were ominous. "This afternoon a baby died across the way, too. I wonder who this time."

Red Leaf had been lying on his stomach with elbows planted and chin nestling in cupped hands. Now he added his bit of news. "There's a whole family down sick over that way," he said and raised his chin momentarily to indicate the direction.

"So many deaths! So much sickness!" Waterlily sighed, thinking of her grandfather far away.

It was long past midnight when she and Sacred Horse walked homeward, hand in hand in the dark. They were both sobered by the sorrowful atmosphere that pervaded the entire circle, by the wailing that started up here and there as the news spread. It was a portentous sound. Anything could happen on the morrow.

Waterlily sat in her tipi doing fancywork. Two days ago her husband had taken some horses that his father had promised sometime during the summer to a relative in a distant camp circle. He had left before sunrise the day after their visit with the social parents across the circle. His elder sister Echo could be heard just outside. "No, no, daughter, you may not go along! Stay here with your aunt. I shall be back soon." Then she looked in at Waterlily, "Sister-in-law, I am going to a tipi yonder, where a kinswoman has just died. Your little niece Robin will stay. I do not like to take her to a death because she always screams so, whenever I wail, trying to help me."

"Of course," Waterlily answered. The little Robin came inside and stood there, pouting her lips and frowning to keep back the tears. Then, all of a sudden, apparently having conquered herself, she went limp where she stood and crumpled to the floor, all joints giving way at once. When finally settled, she was in perfect sitting position as became her sex, with both legs flexed toward the right, a prim little copy of the women about her. Already, at four years of age, it was habit.

Before Waterlily could think how to interest her in something, other mothers had come with their little ones and turned them in. They too were going to the death. "Sister, this one will sit with you.—Now, you mind your mother!—If she does not mind, sister, tell when I return." "Cousin, I am leaving my youngest. He hears very well, the little thing; he will be no trouble. Just tell him to be still. He hears very well." She meant he was quick to obey.

Thus before long Waterlily had eight small children on her hands while their mothers went off to wail over the dead. She had no trouble in keeping them happy. Actually, they managed that themselves, playing quietly at various pastimes. At the start they were politely aware of her and stopped, every time she glanced at them, to explain in full detail what they were playing. But after a while they forgot her and went into their activities in earnest, leaving Waterlily to work uninterrupted.

At noon she fed them all as they sat around her outdoor fire, and in the afternoon she took them for a walk to the wood. They found many tree mushrooms that stuck out from the trunks or branches like immense white ears. It was because of this that they were called tree ears. The tree ears on boxelder and cottonwood were especially preferred, in that order, so succulent and flavorsome were they when cooked with dried buffalo meat. The children pried them off with poles and let them fall, unbroken if possible, into the blanket that Waterlily held below to catch them.

When the little party reached home late in the day, they found the mothers back, cooking for their families around their outdoor fires. Red-eyed and weary, the women sighed and sniffled eloquently now and then. Otherwise they refrained from needless conversation, as became their mood after weeping over the dead.

Only the senior wife, Taluta, was articulate. "So many deaths lately! So many, that I must wail again and again until my eyes are dimmed! My head too, how it throbs!" And she commenced binding her head tightly with a strip of doeskin. But she was not complaining. The truth was that she took a certain pride in fulfilling all her kinship and social duties well, down to commiserating the bereaved and wailing for the dead, for the good woman had a reputation to uphold. "She never misses a death, no matter how humble the one who has died. How good she is! Humans should care for each other so, and should take time to honor one another's passing. Oh, may great crowds throng her tipi when it comes her time to go. It is as she deserves," people often said of her. She was not going to let them down.

Instead of one death there had been several, and the woman had gone about wailing, from one to another. "Oh yes, I know I overdid today. After three places I was coming home to rest. But when I passed a tipi where a strange young man lay unmourned, I had to stop and wail over him, too. I always say that while I live, no human being shall go out in utter stillness, like an animal," the senior wife declared, lying down after binding her head.

The fact was that the epidemic was spreading and that the new blankets which the sons of Buffalo Boy had brought home were infested with deadly germs, against which the people had no immunity. Through give-aways and also as simple courtesy gifts, those blankets had been changing owners and carrying smallpox from tipi to tipi. The people, however, did not connect the sudden series of deaths with the new blankets, and at the same time that they were frightened by the disease, they welcomed the carriers of it.

Good Hunter returned from the council tipi and went straight to his daughter Echo. Waterlily, who owed him avoidance respect, slipped quickly into her own tipi when she saw him coming, so as not to hamper him in what he might have to say to Echo. But tipi walls being only skin deep, she could not help overhearing him, for Echo's home was next to hers. "Daughter, too many people are dying too fast," he said. "It is now plain to the council that the matter is grave, and likely to grow worse. Once before this same many-sores sickness visited other camp circles, and many, many people died of it. So before any of our group gets it, you must leave and stay in the wilds until it is safe for you to return. That way you can escape the sickness. Stay somewhere along Buzzard Creek. I will send for you when it is right."

"Of course, father, since you say so," Echo replied.

"Tell my son-in-law to have the horses ready so that you can leave at dawn. Take your sister-in-law with you, and your mother also. Already she has partly sickened herself from wailing so much. It will be best for her to get away. Take what you will need of food and clothing, but travel light. Luckily, there is always plenty of game along the Buzzard. In the hills on either side there are deer. When your brother returns I will send him out to you. He and his brother-in-law will get all the food you need until this danger passes."

Through all this Echo kept up a wordless lullaby to the infant in her arms, whistling it between her teeth, as women did to put a baby to sleep. But she was also considering the matter. She asked, "And what of the others? My brothers, sisters, and cousins, and their families? What of my middle mother and my youngest mother—and what of you, Father?"

"They must all go, but in different parties and in different directions. Each group is better off alone. Your mothers will take their own children. As for me, I am staying here. For myself I have no fear of the sickness, and I shall not be sick. Do not be concerned for me, my daughter."

When Echo came in to tell Waterlily, she repeated what her sister-in-law knew already and was planning for. Echo told her not to bother about a tipi. Her travel tent was big enough for the five adults in the party, herself and her husband, Waterlily and Sacred Horse, and the mother. Echo's four children would fit in wherever they could. She would, of course, keep the baby with her. Robin could stay with her grandmother, and the lad of nine, whom they called Little Bear, could occupy a small space with his younger brother, who was Robin's twin. "We can leave our home tipis standing and our things just as they are," Echo went on. "Close your entryway and tie down the door flap against stray dogs. Everything will be safe then. Your father-in-law is staying and he will look after our tipis and weight them down in case of storms or high wind. If my brother returns tonight, tell him at once that we leave at dawn."

"He should get home tonight; he has been gone two nights and three days already. Yes, I shall tell him first thing." Waterlily said this for something to reply. To herself, she was making rapid calculations on what to take.

Around midnight Sacred Horse did come in. When Waterlily wakened, she heard him sighing from weariness, and she could tell from his movements that he sat smoking in the honor-place. Her first impulse was to ask about his trip and tell him of their urgent plans to run away in the morning, but something checked her. This was no time to question him; she must wait until he volunteered to talk. Her own mother's wisdom in all wifely conduct was her guide.

Blue Bird never chattered idly on when Rainbow first got home. In a matter-of-fact way she always went about making him comfortable and providing a meal for him, speaking only if he asked a question of her, and then briefly. Not that she feared him; not that he was ever domineering. But she sensed when not to get in his way. When he was tired, let him be. Once she silenced the always eager Ohiya when he began flooding his father with questions. "Son, remember this," she told him then. "When a man toils all day for his family and comes home tired out, he does not feel like talking at once. Wait until your father is rested and his hunger satisfied, and then maybe he will tell you things."

Remembering that advice, Waterlily sat up slowly and said aloud to herself, "He is back. I must get him something to eat."

So she did not oblige him to answer. But when she started up her fire in the middle of the tipi, working easily from where she was, he said, "No, don't cook anything for me—just some broth if any remains in the kettle." He sipped it slowly, drawing it in audibly at each sip, as though it were an effort. He had ridden without rest all the way. When he finished the broth, he told her about his trip and gave her the presents that his distant relatives had sent to her.

"And now for some sleep," he said, "I'm completely exhausted." And only then did Waterlily tell him the news. "There is something you must hear first—something your sister said to tell you as soon as you returned." She proceeded to relate everything that had happened since the night they went visiting together, when a few people died. And now more and more were sick, many had died, and more were dying, she said.

He listened without comment, and she went on. "My father-in-law has ordered us to scatter in small groups and stay out, away from other people. We are to form one party, with your sister and her family and your own mother."

"Very well. When do we start?"

"As soon as it is light enough to see, we are setting out, and I think it would be well if the horses we need were to stand ready outside."

"You think right." And then he began planning aloud, "Two horses . . . more would be a bother . . . one is not enough. The bay can carry the drag with the things we need . . . you will ride it. The sorrel for me. He is fast and I can move on him quickly if necessary . . . Yes . . . the bay and the sorrel." So saying, and suddenly unmindful of his weariness, he went swiftly back out into the night.

CHAPTER 16

As it turned out, the little company escaped nothing by running away. Echo and her mother had thoroughly exposed themselves to the disease in their zeal to comfort the sorrowful. They had visited the stricken homes without fear, unaware of the contagious nature of the affliction. Now, ironically, they were carrying along with them the deadly thing from which they were fleeing. Soon it was to break out in all its ravaging fury, and their stay in the wilds was to become a series of unforgettable horrors. Conceivably, there might be days just as bad in the future; it was hard to imagine that any could be worse. "It was like an evil dream" was the way it would be recalled in after years.

Starting with the senior wife, Taluta, mother of Echo and Sacred Horse, everyone in the party had the disease. Once begun, it was inevitable that it went the round. All nine persons were occupying the one tipi, sick and well side by side. They were resigned to this. Certainly nobody dreamed of isolating the first case as a check against further spread. Had one dared suggest doing so, it would only have shocked and hurt the others. They would have thought and said, "Our relatives are precious to us, sick or well. However loathsome might be their malady, should we separate ourselves from them, as if they were animals, just to save our selves? It is unthinkable! It is unworthy of kinship! There is something wrong with whoever proposes such a thing." They would have seen it as a gross repudiation of fellow human beings.

Mercifully, the cases were staggered. The severest ones improved before others worsened; at least it was so with the adults. Thus there was always at least one woman able to prepare food and watch by the very sick ones, to do for them the simple things they could do—handing them a drink of water or rearranging the pillows and blankets for them. Beyond that, the sick asked nothing but to lie suffering quietly, much as animals might, and let the sickness have its way with them.

Waterlily ministered to them, numb of spirit and body. Too tired to think, she could only feel that here was something hideous to be lived through somehow. And then, one night, little Robin died in her arms. Scarcely had she laid her body down and picked up her twin brother to hold him than he too was gone.

These were Waterlily's first major tragedies, although she had grown up on intimate terms with death—as who did not? In the past whenever she had wept over the dead, unless it was someone in her own family group, it was out of sympathy for the bereaved, or because the whole thing was dismal enough to rouse tears, or simply because it was proper to wail and one could generally work oneself up to it. It was proper to wail lest one be accused of being callous and negligent of kinship. But now she wept because she must, and could not check herself. When she was a very young girl, she had once pulled up her blanket over her head and wailed, utterly dry-eyed, and was at once ashamed of and amused at herself. She could not feel any such grief then as now.

Not long after, her turn came and she lived through the wretched time somehow, indifferent even to the horrid marks that appeared on her smooth young face to mar its beauty. The two men also were sick one at a time, and that was a blessing. Not till Echo's husband was up did Sacred Horse take to bed. Always he lay with his face toward the tipi wall, thus shutting himself away from the others, asking only that Waterlily sit near his head to screen him from them.

At his worst, he crawled out of the tipi without a word and remained under a tree some distance away. When he did not return, his mother grew anxious. "Daughter-in-law," she said, "my son does not return . . . perhaps if you went out to him . . ." Before she had finished the sentence, Waterlily went.

"Your mother sent me. What is the trouble? Can't you get back? Is it that bad?" She did not chide him for coming out. There was nothing else for a sick adult to do so long as he had the strength and was in his right mind. In the interest of sanitation and modesty, adults always went outside to relieve themselves, no matter how they felt or what the weather.

"I could get back well enough," Sacred Horse said, "But I intend to stay out here." He was lying on the grass. She sat quietly by him a long time, until he spoke. "I may as well tell you that I am not going to recover. Even before this pestilence was a manifest thing, I felt, I knew, that I would die before long—of what precisely, I did not know then. You and the others have suffered too much already. I will not cause you further suffering by dying in the tipi where you must sit day and night. Can't you make some sort of little shelter for me here?"

So Waterlily and Taluta set forked posts into the ground and laid poles crosswise on them. They threw their largest bullhide over the poles and weighted the bottom on three sides, leaving the fourth side partly exposed for air and light. When they had brought sage leaves for a couch and spread a blanket over it, with supreme effort he dragged himself over to it and lay down.

"Now go back and rest—both of you," he said. His mother went, because she knew she was needed in the tipi. But Waterlily stayed by and gave him water whenever he asked for it. She brought out some broth his mother had made, but he did not touch it. It was late at night when he said to her, "You must go now and get some sleep." She was crying softly in the dark. When she could control her voice, she answered, "But . . . but you might die. You might die in the night all alone."

He was gallant all the way. "Could you prevent that by staying here?" And it was in him to chuckle a little, sick as he was. Again, after she made no move to obey him, he said, "Look, I mean it. Leave me to meet this thing alone. I am very curious. Others die by themselves, and so can I." And then, with a touch of flippancy he added, "This is a *real* male you have married, don't you know!"

After that Waterlily could not protest. Since it was his wish, she must obey. To insist still would be to insult her husband, as though he were a child or a weakling whose mind could be changed for him. (Dakotas always resented that.) Quietly she withdrew, in tribute to him. "He ordered me back," she told her mother-in-law, who accepted her son's wishes, "Very well. He always knew what he wanted. Very well—since it must be so."

Waterlily did not sleep. She spent the night listening, worrying over him from a distance. As soon as it grew light enough, she went to him. Already he was stiff and cold. Weeping low, she drew his blanket up over his face very gently.

It was a problem to lay the body away with anything like the tenderness and decency the matter required. Sacred Horse had been a tall, well-knit man, whereas his brother-in-law was slight and short, and not yet strong enough after his illness to handle the body alone. The women had to help him bind it to an improvised stretcher and hoist it into a tree that overhung the shelter where death had occurred. By means of rope pulleys they raised the body and laid it across two branches. Then Echo's husband managed to climb up and make the ends of the bier secure to the tree. Ordinarily men handled a man's body and women a woman's. But here, under grim necessity, the mother and wife and sister of Sacred Horse all had to help. They worked dry-eyed and stoical until it was done.

It smote their hearts, by nature so tender with their dead, to see, on looking up, that the body did not lie level, that the head was considerably lower than the feet. But at least it was there to stay, well beyond the reach of animals. In that they found some comfort.

After two days of mourning, Echo's mother proposed that they move to another spot along the stream, away from the scene of so much grief where her son and two of her grandchildren had died. If they had remained there, they might have avoided further disaster. But they struck camp and traveled one entire day. There were now but six in the party—Waterlily and Echo, Echo's husband, her mother, and her two children, the boy Little Bear and the babe-in-arms. On level ground, well protected on the north and west by hills rising away from the valley, they made their camp, with Buzzard Creek flowing below the steep bank not far from their tipi entrance. The woods were thick here, and rich in autumn colors. The view was exceedingly beautiful and lonely, but there were evidences of game in the wooded ravines running down between the hills.

Taluta roamed the woods and returned with more fuel than they could ever use. "Oh, but I marvel at the abundance of dead wood hereabouts! I cannot stop gathering it. Would that this were within reach of our camp circle!" she exclaimed from time to time.

Everyone was well now, and waiting to be sent for. They were impatient and even debated the wisdom of starting homeward anyway. Echo said, "Mother, the nights are getting very chilly. It might snow on us out here. And then if they missed our location, how could we find our way back? Even now all the land looks the same to me. With snow on the prairies we would be lost."

"No!" Her mother was emphatic. "Your father said he would send for us when it was safe, and he will. He knows where we are. From boyhood he has roamed over all this region. We will wait." Echo could not budge her, and she did not try. And of course Waterlily and Echo's husband would accept the decision out of respect for their mother-in-law, even if they disagreed with her.

But one day it was she, the mother, who came home worried. In the wood she had seen a fresh track. It was much longer than Echo's husband could have made, and the imprint did not look like that of a Dakota moccasin. The three women put out the fire and sat in the tipi, growing more and more apprehensive as twilight came on. They spoke very low and only when they must. The worst of it was that Little Bear was still out somewhere, and his father had not yet come in from hunting. The boy never went beyond call, but to shout to him was out of the question. They could only rely on his training to move stealthily whenever he was out alone, as he had been taught by his uncles to do.

After a long, tense wait they relaxed a little, since nothing had happened, and Waterlily said, still whispering, "I will go to the bank and call softly. Perhaps my nephew is down by the stream."

"Please do, sister-in-law," Echo said gratefully. "He may be fishing again—though I can't see why he bothers, when none of us care for fish, being plains people. How I dislike the smell of fish—so nauseating!"

Waterlily moved cautiously, going straight out of the tipi toward the bank. She crouched low and peered into the dark shadows below for a sight of the boy before she would call. And it was lucky for her that she waited, for suddenly there were loud warwhoops from behind the tipi. Another raid! The cries and the din were designed to confuse the inmates of the tipi. The enemy were attacking from behind, apparently having crept up under cover of the buffaloberry bushes that studded the land clear back to the hills. Waterlily, in line with the tipi, had not been seen.

In that sudden uproar she started to run along the edge of the bank but missed her footing and sprained an ankle. Next instant she was rolling into a narrow gully that cut into the bank from the stream. Too frightened to act, she lay motionless. The screaming and yelling and the shooting of white men's guns—all the tribes were using them more and more—and the clatter of tipi poles being struck and broken continued. Her heart beat so loudly that the attackers must hear it, she thought, except for their frenzied racket and their shouting at one another in an unknown tongue. Urging and exciting each other to more and more havoc, no doubt.

But at last the tumult died away as the enemy withdrew in the direction from which they had come. Now Waterlily might safely come forth from her hiding place, were she not too stunned to make the effort. The gully fitted her body snugly. Looking up, as though from an open grave, she could see the stars. The whole constellation of "man-being-carried" (the Big Dipper) was in sight. At first it was over on one side of her fragment of sky. Not until it had swung around and was disappearing on the other side—however long that would take—could she work up enough courage to utter a sound. Even then, she could call only in low voice, "Is anyone left alive?" There was no reply. After a good while she tried again. This time Echo's voice moaned, "Sister-in-law, I alone am alive, alas . . . but I am like one dead."

Waterlily managed to climb up the bank. Able to walk though her ankle was swelling badly, she limped back to the tipi. In the darkness she felt Echo's head and wept to find that the scalp had been cut away, leaving a raw, wet spot on her crown. Elsewhere on her head there were ugly gashes, too. Her baby, clasped in her arms still, was dead from an arrow that just missed Echo.

Echo's mind came and went, and there was nothing to do but wait for daylight. Whenever she grew faint and cold, Waterlily rubbed her wrists and dashed cold water in her face. It was all she knew to do. Sometime after the attack Little Bear had stolen into the tipi all atremble. Young as he was, he had had the sense to lie low and thereby had saved himself. His father and grandmother were missing. It added to Waterlily's distress that he kept threatening to go out and look for them, and she had to keep begging him to stay in. When it grew light enough to see, they found Taluta lying dead some distance out, having been scalped and knifed savagely.

In one of her lucid moments, Echo asked Waterlily to help her down to the stream. "I try to remember, but I keep forgetting," she explained, meaning she kept losing consciousness. "If I could just wet my face and head in living water, I might remember permanently." Waterlily was small-boned and of delicate build. The weight of the heavier woman leaning full against her put such a strain on her ankle that she could hardly bear it. But she managed to get Echo down to the water and seat her at the shallow edge.

Echo apparently had the right idea; living—flowing—water was good medicine. Moving along with a will of its own (so it was said), a stream carried life-giving properties to everything that it touched along the way. As it could revive all manner of grasses and trees, so also it could revive mankind. Water was holy. From then on Echo was able to retain her consciousness.

On her way back, she paused by the body of her mother, still lying where it had fallen, and talked to the dead woman in the customary way, chiding her affectionately.

"Oh, Mother! Mother! Alas, is it thus that you must lie, with me helpless? Once too often have I obeyed you, my mother, from force of habit, grown woman though I am, as though I were still a child. Oh, Mother, if only we had started homeward when I wanted to go. But no. 'Wait for your father,' you said. 'He will not fail us,' you said." And she sat down for a long, unhindered cry beside her dead.

Meantime Waterlily prepared to lay her mother-in-law's body away. There was nothing to do but drag it on a heavy buffalo skin to a place sufficiently removed from camp and out of sight. There she and the boy Little Bear carried stones to cover it. This they continued doing whenever they were at liberty, until the mound was so large that no marauder lacking hands and the intelligence to remove stone after stone could molest the body. Waterlily was thankful that she had thought in time to lay Echo's baby in its grandmother's arms, and so to finish the burial of both at once.

The days that followed were a time of utter dejection. The wretched tipi, though Waterlily had mended it to the best of her ability, was no longer stormproof and no longer in shape to stand firm, being short of poles. When it rained, their things were soaked; and when winter came, it was plain, they would suffer cruelly from the cold. The problem of food also became desperate, until all they could rely on was an occasional rabbit that the boy snared or a bird that he killed with his blunt arrows.

Yet Echo made no further reference to going home, and Waterlily did not discuss the possibility of their trying it. She knew what Echo waited for—her husband's return. It was a futile hope—if he were alive he would have been home long ago—but yet she clung to it in silence for many days.

At last she could talk casually about their situation. "We must stay here—until he gets back. Well, we have to stay here, anyway, seeing that the enemy took all our horses. We are afoot; how *could* we go?" She was at last facing facts. But again there were times when her fortitude failed her. Then she would weep—always for her children. "Oh, if only they had been sick long enough to cause me weariness in watching over them! Oh, if only I might have suffered for want of sleep and felt fatigue in caring for them! How satisfying that would have been! If, in their illness, they had been whimsical and petulant with me, how gladly I should have stood it! But no. They had to die quietly and quickly, without being any trouble. And that littlest one—she even died for me, in my stead. Oh, if only I had been able to make pretty moccasins for their dear feet, that they might lie buried wearing them! These shall be my regrets till I die!" At such times she would not be comforted, and Waterlily was too wise to try.

And then, when things were their blackest, when not a morsel of food remained, a rider stood on the hill above their camp, looking down at them. "Quick! Come inside! He may be an enemy scout!" The three survivors huddled in the tipi, fearing the worst, until the man began to sing a dirge—in Dakota. They knew then that whoever he might be, he realized their plight and would rescue them.

He turned out to be a cousin of Echo, from a camp circle along the Missouri. Unaware of the pestilence, he had come to visit his uncle Good Hunter, who, in the same breath with which he greeted him, had sent him out after his aunt and her party. "Ah, my nephew, it is well that you have come. Go at once and find your aunt and cousins and their families and bring them home. Tell them it is safe for them at last." And he had given him specific directions.

The cousin, immediately upon his arrival, went out to hunt and returned shortly with a deer. It was the first real food they had had in many days. And so he saved their lives. But Echo still showed no disposition to hurry home, and he, understanding why, said nothing, only caring for their needs and protecting them from day to day.

But one morning he came straight to Echo and stood near her as she sat on the ground. "Alas, my cousin," he said, "I have waited here with you, hoping your husband would one day return. I was prepared to wait all winter if need be. But now, alas, my cousin, I have to tell you that he will never return. Last evening I found his body, out in those hills yonder, where he met the enemy like a man." Echo heard this without tears. She seemed resigned. It might be that she had expected it all along. After a decent while she said to Little Bear, "Son, find your aunt and tell her we will go home now."

The cousin improvised a travois and Echo rode on the seat behind. Waterlily rode the horse, which he led along. The boy walked by him or rode behind his aunt, by turns. Before they left they burned everything, including the tipi, each person saving only one fur robe for a wrap by day and a cover for sleeping. They kept the barest of cooking necessities for the trip homeward. It was not wise to spend whole nights sleeping on the way. They rested for short periods or for a nap or some food, and pushed steadily on, as much as the one overburdened horse could stand.

A pitiful sight they were, all brown and tawny and gray, their drabness almost indistinguishable from the sere prairies over which they crawled. They were wearing the last of the clothing they had brought out with them, long since bedraggled and soiled, ripped and torn. Even the last of the extra pairs of moccasins were now in holes. Their faces were blotched here and there with the marks of their disease, and their hair hung loose and neglected, though that was partly in mourning.

Though homeward bound, they were not excited or happy.

Already they had learned from the cousin what the state of affairs was at home. Many familiar faces would be missing, for the cruel scourge had touched every family. In Good Hunter's *tiyoṡpaye* several had died, including the youngest wife, who was a cousin of the other two, and whose children were still small. Thus only the middle wife was left to Good Hunter, as he would soon know.

He himself had come through untouched by the disease. He refused to accept it and therefore he did not take it, the people were saying. He had gone everywhere unafraid and had laid many a child's body away unaided, thus helping those families whom circumstances had compelled to stay in the camp circle the entire time.

Having learned what they would find, the two women were aware that they must weep again when they got home—as if they had not done enough weeping already! Long since wearied to exhaustion, Waterlily thought she could bear no more of it. "Weeping, weeping, always weeping! Will a day ever come when I can be truly happy again?" she asked herself. She doubted it.

It was to a camp circle of ruin and desolation that they returned. And it was deserted. After Echo's cousin had set out to find them, the people, finally suspecting the contagion in their material goods, had burned everything they could do without, including their tipis. Then they had withdrawn to another site, in a wide valley nearby, where they were now settled in winter quarters.

From the hilltop where the returning party stopped and looked down they could see nothing at first. Only gradually were they able to delineate little makeshift dwellings set in clusters hugging the timberline. These were of grass or of skins thrown over dome-shaped frames of willow, and the people living in them had now been reduced to the very lowest poverty. They were in fact right back where their ancestors must have been before the advent of the horse. So they must live until spring, if possible. They must endure either cold shelters or smoke from the fires kindled inside to keep them warm. The wind flaps that controlled the draft in a conventional tipi would be sorely missed.

But at least they still had their horses. With them, the people could rehabilitate themselves when hunting was possible again, when the sick were well and strong once more and sorrowful hearts were healed. And then they would be happy as before, and feasts and ceremonies and play and warfare—all the elements that constituted their life—would be resumed. The industrious and the skillful would soon be well-off again; it was always so. But at present all were leveled very low. Every family was forlorn.

CHAPTER 17

With Sacred Horse gone, Waterlily felt that she could not stay on with her relatives of marriage. The link that held her to them was broken. Kind as they were, she suddenly felt herself a complete stranger in their midst. They said to her, "His going makes no difference. You belong here." She did not think so, though she did not, of course, contradict them, for she still had a respect attitude to maintain. When her parents came for her, she would go home, for that was where she really belonged. Home! The very word thrilled her. But already it was beginning to snow—not serious snowstorms, but an occasional flake for a sample. Soon they must be winterbound, and then she would be trapped here inside a small shelter, with only formal relatives, and she would have to be self-contained and restrained. In such a confine, how could she sustain that manner until spring? For she knew well enough that her parents could not possibly arrive before then.

But the next best thing happened to her in a few days. Her social father and mother claimed her. "Come home, daughter," they said. "No wife needs to stay on where there is no longer a husband to draw her. You shall live with us, poor as our lodge is. At least it is no worse than anyone else's, and it shall be your home until your people come for you." Here was comfort beyond words. This was what auxiliary parents were for—to step in and take over in place of one's own parents in their absence, to reach out and extricate one and surround one with homelike tenderness. How all-sufficient kinship was!

Waterlily felt that with these social parents she could endure anything. Their shelter was, if anything, even smaller than that of Good Hunter, and would certainly be just as cold and smoky. But it was occupied only by the parents and the brother, Red Leaf, and herself. The atmosphere was one that allowed freedom from kinship taboos. She could stand the winter here.

It was entirely proper for Waterlily to go with those she called father and mother, since her husband was dead. The family of Good Hunter knew this and did not try to hold her. Yet, because she went, they did not therefore sever their ties with her. Their sense of responsibility for her remained—increased, in fact, for there was a child on the way, and it claimed solicitous interest in its mother. Particularly was this interest felt by the male collateral relatives of the dead Sacred Horse, his brothers and cousins.

Already they had conferred in secret about Waterlily. And when that cousin who had brought them back from the wilds took leave of her, he said, "May I see you in health some day, wife-of-my-cousin!" Then he added, "I have something I must say to you before we part. We in our group do not neglect our own. You are ours, wherever you go" (a delicate reference to the child she carried, who would be son or daughter to its father's brothers and male cousins). "Most of us already have our wives and families. And none of us is in a position to take a second wife, being still not of that age and prestige when such a step is suitable." Then he paid her a compliment. "Nor would we consider your being anything less than first wife to any man."

Waterlily told him she had no thought of remarrying. But the man continued: "Do not vow that. You are just a girl; your life is only beginning. You will marry again, and that is right. Back home I have a young brother who is still alone. He is the likely one for you. If perchance he pleased you for a husband, it would be well, for the coming child's sake. Wherever possible, a child should have for father one who is father to him already, and not a total, unrelated stranger. For the child, then, I entreat you to stay as you are. Young as you are, keep steady. Be not overhasty to remarry, but wait for my brother, whom I shall send to you." He spoke earnestly, "Wait for Lowanla."

Waterlily might have known. Once when Sacred Horse was telling her about his relatives in other camp circles and had spoken of his brothers and cousins, he had referred to one who was a very fine singer and who had entered the Sun Dance at an early age. But he had neglected to name the cousin, and Waterlily could not bring herself to ask, even casually, "What is his name?" for fear it might appear as though she were interested in other men. She had blushed to remember how once she had been carried away by a charming stranger who also was a singer and a very youthful Sun Dancer—so much so that she had taken water to him secretly. "But that was long ago, when I was very young," she told herself, though she knew that only four winters had since passed. Out of loyalty to her husband and a willed indifference to that once charming singer, whose appearance had become but a blur in her mind, she had had no difficulty in shedding the whole matter.

And now here he was, turning up again—she was sure it was the same man—as a candidate for her next husband, without his knowledge! Ordinarily it would have been an exciting prospect, and certainly an odd coincidence. But now, so lately overwhelmed by tragedy, a confused and homesick young widow with child, Waterlily heard the cousin's proposal, and even the name Lowanla, with complete passivity. She simply thanked the cousin of her dead husband for his concern and turned away.

The long winter in the cold, semidark hut was conducive to nothing but waiting with idle hands. Waterlily could not see to make anything beautiful for her coming baby. And she fretted under the enforced waste of time, with so much she wanted to do. Under such adverse circumstances it was impossible not to be homesick, but she must not let her kind parents see, lest it seem ungrateful of her. The concealing of her homesickness thus became a preoccupation, and she thought she was successful at giving an appearance of complete contentment. Therefore it came as a surprise when one day her mother returned from another hut down the timberline and said to her, "There, daughter, it is all fixed!"

"What is fixed, Mother?"

"That you shall go home. Yes, right now, even though it is winter. A winter trip for you toward a place for which you yearn is better than safety here where you try in vain to be happy." She had guessed it. "You could become sick, doing that. But now your father has found a way for us to take you home."

Then she explained. A war party was starting out toward the Blackfeet country, far off to the northwest. When Waterlily's social father had heard of this, he had enlisted the warriors' protection on the way, as far as the camp circle of White Ghost, which would be only a little east of their route. They had agreed to travel slowly that far, to escort the young widow to her home.

But the neighbors advised vehemently against the trip. They came in with stories of how so-and-so was snowed under for many days and was almost suffocated until he worked his way out, and of how a woman had once died in a blizzard and was found in the spring, having perished in the act of giving birth. "Do not expose this young girl to that risk," they begged. "She has already been through too much." And they pointed out that this, the Moon of Raccoons (February), and the Sore Eyes Moon to follow were always marked with the trickiest of weather. "Why, out of nowhere a blizzard can come up, catching people unaware," they warned. The parents were disturbed by these stories, but once a way was indicated to her, Waterlily was determined to go home, come what might.

The women rode separate horses, and followed certain of the warriors who were assigned to vanguard duty. The others, including the social father, kept on either side of them and in the rear, much as they did when a camp circle was moving.

"Take plenty of robes," the war chief had advised. "Then, if we should run into a storm, we can set up willow poles anywhere and piece a tent out of the robes." As had been predicted, there was a big blizzard on the way, forcing them to stop. They hurriedly improvised a tipi in the lee of a high cliff and there they stayed for two days, waiting for the storm to spend itself. From long practice the warriors quickly arranged everything and prepared the food, which they served to the women.

While they waited there, some strange people came in one

evening, a surprise because it was far from any human habitation. There was a man and his wife, both well over fifty, two girls, their daughters, and three small children. One of the daughters was with child. As if she were their mother the little ones kept close to the man's wife, a stupid-looking woman who said not a word more than necessary. Only the man talked, plausibly enough, accounting for their unexpected presence out there. But he was plainly evading the truth.

After they had gone, the warriors agreed that the man was probably a degenerate character who lived away from civilization, that is to say, the camp circle, because of some crime against society. It was impossible that his wife at her age could be the mother of those small children, and since the man was the only male, the conclusion was inescapable. "Something very bad" was the way the warriors voiced their suspicion, carefully avoiding the ugly equivalent of "incest."

"It is unspeakable," the war chief went on. "No wonder that those who offend so heinously against kinship do not have the courage to mingle with decent folk, preferring to hide out where the other beasts are. He would not have ventured here, but hunger drove him in."

But while the visitors were there, the warriors nevertheless extended hospitality to them and, out of human decency, sent them away with quantities of jerked meat and other foods. They included the man in their conversation, even handing him the pipe. They must do this, for their own reputations as hosts. The rule said in effect, "Treat as a man any stranger in your tipi who bears the physical semblance of a man." What sort the man might be was not the determining factor for extending such courtesies.

Both man and wife seemed to be hiding something, never once looking candidly at anyone. It was, of course, customary to avert your gaze when speaking to one of the opposite sex. That was a matter of decorum. But here was a man of shifting eye, who could not look straight at other men without flinching, and a woman who avoided the eyes of women. Something was surely amiss.

As for the daughters, they had no manners at all. Looking boldly into the warriors' faces and grinning foolishly, they sat down cross-legged in the manner of men. But soon they were devouring the food offered them, forgetful of their surroundings in their eagerness to eat. When finished, they whispered together a while and then went stumbling out the entrance without one word of thanks for the food, and without returning their bowls to the hostess. They were quite incredible.

It was the little ones, however, who excited Waterlily's real pity. When there was an awkward silence, after she and her social mother had tried in vain to chat with the woman, she turned to the children. With a smile she reached out a friendly hand to them and was shocked by their sudden reaction. All together they shrank back and began wrinkling up their noses belligerently at her with a lightning rapidity and a precision that made it comical. Then they settled back against their mother, who made no show of correcting their unfriendly actions. And next, from the folds of her wrap, they stuck out their tongues repeatedly while Waterlily gazed on them in amazement. Instantaneously they had turned into wild cubs, ready momentarily to resist being picked up and carried away. After such a complete rebuff, Waterlily sat listening to the men's talk and forgot the strange children for a time. Much later when accidentally she again looked their way, there they were, all quietly staring at her with fear and hostility in their shining black eyes, which never wavered once, lest she make another attack and they be caught off guard. Friendship had been omitted from their experience, along with everything else that makes life warm and pleasant.

Here were unbelievably wild, untutored children. No one had ever said to them, "No, don't do that . . . see, nobody does so!" and thereby shamed them into good behavior toward those about them. There were no others about them from whom they might learn by imitation. And so they were growing up without civility—and the results were terrifying to see. Camp-circle people were civilized; they knew how to treat one another. They had rules. These children were wild because they lacked any standards of social behavior.

It came over Waterlily as she observed the unfortunate children, so unkempt and so hostile, how very much people needed human companions. It was the only way to learn how to be human. People were at once a check and a spur to one another. Everyone needed others for comparison, for a standard for himself. This measuring and evaluating of self was only possible in camp-circle life, where everyone was obliged to be constantly aware of those about him, to address himself to them in the approved ways. Thus only did people learn to be responsible for and to each other and themselves.

Waterlily used to think that critics and gossips were a public nuisance. But now, seeing these wild people with nobody to criticize them, she decided that perhaps they were an actual necessity, that maybe they could not be spared. If it were not for the critics, people could never know whether they were being at their best or their worst. Here were people unquestionably at their worst—and they did not know it! They did not know enough to care how they must appear to the party they had evaded; they were unconscious of being judged by them. It was a tragic thing, to stay alone like this, in a benighted state. It was better to stay with other people and try to do your best according to the rules there. Waterlily of course did not say this in so many words, to herself; nevertheless, it was what she sensed keenly as she sat watching the children.

Late that night the storm abated and the moon broke through, shining with a diffused light through the air still dense with flying particles of snow. It gave an unearthly quality to the scene. The weather judge stood outside. "By morning it will be possible to start out. We must avoid the ravines, which will be packed with snow, and keep along the ridges where it is windswept, for then we can travel right along," he said.

He was right. The morning was clear and crisp, sunny and cold. The sky was a blue of the deepest intensity, and as far as the eye could see, frosted snow glittered like stars—on trees, bushes, shrubs, and rocks, and over the mantled prairies. Everything was pure white, except for a dark patch here and there in the shallow dips of the land, where tall stalks of yellow grass stiffly perforated the crust. It was a perfect winter day, and the party traveled contentedly. All day long, it seemed to Waterlily, the only sounds were the crunch, crunch, crunch of breaking crust and the rhythmic squeak of soft snow underneath with every step of her horse.

So they continued for three more days, before they found White Ghost's winter quarters. The war party escorted Waterlily and her social parents directly to Rainbow's tipi. After they were well feasted, they went on. Waterlily's social parents were invited to remain as guests until spring, and they could accept in good conscience, knowing that Red Leaf was safe in the care of his uncle and aunt and other relatives back home.

Before she was twenty years old, Waterlily had crammed into a single year enough of life to last her a long while. It was only after the last Sun Dance, in the Moon When Animals Fatten (June), that she had ridden away to be the wife-by-purchase of Sacred Horse the boy-beloved. And now, the following Moon of Raccoons, here she was, back again among her own people, a widow and a mother-to-be. Everyone was there to welcome her back into the environment that was hers by right of birth—that is to say, everyone but her brother Little Chief. He too had married and was at the time visiting his new in-laws at some distant camp circle, though not too far.

"But he will return as soon as he hears that his sister has come home to stay. You mark my word he will!" Black Eagle knew the deep loyalty between Waterlily and her brother. She, for her part, was quite aware of her prerogative to honor Little Chief by giving to his wife some especially beautiful item of dress, a handsome gown or a wrap perhaps. For it was the custom, part of the ancient ways of doing.

"Just what can I give my new sister-in-law?" she asked herself. "I brought back nothing to speak of—how could I under the circumstances?" She would have to get something from her mother or a relative in the group. Nor would she have to ask; they would offer it, she knew, because they would realize her obligation.

It was not that Good Hunter's family had neglected her, but that they literally had nothing for her to bring home after the pestilence and many deaths. As she took leave of her father-in-law he had for the first time addressed her directly, always having avoided doing so before, out of his respect for an avoidance relative. He had said to her: "Go in peace, wife-of-my-son. I shall come north to see my grandchild as soon as I can appear with something worthy in my hand. At present, well, you know how it is with us. But were it possible to send you home according to your worth, a herd of American horses should be going with you." That was a high compliment, for he thought a great deal of his daughter-in-law.

Only too grateful to get home under any conditions, Waterlily had been satisfied to go without presents for her people. Only too happy to have her back, they were not looking for any. Her cousins Leaping Fawn and Prairie Flower were especially delighted, and told her over and over how constantly they had missed her. But Prairie Flower had certainly had time for other matters, too; she had married shortly after Waterlily went away, although she was almost two years younger. Leaping Fawn still gave every promise of becoming a perpetual virgin and was content, apparently, as she moved about with her customary assurance and dignity.

Smiling One was noticeably taller and was such a sweet young girl, with gentle manners and a shy way that was charming. A little listless and languorous she seemed, except when she spoke of the baby coming. And then she was all eagerness. "Sister, I shall take care of him all the time and never get tired!" So she had already pledged her days away.

And then there was Waterlily's young brother, Ohiya, whose early imitating of adult ways had resulted in her acquiring some parents in her time of need for home people. Now he was the elusive adolescent, always out riding with other boys, coming in rarely, only to be off again. "Every boy goes through this stage; it is natural," Blue Bird told her. "He is glad you are home." It did not disturb Waterlily that after their initial greeting she scarcely saw him.

The old grandfather lingered on, with good days and bad days alternating. At the end of summer they had been sure he was dying after his crony's death had left him entirely alone. It was because of that illness that Rainbow and Blue Bird had postponed their visit to Sacred Horse and his people.

The old grandfather lingered on, though he longed to die. "All my friends are gone; why must I live on?" he would cry out pitifully. And at such times only Waterlily seemed able to beguile him, with stories of her experiences and the people she had met down south. Ah, yes, he knew that region, that stream, that prominent man of whom she spoke; years ago he went everywhere. Had Waterlily also met so-and-so perhaps? Meantime she worked steadily on fancywork in order to have nice things ready for her baby. Already in that dark hut she had lost much valuable time. She must make it up.

Her mother, aunts, cousins, and others also made things for the baby. Even though he was getting no fancy cradle from his father's sisters, who were the proper relatives to provide that item for him, Waterlily knew that in a year or two they would send or bring gifts to him. He could afford to wait.

The Moon of Bursting Buds (April) was in the last quarter when Waterlily's baby was born, at the very place she used to dream about but hardly dared hope to be—at home, in a private tipi, with her own homefolk to help her through. It was nearly perfect but for one sad fact: her grandfather lay dying in one tipi while she gave birth in the one next to it. Simultaneously and with perfect timing the baby came and the old man went, at dawn.

Many came to mourn at one tipi and rejoice at the other. Among them was one wise man who thought fit to harangue the crowd regarding the remarkable event. "Life never ends; it slows down but to pick up and go on again," he said. "The boy is the old man; he is privileged, for he has acquired the qualities readymade for him from the old one. He is strangely blessed. His grandfather has left him those traits he made for himself through a long life—gentleness, kindness, fortitude, patience. The boy should carry his name."

But his naming rite was still in the future. Even before he was born, Waterlily had given her son a name and called him by it in her thoughts. It was Mitawa, which means My Own. The following two months sped by unnoticed by the young mother absorbed in her baby. Her cousin Prairie Flower had also given birth to a boy, and the two girls who had always been congenial now had another common interest in their new and happy role of motherhood.

Waterlily's past griefs now seemed like a dream that grew daily more dim. And then, one day while she sat alone outside her mother's tipi, which was again her home, her attention was suddenly caught by a young traveler coming toward her and leading his horse. There was something about him so like her dead husband that for a moment she gasped. Then it dawned on her. This was the man Lowanla of whom she had been told. Yes, it was just as she had thought; there couldn't be two Lowanlas, both skillful singers, both youthful Sun Dancers. This was the one to whom she had once given water to quench his thirst. He was older by five years, but he appeared just as youthful and handsome as then. Her heart beat fast, but she managed to be composed as she greeted him.

As he ate the hospitality food she set before him, their conversation was placid enough, and conventional. He told her who he was, the cousin of Sacred Horse, and that he had come "to take care of my son—if that should be agreeable to you." And Waterlily said, just as matter-of-factly, that if that was his wish truly, and not because someone sent him, it could be so. And thus they became engaged. With a babe in her arms, the only way to meet a new husband was with dignity, and with a touch of sadness over Sacred Horse, whose untimely death had brought them together, and to whom they were both loyal.

All the relatives were happy for her and for the child. While kinship law did not demand that a widow marry a brother or cousin of her husband, it was always desirable for the child's sake, that he might have for a father one who was his father already. All the relatives helped to get a home ready for the two, and there they took up their common abode; and that was the marriage.

Waterlily had been elaborately bought once; this time she married in the other sanctioned way, the way most women married who had the good sense not to elope—the way of mutual agreement openly declared. Back when Lowanla had first charmed her, she might have lost her head and eloped with him, being very young and much infatuated with his graceful movements and attractive ways. But that was all in the past. She was older and far wiser now; she had herself well in hand. She was marrying in a quieter mood and with tribal approval. For the Dakota woman nothing could be better than that.

After the sudden death of her husband, Waterlily used to think over her brief life with him and the memory would stab her heart. "Was it so difficult to feel at home with him? Did I have to remain shy forever? Oh, if only I could have seen what was coming!" For too late she knew that she had been much too self-contained and uncommunicative and that to that extent she had been inadequate as a wife. Remorsefully she recalled a fleeting wistfulness in his patient eyes, as much as to say, "Oh, why can't you be more sociable with me now?" What had ailed her anyway, that she had felt too tongue-tied to say anything? It was so unfair to him. Well, she saw how she had blundered then. Now it was too late to rectify that error. "But," she vowed, "if I ever marry again, I will be better company much sooner, I will!"

And now here was her chance to keep that vow, with Sacred Horse's own cousin. It seemed more appropriate, more just, than she thought she deserved it to be. From the outset life with Lowanla proved easy and pleasant, largely because of Waterlily's changed attitude and behavior, and she was completely happy in her role of wife to him.

And now it was autumn. The time was right for gathering buffaloberries for winter use. The fruit was exceptionally plentiful this year; the getting of it would be rapid and easy. The berries grew each on its own short stem, but they clung in tight clusters to the twigs and larger branches of the bush. They were protected by long, thin spikes that made hand-picking tedious, if not impossible.

As everyone knew, buffaloberries were best left alone all summer, when they were acrid and puckery, hard and a dark, opaque red. It was not until the first autumn frost had worked its magic that, almost over night, they became tender and deliciously sweet. Then they glowed a yellowish red, as if from an inner light. There were always a very few bushes that bore all yellow berries. But red or yellow, they tasted the same and were sweet only after the first frost. They were no bigger than a small pea, or, at best, a middle-sized one. Because of their smallness and of the spikes that got in the way, the berries must be gathered wholesale by a method called "knocking off small things that fall readily."

The women had organized into *tiyošpaye* groups, or into congenial parties of friends from here and there who wished to spend the day together and make of the communal enterprise a sociable excursion as well. At sunrise they went out and set up their awnings all along the first shelf of land above the valley floor where the silvery-leafed bushes grew thick. They spread blankets about and set their drinking water and food under the shades. There they left one or two of their party to look after things and keep an eye on the babies and small children who could not walk far. These women would get the noon meal for their groups when the sun stood overhead.

The workers wrapped their blankets about their hips skirtwise and rolled and tucked the tops in about their waists. This left their arms free for action. And so, with each woman carrying a club of stout wood to knock off the berries, they dispersed in all directions among the countless bushes dotting the valley on both sides of the river as far as one could see.

Blue Bird, Leaping Fawn, Dream Woman, and First Woman set out together, leaving Waterlily and Prairie Flower, whose baby was hardly one moon old, to preside at their headquarters. The youthful mothers put their infants to sleep and then prepared to receive the berries as soon as the others would be filling their containers and bringing them up.

They sat working quietly for a while, processing the first of the fruit. But because the day was so mellow and peaceful, with autumn haze over the land, they must stop from time to time to admire it. Waterlily sighed deeply. "Oh, cousin," she said, "once, after that awful time in the wilds, I said to myself, 'Will a time ever come when I can be truly happy again?' And I was sure it never would. But I was wrong. Such a time has come, and this is it."

After her year away and her bitter experiences in that time, the day and the setting were poignantly beautiful. All the familiar friends and relatives of her childhood were nearby, the women working below and the members of the men's military societies stationed for the day out in those hills and distant peaks, ready to head off anything untoward that might otherwise endanger the women. Somewhere in those hills her new husband was hunting game for her and for her baby, who slept at her elbow, while she worked at this task that seemed no task at all. She felt infinitely content.

And as she worked she smiled now and again, delighting in the dear sounds rising from the women below: unrestrained feminine laughter and good-natured banter, occasional mock scolding or lusty joking by those with an earthy and robust bent, sudden cries of happy surprise upon the finding of another bush even more lavishly laden or with still bigger and sweeter berries, shouted warnings to mobile children forever gravitating toward danger or mischief the instant backs were turned. A piercing shriek because a startled hare sprang away from a bush, startling in turn the women who had disturbed it; the hue and cry when someone nearly stepped on a rattlesnake, and the excited advice from all sides—until it was safely dead—on how to kill it. All these sounds rose against a background of incessant clatter, clatter, clatter, of wood against wood, resounding up and down the valley. The berry pickers were beating the branches with their clubs and knocking off the ripe fruit, which hung by practically nothing and rained down in sheets readily at each blow, onto the hides spread below to catch it.

The two girls worked all morning without rest because the fruit came in so fast and there was so much of it. With a wooden mallet Prairie Flower crushed the berries lightly while Waterlily shaped the mash into small cakes, patting them firm with delicate fingers before laying them on fresh leaves to dry in the sun. At noon they stopped to build a fire and began cooking for their party. All the workers, seeing smoke curling up from their respective headquarters, began making their way back.

Presently they were seated in jovial groups under their awnings, and while they ate, they told funny stories on one another and laughed and joked heartily in a holiday mood, sharing their fun by shouting across from group to group till nearly all were laughing at the same things. After the meal they said, "Let's rest a while through the heat of noon. Later we will go back to work again." So they lay about in the shade of their awnings and slept.

Only Waterlily did not sleep; she lay gazing idly up into the tender blue sky, thinking many things. A fresh sense of security swept over her and her future looked very good. She had everything, she thought. Her brothers, Little Chief and Ohiya, would give her all the social backing a sister could desire. Already both had honored their little nephew by giving gifts away in his name. Soon they would be teaching him to ride and hunt, and to protect himself and grow up to be a real man.

Her younger sister, Smiling One, was lovely in Waterlily's eyes, and her parents, so active and vigorous at their prime best, were ever selfless and adoring of her—as she was of Mitawa. There were also her aunts, the blunt but well-meaning First Woman and the more delicate and sensitive Dream Woman, so mysterious and so good—they would always stand by her. It was the way of father's sisters and women cousins to overlook even one's faults out of loyalty to one's father, their brother, believing the best of one even when the worst was undeniably clear. Her uncles, Black Eagle and Bear Heart, out of loyalty to her mother, their cousin, stood second only to Rainbow in their readiness to help and protect her, should she ever need them.

"All my relatives are noble," she thought. "They make of their duties toward others a privilege and a delight." It was no struggle to play one's kinship role with people like them. When everyone was up to par in this kinship interchange of loyalty and mutual dependence, life could be close to perfect.

She went on with her reverie. There was her new husband, Lowanla, who had come so humbly, for all his own achievements and natural endowments, offering "to take care of my son." That was the usual, dignified way of proposing in a situation like theirs, and people praised him for his fine kinship sense toward his dead cousin's son. It was so correct.

But it was better than that for Waterlily, though of course no one could guess, from her sober acceptance of him. And now she was beginning to believe, from hints he had dropped, that it was better than that for him, too. She knew well enough that if the kindly Sacred Horse had picked her on first sight, she had picked this cousin of his long before, also on first sight. Now she almost dared to think that perhaps he had even wanted her first, if not at the same instant. "When I was leading the singing for the Omaha sitting that time, I first saw you standing there, in the crowd of onlookers," he had told her a few days before.

Her mind skipped about. Now she was thinking how she would always keep her baby's father in grateful, even affectionate, memory. How could she ever forget how kind he was? How easy he tried to make life for her in that far-off place. He was never domineering; what he wanted was always and only what he thought she wanted. And of course even if they were to have lived together for a lifetime, never would he have struck her as some men of short patience struck their wives. She was certain of that. She must tell Mitawa as soon as he could understand how his father was handsome and strong, gentle and kind, modest of his abilities as a hunter, thoughtful, and, above all, fearless—even unto death. Mitawa must be proud of him!

Then it occurred to her that she could begin at once to tell him, whispering it into his ear while he slept, creating about him an aura of the man whose child he was. Maybe somehow he would absorb it into his being; he could hardly do better for himself than that. She remembered how almost from the day Ohiya was born, her grandfather used to sit where he lay asleep, a tiny bundle of a child, and harangue on the making of a man. No doubt that was what made Ohiya grow up prematurely self-reliant, eager to attempt adult and manly responsibilities before his time. Imagine it—he had even made a friendship pact and gone into fellowhood with a visiting playmate. And look what it had meant for her when she was far from home and lonesome!

Next Waterlily recalled the figure of a woman that Lowanla had on his little finger when he underwent torture in the Sun Dance. And again the plaguing question: Whom did it represent? Her, by any chance? She wouldn't ask him—yet she wondered, especially since he had once spoken of how a strange girl had brought water to him. "I had no girl," he had said, "so naturally I was not expecting to have water slipped in to me. But some girl took pity on me. I don't know who she was. She ran off into the darkness. But she left me a little bucket. I still have it. I'll show it to you. Would you like to see it?" He had looked searchingly at her, but she had contrived to remain cool. "She ran off in your direction," he had persisted when she tried to change the subject. "In the direction of Palani's camp. That was where you were visiting, was it not?" Then he had added teasingly, "Maybe it was you!"

"There were many people at the Sun Dance. As I recall, the tipis stood three deep in our section, one row behind another. Surely in all those families there were many daughters and it could have been any one of them." Secure in her control of her secret, she had dared to needle him later on. "It was too bad, wasn't it, that your water bringer did not care enough to make herself known? After going that far, why didn't she? It was cruel to leave you wondering forever." He had smiled ruefully.

All these things Waterlily ran through in her mind, staring at the sky and the white tufts of cloud and not seeing them. The tired women slept prosaically on but she was wide awake and vibrant with happiness. Poor Lowanla, how much he did want to establish as a fact what he so desperately hoped was so! "Oh, if only I could know that you were the girl who dared do that for me!" he had said over and over.

"If you knew that, then what?"

"Why, if I knew, then I should be perfectly happy all my life." For a moment his wistfulness had stirred her pity and she was almost irresistibly tempted to break down and confess—but she had checked herself in time. For deep down in her heart she knew that she would never tell, never! Not even in exchange for what she would dearly love to know: whether that little figurine represented his prayer for her.

The cumulative wisdom of Dakota women, gained through experience from way back, told her it would never do. Of course she wanted him to be perfectly happy; she wanted everything for him. But also she feared the obverse of the kind of happiness he was asking for. It was suspicion. Insidiously it would start, and grow, and grow, tormenting him with an endless cycle of the same questions, until they would become an obsession. "If she, a well-brought-up girl, could do that for me, then why not for other men? Were there other men? Who were they?" In time a curtain of distrust would separate them, and that was no way for a husband and wife to spend their life together.

"No, never!" Waterlily whispered to herself, her lips tightening with determination. "He shall never know! He must get along with a little less than perfect happiness. It will be best that way."

Biographical Sketch of the Author

By Agnes Picotte

Ella Cara Deloria was born January 31, 1889, at White Swan on the Yankton Sioux Reservation in southeastern South Dakota. Her parents—she was the third daughter of Philip Deloria and the first child of his marriage to Mary Sully Bordeaux—gave her the Dakota name *Anpetu Waśte,* Beautiful Day. Her baptism a few weeks later on Sexagesima Sunday at White Swan's Philip the Deacon Chapel, where her father was deacon, marked her formal introduction to the Protestant Episcopal religion, a faith which was, along with her Sioux heritage, to be a major influence in her life.

The Deloria family was a large and loving one. As early as 1869 Ella's grandfather, Chief Frank Deloria, had requested that an Episcopal mission be established among the Yankton people. His son Philip was accepted for religious training two years later and was received into the priesthood in 1891. Twice widowed—his first wife and two young sons having died of smallpox and his second wife having left him with two small daughters—Philip was married in 1888 to Mary Sully Bordeaux, a widow who also had two daughters from a previous marriage. After Ella, two more children, Susan Mabel and Vine Victor, were born to Philip and Mary. Although only of one-quarter Indian blood, Mary had been raised as a traditional Dakota, and Dakota remained the primary language in the Deloria home, an environment in which Sioux values mingled easily with Philip and Mary's devout Christian principles.

In 1890 Philip Deloria was assigned to St. Elizabeth's Church on the Standing Rock Reservation, a pastorate that served a Teton Sioux community. Ella entered the St. Elizabeth's school adjacent to the church and parsonage on the bluff overlooking the Missouri and Grand rivers. In 1902 she transferred to All Saints boarding school in Sioux Falls, South Dakota. After her graduation from All Saints in 1910 she enrolled at Oberlin College. In 1913 she became a student at Columbia Teachers College, receiving a bachelor of science degree two years later.

Deloria returned to All Saints in 1915 and taught there until 1919, when she accepted a job with the YWCA as health education secretary for Indian schools and reservations. In that position she traveled widely throughout the western United States and became acquainted at first hand with a large number of Indian groups. In 1923 she was employed by the Haskell Indian school in Lawrence, Kansas, to teach physical education and dance. Four years later Franz Boas, the preeminent American anthropologist of the time, asked Deloria to translate and edit some written texts in the Sioux language. She did so, gathering additional material as well, and in 1929 she published an article on the Sun Dance in the *Journal of American Folk-Lore*.

Over the years, until Boas's death in 1942, Deloria assisted him as a research specialist in American Indian ethnology and linguistics. Her work resulted in several books: *Dakota Texts* (1932), a bilingual collection of Sioux tales that stands today as the starting place for any study of Sioux dialects, mythology, or folklore; *Dakota Grammar* (1941), a collaboration with Boas; and

Speaking of Indians (1944), a nontechnical but sophisticated description of Indian (particularly Sioux) culture. *Waterlily,* or at least the first draft of it, was also written during the early forties.

By the 1940s Deloria was recognized as the leading authority on the Sioux. She continued her research, writing, lecturing, and consulting into her later years, taking time off from 1955 to 1958 to serve as director of her old school, St. Elizabeth's. From 1962 to 1966 she worked on her projects at the University of South Dakota. She lived out her last years in Vermillion and died on February 12, 1971.

The unique and irreplaceable quality of Deloria's work is reconfirmed as previously unpublished manuscripts like *Waterlily* come to light. Not only was she a meticulous and knowledgeable researcher; she had a deep and heartfelt understanding of—a true kinship with—those whose culture she both studied and shared.

Afterword

By Raymond J. DeMallie

Waterlily is a unique portrayal of nineteenth-century Sioux Indian life, unequaled for its interpretation of Plains Indian culture from the perspectives of women. The prominent features of Plains Indian lifeways during the middle of the nineteenth century were intertribal warfare and the elaborate system it entailed for encouraging and rewarding individual bravery, and mounted buffalo hunting, by which men pursued the vast herds for the food and other necessities of life that the buffalo provided. In writings about Plains Indians, women have not played a conspicuous part.

The book's focus on the experiences of the heroine Waterlily and her mother and grandmother makes it a major contribution to understanding women in traditional Sioux culture. Yet Ella Deloria surely did not intend the book to be construed as a feminist statement. In presenting her people's past in novelistic form she wrote from the heart in the only culturally appropriate way—as a Sioux woman. This special insider's perspective not only infuses the narrative with interest and insight, but offers ample material for a reexamination of the written record of traditional Sioux life.

In order to understand what Ella Deloria attempted to do in *Waterlily*—and accomplished so well—it is important to appreciate the intellectual context in which the idea grew and the manuscript was written: Boasian anthropology in the 1930s and 1940s. For even though Ella Deloria never undertook any formal study of anthropology, her long association with Franz Boas, Ruth Benedict, Alexander Lesser, and Margaret Mead—all leaders in the field—shaped and directed her studies of the Sioux past.

At Columbia University in New York, from 1899 until his death in 1942, Boas attracted the leading scholars of the first half of the century who were devoted to the recording and preservation of American Indian languages and cultures. Boas's leadership of this diffuse group, whose members spread throughout the country to develop academic anthropology in the universities, was most importantly by example. He facilitated research by finding funds to support it and helped design many of the projects carried out by his students, but in this as in teaching he let the quality of his work set the example and allowed students the freedom to develop their own ideas.

For Ella Deloria, Franz Boas was a charismatic figure. She respected his integrity as well as his scholarship. Writing on July 17, 1939, to congratulate him on his eighty-first birthday, Deloria commented, "I would not trade the privilege of having known you, for anything I can think of." Although some of his students called him "Papa Franz," she addressed him as "Father Franz," acknowledging the closeness of their relationship but marking her respect. (Boas, the prototypical Jewish scholar, would respond to Deloria by saying, "Ella, you make me feel like a Catholic priest!" and she would reply, "Next to my own father, you are the most truly Christian man I ever met.") For Boas, Ella Deloria was the fulfillment of a long search to find a native speaker who could help him in his study of the Sioux language. With her command of Lakota, appreciation for scholarship, sharp intellect, and literary skills, she was the perfect collaborator.

Boas's interest in the Sioux seems to have stemmed from his commitment to bring to fruition the studies of James Owen Dorsey, of the Smithsonian Institution's Bureau of American Ethnology, who died prematurely in 1895, leaving a rich legacy of unpublished manuscripts relating to Siouan languages. Among them was a remarkable collection of stories in Lakota—more than a thousand handwritten pages—composed in 1887 under Dorsey's supervision by George Bushotter, a young Sioux educated at Hampton Institute in Virginia. Boas tried on several occasions to prepare the manuscripts for publication, and he employed Ella Deloria to work with him and his students on a small part of them during the spring of 1915, when she was a student at Columbia Teachers College. She found the process of translation and grammatical analysis fascinating, and later wrote that she had enjoyed the work under Boas, her first real paying job, which brought her eighteen dollars a month!

After Ella Deloria left New York, Boas lost contact with her until 1927. That summer he visited her at Haskell Institute in Lawrence, Kansas, and apparently resumed work on the Bushotter material where they had left off a dozen years before. He stayed there a few days to establish a routine, showing her exactly what he wanted done by way of revision, rewriting, and translation of the texts, and then hired her for the summer to continue the work. This was the beginning of her long association with anthropology.

The next year, 1928, Boas was able to find funds to bring Ella Deloria to New York to begin work in earnest. Although he wished to collaborate with her on study of the language, the project for which she was hired was psychological in nature. Boas wrote to her on January 16, 1928: "The object of your work would be to study, in the greatest detail, the habits of action and thought that are present among the Dakota children and among adults. . . . From an ethnological point of view, the whole study will, of course, be full of opportunities because the investigation implies that you will have to know all the details of everyday life as well as of religious attitudes and habits of thought of the people."

In New York, Deloria met Ruth Benedict, a student and colleague of Boas who came more and more to control the daily operations of the anthropology department at Columbia in Boas's later years, and who was fiercely loyal to his perspectives and methods. In subsequent years Ella Deloria's assignment was to collect specific types of material as suggested by Benedict, who planned ultimately to assist her in editing and preparing them for publication. It was she who suggested, for example, that Deloria should work on the family and tribal structure, and examine kinship and the role of women, recording women's autobiographies as a source of insight.

Ella Deloria continued to work with Boas until his death in 1942 and with Benedict until her death in 1948. During the twenty years of her association with Columbia she worked steadily on Sioux grammar and compiled a Sioux-English dictionary; she also completed her translation of the entire Bushotter collection and translated the manuscripts of George Sword, an Oglala (written around 1908), and of Jack Frazier, a Santee Sioux (dictated to Samuel and Gideon Pond in 1840). In addition, she transcribed and translated an enormous body of texts in the Lakota and Dakota dialects of Sioux on a wide variety of topics, selected to represent the range of variation in spoken language: traditional myths, anecdotes, autobiographies, political speeches, conversation, humerous stories, and aphorisms. A written record of such magnitude and diversity does not exist for any other Plains Indian language.

Although most of her work was devoted to the collection of data, Ella Deloria also spent a great deal of effort after Boas's death in writing syntheses of ethnographic material on the old Sioux way of life. Foremost among the projects was the one suggested by Benedict on kinship and social life, a manuscript that Deloria entitled at different times "Camp Circle Society" or "Dakota Family Life." It is a thorough presentation of Sioux social life, ranging from the structure of society to the workings of the kinship system and the individual life cycle, all copiously illustrated with quotations from her interviews and from the historical writings she had translated.

This manuscript is very much a scholarly study and was intended for publication by the American Philosophical Society, but without Benedict's guidance, Deloria found it difficult to complete. By integrating material from all her sources, she produced a work that may be characterized as ahistorical; it is not grounded in time. The core of the book is a presentation of the values of the traditional Sioux way of life as articulated in the historical manuscripts she had translated and the interviews she had recorded; it is a contrastive view of Sioux society that places it in perspective with modern America. In a word, it is a cultural description in a Boasian sense: an idealized and generalized synthesis of the past, a testament to the old and valued customs of the Sioux.

The work was well under way in 1945 when Deloria offhandedly remarked in a letter to her friend Virginia Dorsey Lightfoot (daughter of James Owen Dorsey) that such research had become old-fashioned; the Second World War had ushered in an era of practical social science, and American Indian ethnology was no longer perceived as an endeavor with high priority. Lacking adequate financial support, she struggled on with the project, finally completing the manuscript in 1954. But no publisher could be found, and the work is only now being prepared for publication.

The dedication that is apparent in Ella Deloria's lifelong quest to preserve traditional Sioux language and culture was deeply rooted in her concern for the future of her people. She articulated this concern in relation to her own work in a letter written December 2, 1952, to H. E. Beebe, who provided her with funds to have the manuscript on social life typed for publication:

> This may sound a little naïve, Mr. Beebe, but I actually feel that I have a mission: To make the Dakota people understandable, as human beings, to the white people who have to deal with them. I feel that one of the reasons for the lagging advancement of the Dakotas has been that those who came out among them to teach and preach, went on the assumption that

the Dakotas had *nothing*, no rules of life, no social organiza-
tion, no ideals. And so they tried to pour white culture into, as
it were, a vacuum, and when that did not work out, because it
was not a vacuum after all, they concluded that the Indians
were impossible to change and train. What they should have
done first, before daring to start their program, was to study
everything possible of Dakota life, and see what made it go, in
the old days, and what was still so deeply rooted that it could
not be rudely displaced without some hurt. . . . I feel that I
have this work cut out for me and if I do not make all I know
available before I die, I will have failed by so much. But I am
not morbid about it; quite cheerful in fact.

Clearly, a scientific monograph would establish credibility
and present the social foundations of traditional Sioux life in a
context where it might be beneficial for government officials,
missionaries, and teachers who dealt with Sioux people. But it
was not a vehicle suited to reach a wide audience. As she wrote to
Virginia Lightfoot on February 3, 1946, "Ethnology has to be
objective and impersonal." Perhaps she was thinking of the chap-
ter based on her manuscripts that was written by Jeannette
Mirsky, a student of Boas, and published in the volume edited by
Margaret Mead, *Cooperation and Competition among Primitive Peoples* (1937). While an excellent summary of the fundamental features of the traditional Sioux social system, it gives little sense
of the dynamics of daily life. The lead sentence of the conclusion is indicative of the tone: "The Dakota have a culture that
rests solidly on a constant interplay between the individual attain-
ment and group participation, with prestige accorded a place in
either" (p. 426). Such flat generalization vitiated Deloria's rich
source material and reduced human emotion to statistical patterns.

Ella Deloria herself always chose to take a directly personal
approach. Throughout her career, beginning as a student at Columbia Teachers College in 1913, she made it a practice to lecture
and give presentations of Sioux songs and dances to white audiences of all kinds—church groups, schools, the YMCA and
other organizations—both to earn money and to reach the public

and promote understanding of Indian people. It was in this spirit that she developed some of her material into a popular book on the past and present of American Indians published by the YMCA in 1944 as *Speaking of Indians*.

Ella Deloria was not alone in regretting that anthropological approaches to the American Indian seemed to preclude a personal dimension to the presentation of the American Indian past. In 1922 Elsie Clews Parsons—an anthropologist who was herself a student and colleague of Boas, as well as one of the main financial supporters of the field research of Boas's later students—edited a volume of fictional sketches of American Indian individuals set in historical times under the title *American Indian Life*. Boas and many of his prominent students responded to Parsons' call, for some of them, perhaps, their first and only experiment with writing fiction. Parsons conceived of the book as popular literature and expressed in her preface the hope that it would be read, as an antidote to prevailing stereotypes, by people everywhere who were interested in American Indians. By focusing the sketches on what she termed "the commonplaces of behavior" in daily life, Parsons designed the book to present impressionistic pictures of the variety of American Indian traditional cultures, drawing attention to the psychological dimensions of common human experience that were so notably lacking from professional anthropological monographs.

Perhaps it was this book that inspired Boas and Benedict to suggest to Deloria that she undertake to write a novel about the life of a Sioux woman set a century in the past, before traditional culture had been significantly altered by contact with American civilization. It would provide the opportunity for her to explain the workings of kinship and the social system in the context of daily life and in a format that would appeal to the general public. She could work from the same material she was using to write her ethnographic monograph on Sioux social life, but take a freer perspective, situating her cultural description in the context of daily life and revealing the social patterns and emotional overtones of the kinship system in action.

Deloria was hard at work on *Waterlily* in 1942, but how she developed the plot seems not to have been recorded. A passage from George Sword's manuscript may well have served as one inspiration for Deloria to focus her novel closely on the female characters as a vehicle for presenting ethnographic description of the women's share of traditional life. Although Sword had been an accomplished warrior, epitomizing the manly virtues of Sioux culture, in describing the old way of life he went to great length to point out the crucial importance of women's roles, and wrote as follows (Deloria's translation):

> The work of men was as follows: They took part in fighting the enemy; that was a great honor. They hunted buffalo; they shot deer; they hunted for wild animals for food; they went to the hill to scout for buffalo.
>
> The women's work was: They packed every bit of household equipment each time the camp moved; they alone guarded all these things during the march. When they stopped to make camp, the women again unpacked everything alone and erected their tipi. They laid out all the bedding; they gathered and brought in firewood; they brought water; they cooked; they passed out the food; they took care of all the children. They used all the utensils incident in managing the household. They even made the tipis; they themselves dressed the robes for their tipis; they made all the bedding; they were in entire charge of all food, once it had been obtained and brought home by the men.

The letter from Ruth Benedict to Deloria of November 7, 1944, indicates that the original version of the manuscript had been completed by then. Benedict encouraged her to shorten it for publication. With Benedict's help, Deloria cut and revised the manuscript in 1947 and by the summer of 1948 had completed the final copy. Benedict planned to help in obtaining its publication, but her sudden death in September 1948 deprived Deloria of the professional assistance she needed. *Waterlily* was to suffer the same fate as the monograph on social life. In a letter to H. E. Beebe, February 7, 1954, Deloria outlined her attempts to get the work published. The critics agreed that the work was "rich

in material, and racially and ethnologically accurate. But Mac-
Millan's turned it down, saying it was all of that but they feared
the reading public for such a book would not be large enough to
warrant their publishing it." She had recently submitted it to the
University of Oklahoma Press, only to have it returned with
similar comments.

Ironically, the very qualities that made *Waterlily* unpublishable
at the time it was written are those that make it of such interest
today. It represents a blurring of categories: in conception it is
fundamentally a work of ethnographic description, but in its
method it is narrative fiction, a plot invented to provide a plausible range of situations that reveal how cultural ideals shaped the
behavior of individual Sioux people in social interactions. The
correct attitudes and behaviors for kin relationships are the focus
for much of the narrative, reflecting Deloria's interpretation of
the supreme importance of kinship in structuring Sioux life.

In the novel, Deloria writes of traditional Sioux women's life
without apology or explanation. Her female characters reflect
their preeminent concern for the welfare and reputation of their
brothers, followed by concern for their children and husbands.
The women's role in achieving honor for themselves by honoring their relatives, especially their male relatives, is clearly portrayed in a social environment in which differences in activities,
status, and all aspects of life are rooted in the differences—culturally perceived by the Sioux to be the natural state of affairs—
between the sexes. Men's and women's worlds were comple-
mentary but very much compartmentalized. Women, for example, are portrayed in *Waterlily* as playing only peripheral (but no
less essential) roles in religious activities. Blue Bird, as a young
mother, has only a vague notion of proper procedure in prayer
and sacrifice as she seeks to save her baby's life, and Deloria goes
to some length to suggest how vague her character's notions of
the Powers of the Universe are. Gloku, the aged grandmother,
prays more confidently on Box Butte for the welfare of her
grandchildren, suggesting increasing experience of the sacred as
a woman matured. Importantly, Deloria presents such inequality
between men and women as a normal and accepted part of the

differentiation of Sioux society by sex. Women are portrayed not as exploited, but as comfortably situated in a cultural system that provided them with security and a sense of well-being.

Ella Deloria wove into the narrative of *Waterlily* materials garnered over more than two decades of study. Many of the customs mentioned or described incidentally in the plot—the burial of baby teeth in the earth at the side of the tipi door, Gloku's prayer and offering of rocks on Box Butte, the fellowhood established between Rainbow and Palani, the ghostkeeping ceremony, and the Virgin's Fire, to name a few—are subjects of the writings of George Bushotter. Most of the description of the Sun Dance, including the prayers and detailed discussion of the cutting of the sacred tree, as well as the customs of war, are taken from the writings of George Sword. Deloria had translated this material and studied it, reviewing details with living elders for so many years that she had clearly made it her own. Other parts of the narrative, such as the presentation of the treatment of murderers, the long admonitions to young women about the dangers of courtship, the discussions of types of marriage, the honor bestowed on a girl who was "bought" as a wife, the mechanisms of polygyny, the details of getting along with one's in-laws, and the description of how the space inside the tipi was designated for various functions, were taken directly from her transcripts of interviews. Finally, some aspects of the manuscript—for example, Deloria's comparison of the repetition of the pipe ceremony in the Sun Dance to the recitation of the Gloria Patri, the unequivocally negative stance toward warfare, the exceptional adherence of the protagonists to the spirit and letter of kinship law—may mirror Ella Deloria's own personality rather than her reconstruction of nineteenth-century social life. But that is as intended: This was to be a personal statement, in contrast to the objective stance of the anthropological monograph.

Although Ella Deloria mused once in a letter to Boas (dated December 5, 1935) that perhaps she should have tried to earn a degree and become a professional anthropologist, she stated flatly, "I certainly do not consider myself as such." In later years she was content to call herself a linguist. Doubtless she would have found the anthropology of the 1980s much more congenial than that of the 1940s. That ethnography is as much literature as science, that ethnographic reportage should focus on meaning as much as behavior, and that the anthropologist's role is to serve as interpreter between cultures, are increasingly-accepted tenets of what has come to be designated "symbolic" or "interpretive" anthropology. This anthropology has grown out of the same concerns that led Ella Deloria—and doubtless Boas and Benedict, as her advisers—to experiment with the medium of fiction as an effective way of explicating ethnographic fact.

Readers will appreciate *Waterlily* as a novel that guides them into the mental as well as the historical world of the nineteenth-century Sioux. The twists and turns of plot are no more fantastic than the true-life autobiographies Deloria recorded from living people. The story is charged with universal human interest, set firmly in the matrix of Sioux cultural practices and understandings. Some readers will want to compare this work with the writings of anthropologists and historians as a means of critique, particularly of the adequacy of published representations of the role and status of women in Sioux society. A few readers, like myself, will find it a useful commentary on the development of anthropology during the past century, in terms of both its methods and its goals.

Waterlily forms a valuable part of Deloria's legacy, the treasure trove of material preserving the Sioux past that she has bequeathed to us all, Indian and non-Indian alike. Today, fifty years after most of her interviews were recorded, we realize how irreplaceable those records are, and how fortunate we are that Ella Deloria devoted her life to their collection and translation. As more of her writings become published at long last, we can appreciate how splendidly she achieved her life's mission. For above all, Ella Deloria's work of transcription, translation, and cultural interpretation has provided the data and insight from which we can come to understand the Sioux people of the last century in the way that she intended, as fellow human beings.

The fullest account of Ella Deloria's life is Janette K. Murray, "Ella Deloria: A Biographical Sketch and Literary Analysis" (Ph.D. dissertation, University of North Dakota, 1974). Most of Deloria's unpublished manuscripts, including her voluminous correspondence with Boas, are housed in the Library of the American Philosophical Society, Philadelphia, Pennsylvania. Other manuscripts—including "Waterlily" and the accompanying letter from Ruth Benedict—are in the keeping of the Dakota Indian Foundation, Chamberlain, South Dakota. Deloria's correspondence with H. E. Beebe is in the Southwest Museum, Los Angeles, California; her correspondence with Ruth Benedict is in Vassar College Library; and her correspondence with Virginia Dorsey Lightfoot is in my possession. The anecdote about "Father Franz" was told to me by Ella Deloria in 1970. I wish to express my gratitude to Father Vine Deloria, Sr., and to the entire Deloria family for sharing with me remembrances of Ella Deloria and her work.